MUSIC IN AMERICAN LIFE

Oscar Sonneck and American Music

*A Gathering of Those Writings
on American Music by Oscar Sonneck First
Published in Scattered and Sometimes Obscure Sources,
Followed by Comments on His Life and Work by
Herbert Putnam, Carl Engel, Otto Kinkeldey,
Gilbert Chase, and H. Wiley Hitchcock.
With a Bibliography of His Writings and
Musical Compositions, and of Writings
about Him, by Irving Lowens.*

Oscar Sonneck
and American Music

EDITED FOR
THE SONNECK SOCIETY BY
William Lichtenwanger

With a Foreword by
Irving Lowens

University of Illinois Press
URBANA and CHICAGO

This book has been published with the aid of grants from the Sonneck Society and from the Sonneck Memorial Fund administered by the Music Division of the Library of Congress.

Grateful acknowledgment is made for permission to use the following material:

H. Wiley Hitchcock, "After 100[!] Years: The Editorial Side of Sonneck" [Louis Charles Elson Memorial Lecture] (Washington, D.C.: Library of Congress, 1975). Copyright © 1974 by H. Wiley Hitchcock.

Otto Kinkeldey, "Oscar George Theodore Sonneck (1873 – 1928)," *Notes* 11 (December, 1953): 25 – 32. Copyright © 1953 by the Music Library Association, Inc.

Irving Lowens, "Oscar George Theodore Sonneck: His Writings and Musical Compositions; A Bibliography," published with H. Wiley Hitchcock, "After 100[!] Years" (Washington, D.C.: Library of Congress, 1975). Copyright © 1974 by Irving Lowens.

This book is printed on acid-free paper.

Library of Congress Cataloging in Publication Data

Sonneck, Oscar George Theodore, 1873 – 1928.
  Oscar Sonneck and American music.

  (Music in American life)
  "A gathering of those writings on American music by Oscar Sonneck first published in scattered and sometimes obscure sources, followed by comments on his life and work by Herbert Putnam, Carl Engel, Otto Kinkeldey, Gilbert Chase, and H. Wiley Hitchcock. With a bibliography of his writings and musical compositions, and of writings about him, by Irving Lowens."
  Bibliography: p.
  Includes index.
  1. Music — United States — Addresses, essays, lectures.
2. Sonneck, Oscar George Theodore, 1873 – 1928.
I. Lichtenwanger, William, 1915 – . II. Title.
III. Series.
ML200.1.S65 1983 780'.92'4   82 – 13670
ISBN 0-252-01021-3

. . . and we need a little more fun in music.

Sonneck, "Guillaume Lekeu"

Contents

PART 2

Writings about Sonneck

Foreword

⌣

Although Oscar Sonneck was born in Lafayette, New Jersey, in 1873, he did not live in this country long enough to become an American patriot. His father died when he was fifteen months old, and within a year or two his mother returned to Germany, taking her son with her. In Frankfurt-am-Main, and later in Kiel, Munich, and Sondershausen, he received the education of a well-to-do German youth. His earliest scholarly work dealt with Méhul's *Joseph* and Spontini's *La Vestale;* in 1895, the Frankfurt firm of Gebrüder Knauer published a collection of his poems under the title *Seufzer.* In the following year, his first articles about music appeared in print, in the *Kieler Zeitung,* the *München Allgemeine Zeitung,* the *Neue Musik-Zeitung,* and (Sonneck was coming up in the world) the *Rivista musicale italiana.* He continued his musical journalism in 1897, and the Gebrüder Knauer brought out *Ein kritisch-polemisches Referat über die Musik-ästhetischen Streitfragen u.s.w. von Friedrich Rösch, als Protest gegen den Symbolismus in der Musik,* followed a year later by another book of Sonneck poetry, *Eine Totenmesse.* In 1899, he blossomed out as a composer, with the Frankfurt music publisher B. Firnberg issuing some of his original compositions. He spent much of the year in Italy, continuing his work as a scholar. He finally returned to the land of his birth about the beginning of 1900, pursuing his musical research in the principal libraries on the American East Coast.

Just how and why it was that Sonneck became interested in the history of American music is something of a mystery, but once he arrived back on this side of the Atlantic he quickly abandoned his previous, rather esoteric musical interests in such figures as Friedrich Rösch. Among the first of his articles to appear in American periodicals was

"Benjamin Franklin's Relation to Music," which appeared in *Music* (Chicago) in 1900, and his contributions to European journals began to take on a much different aspect. To the *Kieler Zeitung* he contributed a piece entitled "Ein Indianer-Konzert"; to *Die Zeit,* "Zum Verständnis des amerikanischen Musiklebens"; and (most significantly) to the *Zeitschrift der IMG,* "Die musikalische Zeitschriften-Litteratur: Ein bibliographisches Problem," the first indication that he had been bitten by the bibliographical bug.

The problem that had seized his imagination, and that continued to fascinate him until the end of his life, was the early history of white men's music in the land of his birth. In the preface to his *Bibliography of Early Secular American Music* (Washington, D.C.: Printed for the author by H. L. McQueen, 1905), he wrote that the most serious obstacle he encountered in his attempt to solve the problem was

> the deplorable lack of interest taken in the history of our early musical life. To some extent this indifference is due to the superficiality and prejudice with which the subject has repeatedly been approached. Historians, popular and unpopular, have steadily (and with surprisingly uncritical methods) guided the public into the belief that a secular musical life did not exist in our country during the eighteenth century. To be sure, these pages throw little more than side-lights on the formative period in our musical history, but possibly they will help to undermine an absurd theory and strengthen the opposite position correctly held by a few writers, as, for instance, Henry Edward Krehbiel.

Sonneck was keenly aware of the fact that before one can chart the history of music accurately, he must know what music was available to those who practiced the art. As a consequence, a bibliographical guide to what was largely *terra incognita* was essential if an accurate view of music in early America was to be projected. This he attempted to provide with his first American book-length contribution to musical scholarship. He had no illusions about the romantic nature of bibliography. "Bibliographical work," he wrote many years later, "is fascinating for him who happens to be afflicted with the disease. It is stupid work in the eyes of him who is not, but it becomes useful work in the eyes of even the scoffers if circumstances compel them to depend upon a piece of bibliographical work well done." And the *Bibliography of Early Secular American Music,* despite the extraordinary obstacles in the path of Sonneck as pioneer bibliographer, was superlatively well done.

The bibliography also determined Sonneck's future career. It so happened that Herbert Putnam, since 1899 Librarian of Congress (and considered by many the greatest of all Librarians of Congress) was looking for someone who could take the miscellaneous accumulation of music that had piled up in his institution over the years, mostly as a result of the copyright requirement for deposit, and transform it into a useful research tool. He had been looking for the right person for three years when, one day in 1902 (to quote Putnam), "there strolled into my office a young man who introduced himself as Oscar Sonneck, and his interest as Music. He had under his arm a packet of manuscript which he proffered to me — without recompense — for publication by the government. The explanation of it — very simple and modest — [was] . . . that for the several years preceding he had been writing criticisms and reviews, during the last two, however, concentrating upon the preparation of this manuscript. And the manuscript proved to be 'A Bibliography of American Music in the Eighteenth Century'!"

It was, of course, highly unrealistic of Sonneck to expect that the United States government could be interested in anything quite so inconsequential as a bibliography of eighteenth-century secular American music, and Putnam gave him absolutely no reason to believe that his bibliography could or would be published. But perhaps more important was the fact that Putnam saw in Sonneck a man who could accomplish the miracle of transforming a pile of miscellaneous junk into a major resource for scholars. "I talked to him of the task with us, asked him if he would consider it," wrote Putnam. "He thought it might interest him. There were some adjustments — of our roll — involved for which I had to look to the Appropriation Committees in Congress. I sought them, describing the opportunity, and, very frankly, the man himself. They were granted; and he came."

He came, but he did not quite conquer. Three more years were to pass before "the packet of manuscript" achieved the respectability of publication; even then, he had not succeeded in persuading a publisher to bring it out in a trade edition. Sonneck finally approached the Washington job-printer H. L. McQueen and asked him to print up two hundred copies of the work, the tab to be picked up by the author. Meanwhile, Sonneck had not been idle. Between 1902 and 1905, he had done some intensive research on two key figures in eighteenth-century American musical life, Francis Hopkinson and James Lyon, and he had a magnificent monograph ready for publication. Nobody would publish it, so again Sonneck went to McQueen, ordered a two-hundred-copy edition, and created another milestone in the history of American music despite the "deplorable lack of interest" in the subject manifested by his fellow countrymen. As late as 1907, Sonneck could still find no American publisher for his work. He had to go as far as Leipzig to find a publisher for his definitive *Early Concert-Life in America (1731 – 1800)*; there the respected firm of Breitkopf & Härtel found the study of sufficient consequence to merit publication.

Meanwhile, Sonneck had been hard at work transforming the Music Division of the Library of Congress into a respectable institution. Since it was impossible, for financial reasons, to buy the rare scores of eighteenth- and nineteenth-century operas available in European libraries, and since labor was cheap, he developed a copying program that ultimately made the Music Division an international center for the study of opera. As early as his second year of service, Sonneck became keenly aware of the lack of music periodical indexes, a lack that masked the quantity and quality of the work being done in the field of musical research. He personally began to index those periodicals that came across his desk. During each of his fifteen years at the Library of Congress, he prepared between three and four thousand subject cards. He systematically went about analyzing back sets of periodicals, and by 1907 he could report to the Librarian of Congress the commencement of a "Subject List of Articles on Music in American [nonmusical] Magazines"! In addition, with minimal help from a tiny staff he cataloged every piece of music and every book about music that was bought for the division.

Then, in 1908, Sonneck actually won a battle with the government. In that year, the Government Printing Office brought out the first of many bibliographies of music, bound in the dark red buckram familiar to every music librarian today, a volume that represented a part of the fruit of his labors. *Dramatic Music (Class M 1500, 1510, 1520): Catalogue of Full Scores* was hardly the catchiest title in the world, but it proved to be a trailblazer. It was followed by Sonneck's *Report on "The Star-Spangled Banner," "Hail Columbia," "America," "Yankee Doodle"* (1909); *Orchestral Music (Class M 1000 – 1268) Catalogue: Scores* (1912); Julia Gregory's *Catalogue of Early Books on Music (before 1800)* (1913), prepared under Sonneck's direction; the two-volume *Catalogue of Opera Librettos Printed before 1800* (1914); *"The Star Spangled Banner"* (1914), revised and enlarged from the 1909 report; *Catalogue of First Editions of Stephen C. Foster (1826 – 1864)* (1915), by Walter R. Whittlesey and Sonneck; *A Catalogue of Full Scores of Dramatic Music* ("practically completed in December, 1915," according to Sonneck, but never published); and the *Catalogue of First Editions of Edward MacDowell (1861 – 1908)* (1917). All were published by the Government Printing Office in Washington.

Outside the Library of Congress, Sonneck continued to work actively as a historian and a musicologist, exhibiting an extraordinary range of interests. Twice, the first time with *Suum Cuique: Essays in Music* (New York: G. Schirmer, 1916), he assembled between the covers of a book some of the papers he considered of greatest interest. But his *Miscellaneous Studies in the History of Music* (New York: Macmillan, 1921), published after he left the Library of Congress in 1917, while containing a few significant Americanist papers, demonstrates an expansion of his interests that seems to coincide with the commencement in 1915 of the publication, under Sonneck's editorship, of *The Musical Quarterly*. During his last years at G. Schirmer, he was very active in Beethoven research and was instrumental in establishing the Beethoven Association and in seeing to it that Alexander Wheelock Thayer's Beethoven biography finally appeared in at least partial English translation by Henry E. Krehbiel.

Meanwhile, a number of interesting papers by Sonneck dealing with various aspects of American music, papers published in various periodicals at one time or another during the course of his career, failed to achieve the permanence they deserved because they were never issued in book form. When the Sonneck Society was established to celebrate the centenary of his birth, one of the initial projects it proposed to sponsor was to collect some of these papers, bring them out as a book, and add to them evaluations of Sonneck's role in the development of our knowledge of American music history by some of the most prominent Americanists in this field. All of these scholars had, at one time or another, based their own labors on the firm foundations established by Sonneck. It took some years to find exactly the right editor for this posthumous collection of Sonneck's articles on American music, but the delay was worth undergoing. In William Lichtenwanger, retired head of the Reference Section in the Music Division at the Library of Congress, the Society succeeded in finding Sonneck's spiritual son, and his annotations to this volume have transformed it into something more than the Society originally expected. It is not only a tribute to "the father of us all" but an unveiling of Oscar Sonneck as a great human being as well as a great scholar and a great librarian. It is my strong feeling that this book will soon make a place for itself as a fount of information about one of the finest of all American music historians, about a man who has been grievously neglected and unjustly forgotten in the realm of American cultural historiography. This book helps to demonstrate how brilliantly Sonneck blazed the way for those who followed after him, and to explain why the Sonneck Society — proposed in 1973, established in 1974, and incorporated in 1975 "to carry out educational projects and to help disseminate accurate information and research dealing with all aspects of American music and music in America" — flourishes today in its attempt to realize the goals enunciated by Sonneck in the first years of the twentieth century.

Peabody Conservatory of Music   IRVING LOWENS

Editor's Preface

Oscar Sonneck died on October 30, 1928, just twenty-four days past his fifty-fifth birthday. This volume is published in the fifty-fifth year following his death, and it is the first book on Sonneck to appear. Not often is the first book about a figure of public interest published so long after his death — nor a society named in his honor past the centenary of his birth. Perhaps the reason for Sonneck's relative neglect is the fact that he was not granted a long life, with the additional fact that his life encompassed several different careers, which together did not achieve the cumulative force that a more unified professional life acquires.

Sonneck is remembered, for example, as the pioneer American music librarian; yet his edifice in the Music Division of the Library of Congress was reared in only fifteen years and without the help of assistants of equivalent stature. He can also be called the father of American musicology, since he anglicized the French word and introduced it into American scholarship — and at the same time became its first genuine practitioner in the Americas. Before Sonneck, America had only musical journalists along with a few essayists and dabblers in the bibliography of music. If librarianship and musicology are but different aspects of the same profession (a proposition many in each field would deny), the same cannot be said of music publishing. In this activity Sonneck served the last eleven years of his life, functioning as both a responsible businessman and an editor of music — a prophet for contemporary music (as he saw it) as well as its angel.

Yet it is not for his work in these areas that Sonneck is known to the broadest spectrum of readers, but rather for his missionary work as founding editor of *The Musical Quarterly,* and as a contributor to it and to many other music journals. In these capacities he was usually serious (as befits a missionary), sometimes to the point of solemnity; but he could on occasion be humorous in an ironic vein. He likewise could shed the mantle of bibliographic drudge he frequently (sometimes ruefully) wore and turn philosopher or aesthete. In all the activities so far mentioned Sonneck can be seen as a practical, highly organized individual who put the achievement of at least minimal results ahead of roseate dreams. No doubt this pragmatism derived in some degree from his Germanic upbringing and classical German education — yet it may also be significant that his father, George C. Sonneck, was by profession a civil engineer.

Oscar Sonneck showed himself in his career now as engineer, now as artist. We know from his letter of May 27, 1894, to his mother that the artist had been prominent, perhaps dominant, in his earlier years, that he had dreamt of being a famous composer. He even tried his hand at poetry. But the poet is not seen after Sonneck's return to the United States in early 1900, and the composer apparently was dormant during his years at the Library of Congress though glimpsed later in New York. The engineer, as it were, forced the artist to recognize his lack of creative talent and to give up all thought of being taken seriously. It was also the engineer, I believe, who persuaded Sonneck to leave his European home and start a new life in the United States, carefully selecting a field of work agreeable to both his tastes and his talents and — most important — a field lying not only fallow but unplowed: secular music and musical life in North America before 1800.

A formal biographical sketch of Sonneck seems unnecessary here. The main features of his career are evident in the writings about him that conclude this volume, and Irving Lowens's vastly comprehensive bibliography of works both by and about him is the key to more extensive reading. The other articles range from Dr. Herbert Putnam's funerary eulogy to Dr. Kinkeldey's reflections on his old friend's career and personality after twenty-five years — and, less solemn but even more perspicacious, Dr. Hitchcock's study of Sonneck-as-Editor. Two small but nagging mysteries regarding Sonneck's life remain, however, and they are mentioned here in the hope of eliciting information from readers who can help to solve them.

One mystery concerns the date when young Oscar, his father having died of typhoid fever in Jersey City on January 28, 1875, was taken by

his mother to Germany, where he grew up and received his schooling.[1]
Olin Downes, in an otherwise splendid Sunday article on Sonneck in the
New York Times of November 11, 1928, has him growing up and going
to school in this country until he was "about twenty." The phrase
"when he was ten years old" has been used, but without any documentation I have seen. For this guess Sonneck himself probably was responsible: in his autobiographical sketch that ran in *Who's Who in America*
from 1910 through 1928, he jumps immediately from his birth on October 6, 1873, in New Jersey to his formal education begun at Kiel in
Germany in 1883. (One suspects that for several years before that he
had a private tutor.) Carl Engel follows Sonneck in his article on his
friend in the *Dictionary of American Biography*.[2] In neither source,
however, is there any suggestion that Sonneck remained in the United
States until he entered school in Kiel.

Otto Kinkeldey, perhaps Sonneck's closest friend after Engel, wrote in
1953 that Sonneck returned to this country after an absence of "about
thirty years."[3] Even with a generous allowance for rounding off, that
figure implies that Sonneck left the United States when he was very
young. The only bit of evidence on this point supplied by Sonneck himself is indirect but, when taken with Kinkeldey's "about thirty years,"
appears reasonably convincing. In his good-natured but meticulous account of his search for his birthplace, Sonneck shows absolutely no sign
of having any memories of "99 Pacific Avenue."[4] That lack of memories
would be extremely odd — especially given Sonneck's memory as an
adult — if he had lived in his birthplace until he was ten, or even six or
seven, years old. It seems safe to assume that Mrs. Julia Sonneck went
back to Germany and established herself and her infant son in the

---

1. One former mystery, the fate of Sonneck *père,* was solved on January 5,
1982, when Bette Barker of the Bureau of Archives and History, New Jersey
State Library, Trenton, N.J., located there records of his marriage (on December
15, 1872) to Julia Meyne and of his death in Jersey City after only twenty-five
months of marriage. The death record gives his occupation as "maker of math-
ematical instruments."
2. Carl Engel, "Sonneck, Oscar George Theodore," in *Dictionary of American Biography,* vol. 17 (New York: Charles Scribner's Sons, 1935), pp.
395–96.
3. See "Oscar George Theodore Sonneck (1873–1928)" in Part 2 of this
volume.
4. See his article with that title in Part 1.

Frankfurt ménage within some months after her husband's death and when Oscar was in or just past his second year.

The other mystery concerns the fate of Oscar Sonneck's widow, née Marie Elisabeth Ames, to whom he was married at Washington in 1904 — on November 9, according to Engel's *Dictionary of American Biography* article. For years Otto Kinkeldey and many others must have walked this earth with information about her secure in their memories; but by the time Harold Spivacke and others at the Library of Congress tried to trace her that information proved elusive. If some reader of these lines knows what became of Mrs. Sonneck, we hope that he or she will notify the Music Division of the Library of Congress or an officer of the Sonneck Society.

The sixteen pieces by Sonneck in this volume by no means exhaust the store of Sonneck writings not yet published in book form. They do, however, include those that seem most interesting for either their substance or their style. In the first category, for example, are the 1908 progress report to the Music Teachers' National Association on the Music Division at the Library of Congress after only six years under Proud Papa Sonneck; the 1922 disquisition by an American music publisher on "the American composer"; and especially the 1921 letter to Carl Engel, which is extraordinarily revealing of Sonneck's personality and of some early history of the Music Division — not to mention a bit of inside history of the firm of G. Schirmer, Inc. In the second category are, among others, the early paper for the Bibliographic Society of America that shows Oscar George Theodore Sonneck at his most bookish (a modest pun that requires no apology since it is typical of Sonneck's own bilingual punning — see Hitchcock on *Suum Cuique* in Part 2 of this volume). In contrast there is the last paper in Part 1: unfinished but a good example of Sonneck's mature and more fluid style.

In the two short pieces here published for the first time, Sonneck is again seen at two extremes: as a carefully tactful, even *galant*, expositor to the ladies of the Pennsylvania Colonial Dames, and as a frankly outspoken referee or reader delivering a private and privileged opinion to a publisher. The two translations from Sonneck's German are interesting for the outside-inside view they give of American musical life just before World War I, and perhaps even more for their reflection of Sonneck's ambivalent sense of his own nationality. In one paragraph the German-Americans are "we" and all other Americans are "they"; in another it is the German-Americans themselves who are "they." There are, finally, two rather short pieces — the first and the third from last — that exemplify Sonneck's most characteristic vein of humor: tongue-in-cheek irony and satire to the point of sarcasm.

In transcribing and printing "primary sources" it is customary for the conscientious editor to distinguish clearly between the author's original usage and any corrections or emendations made by the editor. In ordinary copyediting of current writing, on the other hand, it is routine for an editor to ensure that the varied contents of a collective volume be made as consistent as possible and conform to the best current practices in spelling, punctuation, method of citation, and other details of printed language. To which category, then, does this volume belong? All but one of the Sonneck items are from a period of fifty to more than eighty years ago and thus are neither clearly old nor clearly new. There is a confusion of "house styles" and "no house styles," of pieces originally edited and pieces edited poorly or not at all.

Sonneck always had definite and often pungent ideas, and in his later years he generally clothed them in proper and cogent English. During his earlier years in this country, however, his written English often showed strong Germanic influences upon his syntax, his punctuation, even his choice of words. His editors in those days were inclined to be overly deferential or careless or both. A majority of his writings in this volume, therefore, have been edited sufficiently to make the rough places plain and to achieve a reasonable consistency — though not, I hope, to the point of erasing Sonneck's linguistic personality. I have supplied first names to surnames that are not household words today, and I have silently corrected occasional errors of fact. Those pieces printed without editing are so identified in their source notes. Footnotes in which I have updated information or otherwise commented have been distinguished from Sonneck's notes by the addition of " — ED." at the end. This practice has been followed throughout both parts of the volume.

I thank my colleague Judith McCulloh, senior editor at the University of Illinois Press and herself a member of the Sonneck Society, for her help in these and many other matters, for her good-natured acceptance of my sometimes stubborn and old-fashioned preferences in matters of style, and for making do with my firm agreement with Oscar Sonneck's dictum (in the introduction to no. 130 in Mr. Lowens's bibliography, below) that chronic consistency is desirable only in mummies. I also give warm thanks to friends — especially Mrs. Edward N. Waters, Mrs. E. Lee Fairley, and Dr. Miloš Velimirović — for help both substantive and stylistic.

The writings about Sonneck in Part 2 also have been modestly edited for consistency and smoothness or where pertinent new information could be added. No effort was made to edit out occasional duplications among authors; nor, on the other hand, to expunge points of disagreement. *Suum cuique,* as Sonneck would say — with Hitchcock to translate him on two different levels.

WILLIAM LICHTENWANGER

PART 1

Writings by Sonneck

Prize Don'ts for the Public

Don't be punctual. If a concert begins at eight o'clock, come five minutes past eight. Others will come ten, fifteen, or twenty minutes past. The noise produced by this custom is a feast for everybody. Moreover, it is very musical, as the essence of music evidently is noise.

Don't wait until the end of the last number of the program, but begin to gather your libretto and rubbers and rush out of the hall as soon as you feel the closing bars near. For the effect see first don't.[1]

Don't stop the conversation you started with your friends before entering the hall, but modulate your voices in correspondence with the dynamical effects of the music. If the orchestra has a sudden "general pause" everyone will enjoy your unexpected melodious solo.

Don't take your hats off, ladies. We all know that those behind do not care for a full view of the stage.

Don't listen to the music, but read the analytical notes. As music is an emotional art, you will never enjoy it without knowing how music is manufactured.

Don't applaud any artist, unless his manager and "his" critic tell you that he is the Siegfried of the piano or the Wotan of the kettle-drum.

Reprinted unedited from *The Etude* 18, no. 4 (April 1900): 124.

1. This piece apparently was Sonneck's first appearance in English print or in his native land. *The Etude* had offered three prizes: "Don'ts for Teachers" and "Don'ts for Pupils" (both full of sober advice) were won by Phebe J. Bullock of Ann Arbor, Mich., and N. E. Craig of Calhoun, Ga., respectively. Sonneck won in the "Don'ts for the Public" category with his tongue in his cheek and his address printed as "56 West Forty-ninth Street, New York City." A note in his hand among his papers at the Library of Congress indicates he received five dollars in prize money. — ED.

Then your enthusiasm should be hysterical. A dignified attitude is especially unladylike, when a Paderewski is the centre of adoration.

Don't go to a musical performance because you love music, but because it is the fashion. Even if you are not musical and even if you are bored, be a slave of the fashion. Pay your five dollars, patronize "Tristan" without cuts. Close your eyes and if possible your ears and take a nap. Nobody will be aware of your peaceful slumbers, but everyone will admire your deep appreciation of music. You will be awakened by the frantic applause at the end of the act in time to applaud more hysterically than the others. Such is your duty.

Don't express your opinion of a production before reading the morning paper. Whenever possible, always air your deep appreciation and knowledge.

Don't say the performance was "good," but say it was "grand." Don't say it was "bad," but say it was "horrible." If a great artist happens to make a mistake and if you happen to notice it, shake your head in disgust and exclaim: "Why, that man has no technic whatever! I never miss that note!"

Don't applaud any composition of any American composer, unless he has studied abroad, unless his score is like a blotting paper of Richard Wagner, or unless he imitates the peculiarities of "Rag-time." Then you may say: "He may not be a Richard Wagner, but he is an American composer."

A Plea for Home Products

Librarians are frequently called upon to answer questions that would baffle the ingenuity of a spiritualistic medium. I have repeatedly been asked questions like these: "Who is the best singing teacher in Europe? Shall I study harmony in Berlin or Paris? What is the most musical and at the same time the cheapest city abroad?" etc., etc. Of course, the correspondents usually forget to submit their biographies and leave the supposedly omniscient librarian entirely in the dark as to whether their teacher at home is equally dissatisfied with them as they are with him.

It would be bad policy to leave such inquiries unanswered, but how much satisfaction these naive persons derive from my advice I do not know. This, however, I do know: that such queries are highly embarrassing, and that they show a surprising lack of information concerning matters musical at home and abroad.

Do our musical students really believe this country to be without educational opportunities sufficient to make a good musician of any person of talent and energy? I fear it is more the commercial aspect of things than this idea that drives so many third- and fourth-grade [third- and fourth-rate?] pupils abroad. To have been "made in Germany" still seems to be a label that will allow a teacher to charge more for his lessons than one who graduated with honors from an American conservatory.

But things have changed during the last thirty years. Before that, or even ten or fifteen years ago, it might have been necessary for Americans to acquire an artistic training in Europe. But today it is no longer

Reprinted from *The Musician* 8, no. 7 (July 1903): [239].

necessary, certainly not for ordinary purposes. What can be learned in music abroad, our best men have imported. A MacDowell and a Horatio Parker are able to teach composition as well as anybody in Europe. With instrumental and vocal technics the case is not different, and only in the higher studies of musical history are we decidedly left behind by Europe. However, as soon as our musicians awaken to the fact that history properly treated does not mean a dry registration of dates but the best introduction into the mysteries of musical form, the most natural means of developing artistic instincts, and the easiest way to acquire a thorough knowledge of the masterworks of all countries and periods — then this last gap will have been filled.

It may be objected that every person has the right to study music where he pleases, and that it makes no difference where we pursue our studies so long as we learn something. Granted, but neither does this "none of your business" policy carry us very far, nor are we confronted merely by the problem of learning something. It is rather the problem of avoiding waste of time, superficiality, and serious obstacles to the healthy development of our musical life.

Most Americans go abroad without understanding foreign languages. To expect the "Herr Professor" to explain his rules and technical tricks in any but his mother tongue would remind me of the English lady who described the Germans as being utter barbarians because a heavy-waisted policeman could not answer her questions in the Queen's English. Consequently the American pupil is at a decided disadvantage from the beginning when studying abroad. He does not understand his teacher thoroughly, nor the teacher him. To make some headway they resort to the language of signs. How in the world can this deaf-mute pantomime result in solid and speedy progress? To be sure, such ridiculous scenes — I have been witness to more than one — would soon come to an end if only our "Innocents Abroad" saw the seriousness of the situation and associated with none but Germans in order to learn their teacher's language. Instead they very frequently board with Americans, associate with Americans, and — play poker with Americans.

The ignorance of foreign languages has still another serious drawback. It is the cause of the astonishing ignorance of musical history that I frequently had occasion to observe in Americans who studied abroad. The history of music, of course, is taught in every European music school. Not always thoroughly, as in Parma, with copious musical illustrations, but sufficiently to give the students at least the primary facts of the development of their art. Not being able to follow the lectures, the Americans are frequently excused from these courses. So, unless they privately spend some time on the subject, they return to the United States none the wiser in this respect. Here they plunge into the business of teaching, etc., and as a rule remain historical ignoramuses; for those are in the minority who read musical reviews, not to mention good books, with an object other than to imbibe critical gossip.

Perhaps even serious-minded musicians are not inclined to attach the same importance to historical studies (practical historical studies!) as I do. But what would be said of an art student who lacks familiarity with the masterworks and styles of Giotto, Mantegna, Teniers, Ribera, Goya, Gainsborough, et al.? It cannot be denied that musicians, generally speaking, take a vastly more mechanical view of art than painters, sculptors, and poets. This state of things is to be lamented, for it degrades us and our art.

Of course the American goes abroad with the ambition of returning as a second Nordica, Mason, MacDowell; and of course he leaves his native shores with the intention of studying with none but Joachim, Sauer, Stockhausen. Alas! He forgets, or rather he does not know, that these men accept but few students (and those uncommonly gifted) as their personal pupils unless forced by the statutes of the institution to do otherwise. Cases are on record where persons studied in Stockhausen's singing school for years without being honored by his presence more than a few times, but they pass themselves off as pupils of the great Stockhausen — and the public is duped.[1] We might admit that a Joachim has not his equal in this country as a teacher — though I know of impartial experts who flatly deny it — but we certainly are allowed, without running the risk of being called chauvinists, to question the absolute advantage of studying with his assistants rather than with a Bendix, Kneisel, or Loeffler here at home.

All in all, no decided advantage can be pointed out for the study of instruments abroad. On the other hand, a decided disadvantage emerges if we study singing or composition in Europe.

If singing consisted merely in producing musical sounds, it would

---

1. "The great Stockhausen" of 1903 was of course not "the great Stockhausen" of eighty years later, Karlheinz Stockhausen of aleatory composition fame. In 1903 it was Julius Stockhausen (1826–1906), noted singing teacher, who was a professor at Frankfurt-am-Main when Sonneck was growing up there. — ED.

make no difference where this art is learned. But the voice is not an instrument that produces absolute music. Singing is the art of speaking musically, and again we are faced by the linguistic problem. To sing in French means to speak French musically, and to sing in English to speak English musically. It is self-evident that the voice will have to be trained differently, once the stage of placing tones is passed, according to the innate principles of the different languages.

To sing in English perfectly, so that every word will be understood and sound like English, can be taught only by persons thoroughly familiar with the English language. They are not to be found in continental Europe, but here and in England. It is, therefore, utter folly to study singing in Paris, Berlin, or Florence, unless the object be to learn how to sing in German, French, or Italian. But the fad for polyglot dexterity is fast approaching its end, and the demand of our public for legitimate English singing increases daily. It will soon learn to discriminate between the art of singing a pure English and the hybrid art of singing English with a foreign flavor — of which the artist, as a rule, cannot rid himself even if he tries, because his entire vocal culture is based upon the principles of a foreign language.

We witness similar evils in our composers. Undoubtedly their technic equals that of European composers, but, a few excepted, they lack an American sound. By this I do not mean those silly African and Indian tendencies, but an unmistakable American character — as Brahms sounds *German*, Rimsky-Korsakov *Russian*, Puccini *Italian*, or Lalo *French*. We are clamoring for an American school of composers, but I fear it will not come if we continue to undermine its possibilities. We send our future composers to Europe for three or four or five years at an age when their characters, the individual as well as the national, are still like wax. Foreign surroundings, foreign ideals, foreign characteristics, and the artistic nationalities of their teachers cannot but leave indelible marks on their styles. They inevitably become "Colonists," as Mr. Hughes so felicitously put it.[2] Only a few succeed in

---

2. Rupert Hughes (1872 – 1956) was best known as a novelist, but he dabbled in the composition and editing of music and was a valuable writer about it. His *Contemporary American Composers* (Boston: L. C. Page, 1900) was one of the first biographical guides to American composers, and one of its largest sections is headed "The Colonists." In the revised edition, *American Composers* (1914; rpt., New York: AMS Press, 1973), "The Colonists" occupies pages 267 – 422. — ED.

gradually weeding out the foreign element in their ideas, whereas the majority continue to write German or French music "made in America."

This phenomenon is due not to the inevitable influence of a great master like Wagner, under whose spell a composer will fall regardless of his nationality, but to the deeper and more subtle characteristics that distinguish French works from German, and certainly should also distinguish American from German. To claim boldly that we possess, to a noteworthy degree, something that in this sense can be called American music would be absurd. We do not have it so far, nor will optimistic confidence alone create it. But we can clear the path for it by removing such undeniable obstacles as those mentioned. Prevent the young American composer from going abroad at an immature age, induce him to study composition with men like MacDowell, Edgar Stillman Kelly, or Arthur Whiting, and the day may come when American compositions will figure on European programs more than they do now on American.

This plea for home products does not, however, contemplate doing away entirely with music study abroad. On the contrary, *after the American has completed his course of study at home*, he should spend a year or two in Europe — less to improve his technic than to hear music. For if one excepts New York, Boston, Chicago, Philadelphia, and two or three other cities, our musical life is still rather provincial compared with that in even smaller European cities such as Frankfurt. Our operatic life, especially, cannot begin to compare with that abroad. Two years spent in professional travel through Europe, in hearing music and good artists, of whom we hardly know the names, in attending the lectures of great teachers more as critical observers than as pupils, in forming friendships with young and talented European musicians — such a course will prove of greater benefit to our students than the method heretofore adopted. It will, moreover, serve them as a healthy stimulus for the rest of their careers.

European Fallacies
and American Music

Europeans think very little of music in America. The reasons are various but simple.

First of all, hardly anybody, outside of England perhaps, takes an interest in our musical life. The few who do are hampered by a surprising lack of information. I doubt whether more than a dozen of their professional writers on music are conversant with its development in this country, or with its present status. This is even true with such writers as Luigi Torchi, who in the *Rivista Musicale Italiana* at least tries to do us justice. If those who ought to know better are found wanting, what can be expected from the average musician or the public? They, as a rule, excuse themselves with saying: "We know nothing about your music because there is nothing worth knowing." Evidently a fallacy, invented ad hoc.

Nevertheless, it contains a grain of logic. We continually pour hundreds and thousands of music students into Europe. They do not always represent our best material, but consist mostly of those people who can afford to stay some years with European masters, either privately or in the innumerable music schools. Today a sufficient reason for their emigration is out of question. Thirty years ago, when the musical opportunities of this country did not equal those in Europe, the comparatively few Americans who sought musical education abroad had a reason for doing so and, if really talented, a moral duty. Today, studying abroad is nothing but an uncritical and chimerical fashion.

Reprinted from *Music* 19, no. 3 (January 1901): 220–25.

I do not deny that among hundreds of mediocrities there are some students of considerable talent. Professor Carl Schroeder in Sondershausen, the brother of Alwin Schroeder, himself a prominent cellist and a remarkable conductor besides, once told me that his best pupils have been Americans. But he forgot to speak about the many others who were his worst.

We usually judge ourselves according to our virtues, and others according to their defects. Therefore, the really gifted Americans have to pass unnoticed in the crowd of their less gifted compatriots. This majority lacks talent, temperament, and sincerity, just as the majority of the native German or French students. Europeans do not take the minority into consideration and claim simply that Americans are not musical.

If you try to convince them of their fallacies, they argue: to stay four or five years away from home means highly increased expenses. It would be common nonsense to undergo them if your folks or your former teachers did not feel sure of your talent. Therefore, the Americans who come to Europe represent the cream of your musical talent. As not even they amount to anything, how unmusical must the rest be! And why does the cream come to Europe? Evidently because they have no sufficient educational opportunities at home. If European music schools and European teachers were not far superior to those in America, again it would be common nonsense to leave home. Of course, two more fallacies, but *dulce est desipere in loco*.[1]

It ought to be easy enough for any American to destroy such fallacies, and to imbue a just respect for the wonderful progress music has made in the United States. Alas! Either they think it a good policy not to rub against the conceit of their European masters and fellow students, or they are not capable of doing so. Most of us go to Europe at an immature age when we ourselves know but little of music in this country.

Comparatively speaking, many Americans win prizes in music abroad. Unfortunately, prizes in themselves prove little. To take a prize in Europe seldom means to be the best man. It means rather to have been the hardest worker. This is true especially in Germany, where in competition academic technic is rated higher than talent and personal-

---

1. Literally, "How sweet it is to unbend on the proper occasion"; Sonneck here probably means "Oh well, how nice to be wrong when it doesn't really matter!" — ED.

ity. Take Hans von Bülow, who certainly knew the difference between good and bad, as my authority. He said, in his paradoxical way, "Je preisser ein Werk gekront wird, desto durcher fällt es."[2] Even if Americans should win every prize offered in the music school, would that bring credit upon them as American composers? Certainly not!

To study composition with a composer of distinct personality — Draeseke, Rheinberger, Ivan Knorr, Martucci, Dvořák, Rimsky-Korsakov — means to become more or less an imitator. There is a great difference, however. An Italian will, for a while, compose à la Martucci, but both are Italians, and the music of both pupil and teacher will be essentially Italian. What does nationality in music signify? Simply the character of a nation expressed by means of its music! Now, take the immature American studying abroad. He becomes an imitator, for instance, not only of Draeseke as Draeseke but also of Draeseke as a German. His American character, from the beginning not yet developed, is in eternal conflict with the foreign character and is systematically eroded. Hence in so many works of American composers we see the unesthetic mixture not only of different styles but, what is worse, of heterogeneous nationalities.

It would be decidedly better for American art if our going-to-be composers would finish their studies with some Anglo-Saxon composers at home before coming into contact with European celebrities. Otherwise it might take them years and years of hard work and self-criticism, as it did one of our best composers, for whom I have in every way a great respect, to get rid of unnecessary European influences.[3]

If this be so, who can blame the continental Europeans for not appreciating our music? To be sure, they often applaud works of their own composers that are inferior to American products in every technical respect. But skill alone amounts to nothing. Formal beauty, too, without a typical character, has little value. Germans listening to American music justly want to hear something typically American, and not German music made in America. Eclectic art is soon forgotten. The typically national character of a work, created by a skillful personality, makes it international and a work of the future.

---

2. "The higher a work is praised, the farther its fall from praise." — ED.

3. Sonneck probably is referring to MacDowell, whom on occasion he called America's greatest composer, and who like Sonneck was a native American but received most of his education in Europe, mainly Germany. — ED.

La psychologie des masses adds another difficulty. Men never cease to be babies in the eyes of their mothers. Exactly so with the alma mater. Just after peeping out of the conservatorial eggshell [*conservatoriums-Eierschalen*], the American composer leaves Europe and usually is not heard of abroad for many years. But the Europeans still remember the academic efforts of his youth and do not care for a second edition of their unfavorable impressions. The idea that the former student might have improved and gained an interesting and independent style never enters their minds. *Menschlich, allen menschlich,* as Friedrich Nietzsche, that sadly abused person, would put it.[4] The fact that most of MacDowell's works, for instance, have been published by Germans has little to do with the internal aspect of the problem; otherwise his works would be produced more often than they are. The names of American composers appear surprisingly seldom on Continental programs, as examination of the concert reviews will prove beyond any doubt — and I believe for the reasons stated above.

The craze for things foreign has had other and still worse effects upon our singers. They learn how to sing in French, Italian, or German, and as this country produces many fine voices, it is comparatively easy for them to become stars on the European stage. If they would sail under their everyday American names, they could soon destroy the prejudice against American musicians. But they love to cover their names with exotic colors, and no European can possibly take a "Madame Maccheroni" for an American. Furthermore, they think it below their dignity to sing in English opera for commonsense salaries. Why? Probably they do not want to risk a fiasco. Their training was in foreign tongues. To sing in English without a special and equally careful training naturally would mean a fiasco.

So far we have discussed what may be termed the export of musical talent. The import has been no less detrimental to the interests, rights, and duties of our native musicians.

Ever since the middle of the eighteenth century, this country has been an El Dorado for European virtuosos, teachers, conductors, publishers, and others active in music. No doubt America owes a great part, probably the greater part, of her musical life to these influences. It would be

---

4. *Menschlich, allzu menschlich* ("human, all too human") is the phrase associated with Nietzsche. — Ed.

narrow-minded and ridiculous to favor expulsion politics. Men like Theodore Thomas have done perhaps more for the cultivation of musical taste in this country than any individual Yankee, with the exception of Lowell Mason and a few others. The same may be said of the Kneisel Quartet and kindred groups.

Without the constant flood of immigrants the United States of today would not be what they are. Among innumerable other occupations, music naturally would draw its share of immigrants. Those who settled here and labored here undoubtedly have to be considered useful American citizens and Americanized musicians. They have helped to give us a musical life of which we have every right to feel proud. In this direction there is no problem to be solved. But the question arises whether, for the future, it is not dangerous to foster open-door politics in music. I believe it is. I claim that the hundreds of newcomers are no longer in just proportion to our needs. Moreover, they continue to keep the native musicians in the background.

Our orchestras mostly consist of Europeans — our young musicians do not care to do orchestra work. But this is a sad fact that Horatio Parker has sufficiently dwelt upon. Chamber music, too, is neglected by them. At least, they do not cultivate it as much as their European colleagues do — where there seems to be no chance, there is no ambition!

Our audiences go hysterical over imported virtuosos, but treat American virtuosos, whether immigrant or native, rather indifferently. Perhaps ours are inferior in personal magnetism. Even then the contrast in applauding is not justified. Of course we want to hear the glories of the Old World, but the natural interest taken in visiting foreign musicians has become a deplorable fashion, or rather has never ceased to be a fashion, unduly protracted by the ever-speculating managers.

There certainly is reason to import, season after season, a number of European stars in order to keep in touch with things abroad; but there is no need today to keep on importing second-class music teachers. And why do these minor lights come here? To make more money than they can at home. Their ambition to make money, however, is no guarantee that they represent the acme of their profession or indeed that they are desirable for the art of this country. In fact, many of them are nothing but adventurers. Being unfit for profitable positions abroad, they emigrate, thinking themselves just good enough for unmusical America. Hear them sneer at us after their return to Europe. They tell long tales about bluffs, self-advertisement, corruptible critics, the low state of musical affairs, *e via discorrendo.*[5]

Prejudiced against us from the beginning, Europeans are apt to trust these adventurers more than the respectable class of foreign musicians who, either in articles or in private conversation, try to be impartial judges by favorably comparing our musical life and its opportunities with those abroad. Two aspects of that musical life, however, even the latter judges cannot deny. The first is a certain anti-artistic atmosphere, derived from the habit and perhaps the necessity of being in America first a businessman and only then an artist. The other point is that, in opera far more than in absolute music, we have remained a European colony.

The orchestra is European; the conductors are Europeans; most of the singers are Europeans; the words are sung in European languages, and the repertoire is European. It reminds one of the eighteenth century, when Germany to a great extent was an Italian colony in opera. But the Germans had German operas besides, and never contented themselves with such a fossil repertoire as our public does or has to do. In the United States of today opera not only is an Italian colony, but a mixed combination of Italian, French, and German colonies without any real novelties. Worse than that, operas made by Americans and sung by Americans in their native tongue have no chance. There are no American operas worth producing? Perhaps, but give our young composers a fair and repeated chance; do not turn the cold shoulder upon them after one or two failures, and things will change surprisingly soon.

In this respect, the recent venture of "grand" operas sung in English means a marked progress toward real American opera, though artistically it is a failure, in spite of the evident zeal of the performers, and Mr. Temple's clever stage managing, which has rendered the *tohuwabohu* staging in the Metropolitan Star-Circus even more laughable than it was heretofore.[6] But if the venture should prove to be a com-

---

5. "And so on and so on." — ED.

6. *Tohu wa bohu,* Genesis 1:2, rendered "without form, and void" by King James's translators; hence, "chaotic." Mr. Temple was no doubt stage manager with Henry Savage, who produced a "season" of opera in English (using some of Maurice Grau's Metropolitan "stable") before the Met's regular season opened on December 18, 1900. See Irving Kolodin, *The Story of the Metropolitan Opera 1883 – 1950: A Candid History* (New York: Alfred A. Knopf, 1953), pp. 158 – 59. — ED.

mercial failure besides, good-bye English opera. For years to come, operas with our public would continue to be a mere pretense for hearing brilliant voices. I fear the true spirit of musical dramas will not dawn upon our public until some American opera conquers Europe and the opera trust considers it a safe speculation to import it. In the meantime we shall remain the laughingstock of Europe. Of course, it matters little what people abroad think of us. Their laughter, however, ought to teach us one good lesson: honor our American masters, and throw off all unnecessary European influences.

The Bibliography of
American Music

When I was invited to read a paper to the Bibliographical Society of America, a paper on "The Bibliography of American Music," I hesitated at first to accept. Not that I lacked interest in the theme — on the contrary — but I felt very much like the student who was called upon to describe a vacuum. Indeed, worse; for a vacuum represents at least an ingeniously positive accomplishment in a negative direction, whereas the present vacuum of the bibliography of American music impresses me as a very negative accomplishment in a positive direction.

The little that has been done is easily recorded. The first to approach the problem in a friendly spirit, though rather timidly, was George Hood. In his *History of Music in New England* (Boston, 1846) he gave, on pages 154–78, a "History of Books, Chronologically Arranged" beginning with the year 1741[1] and leading, on pages 170–78, to a "List of Works Published before 1800" and after 1773 (mainly) in New England. Hood himself called the list imperfect and remarked in a footnote:

This list is made from our own and from Mr. Mason's large collection of old American books,[2] and we are sorry not to have it in our power to give it entire down to the year 1800. With a little attention the friends of music could easily complete the list, which should be deposited in the Massachusetts Historical Library as a

---

Reprinted from *Bibliographical Society of America, Proceedings and Papers,* vol. 1, pt. 1, 1904–5 (New York: The Society, 1906), pp. 50–64.

1. Earlier publications were described in the preceding chapters.

2. Lowell Mason's musical library of about 8,000 titles came into the possession of Yale University in 1873.

relic of the past. [Its contents are] worth preserving, not so much for their intrinsic value, as for their historical character. In the future, they would tell the history of the past far more impressively than the pages of history.

While excellent in spirit, this appeal was woefully characteristic of the historical horizon of Hood and later historians, who, as I have expressed it elsewhere, naively viewed the history of American music through a New England church window. Hood enumerated a number of psalm-tune collections and the like, but paid no attention to secular music. This unpardonable sin of omission, together with the pardonable sin of omitting even many "sacred" titles, renders a perusal of the list today almost useless. The same is true of the list of collections of sacred music for schools and churches in the United States since the year 1810, as Nathaniel D. Gould gave it on pages 231–33 of his *History of Church Music in America* (Boston, 1853). How could it be otherwise if "only such works as contain three hundred pages and upwards are referred to in this list"!

Hood was also mistaken if he thought that with a little attention the friends of music could easily complete the list. Surely he would have changed his mind had he lived to see Mr. Wilberforce Eames concentrate his bibliographical genius on the history of a single book. Though Mr. Eames's "List of the Editions of the Bay Psalm Book" (in Sabin and separately issued, 1885) owed life to a broader bibliographical impetus, it lastingly contributed also to the groundwork in a special field of musical bibliography.[3] This fact notwithstanding, the historians of American music prefer to stagger on without it. For instance, you will not find Mr. Eames's list mentioned in the "General Bibliography" as attached on one page and a half to Mr. Louis C. Elson's clever *History of American Music* (New York, 1904), whereas quite a few of the sixty-odd titles enumerated bear only slightly on the subject of American music.

---

3. Joseph Sabin's *A Directory of Books relating to America, from Its Earliest Discovery to the Present Time* 16 (New York, 1885): 27–39. Sabin's work, more an irregular periodical than a one-man multivolume work or series, is better known under its half-title *Bibliotheca Americana*. Sabin died in 1881, but his work was continued under the editorship of Wilberforce Eames and then others until well into this century. Eames's "List of Editions of the Bay Psalm Book" was issued at New York as an offprint in 1885; was revised and printed as part of Eames's introduction to the first facsimile reprint of the Bay Psalm Book (New York: Dodd, Mead, 1903), which was itself reprinted entire by Burt Franklin at New York in 1973. — ED.

This "General Bibliography" — decidedly the most superficial part of Mr. Elson's work — is exposed to still severer objections by the omission of a book that must be considered indispensable to the historian of American church music. I mean, of course, Mr. James Warrington's *Short Titles of Books, Relating to or Illustrating the History and Practice of Psalmody in the United States, 1620 – 1820* (Philadelphia: Privately printed, 1898; 96 pages).

Mr. Warrington informs us in the preface that for many years psalmody attracted his attention to such a degree that he began to collect material for a "History of Psalmody among English-speaking Peoples." Then the "disturbing element of Puritanism" compelled him to abandon the original design and he resolved to compile, first of all, a "History of Psalmody in the United States, 1620 – 1820." As the contemplated work was to be accompanied by as exhaustive a bibliography as possible, Mr. Warrington, seeing the limitations of individual research, printed his *Short Titles* as a "tentative list issued for the purpose of inducing librarians and collectors to report [to him] any books which are not included in it." To my knowledge this appeal has been heeded, and librarians and collectors should now in turn prevail upon Mr. Warrington not to delay a second edition of his pamphlet, revised on the same basis of professional courtesy.[4] Twice revised, the list would certainly justify the author in dropping the "tentative," and we might reasonably expect a

---

4. Sonneck must have had occasional contacts with James Warrington, a Philadelphia accountant by vocation, and must therefore have known what, from feelings of delicacy and diplomacy, he chose not to mention in this paper: that Warrington's mind had been grotesquely diverted from his "History of Psalmody" by a situation far more disturbing to him than Puritanism. Warrington's *Story of an Unpublished Crime: Being the Court Records (with Annotations) of a Case That Is Not Allowed to Be Tried* was privately printed for him at Philadelphia in 1913. On July 25, 1899, he had sold his existing "psalmody" collection to a group headed by Waldo Selden Pratt for the Hartford Theological Seminary in Connecticut, the sale price being $5,000. One gathers there were differences of opinion as to when and how the collection was to be turned over to the seminary, how much of the $5,000 was to be used for judicious additions to the collection, and other details. On March 27, 1902, according to Warrington, he returned to his modest rooms to find the locks changed and the whole collection gone. His charges were heard in the Court of Common Pleas at Philadelphia in June, 1904. No action resulted, apparently not even a counter suit. For another decade Warrington labored bitterly but vainly to obtain redress for his alleged wrongs. No "History of Psalmody" by Warrington ever reached print. Alas, that so much diligence and learning bore such tasteless fruit! — ED.

bibliography of psalmody in the United States that would stand the test of time. It is to be hoped that Mr. Warrington will then abandon the present chronological arrangement, or, at least, that he will add an author and title index, for the present chronological arrangement without such an index seriously interferes with the usefulness of his admirable work.

Mr. Warrington's effort to cover bibliographically the wide field of American psalmody was preceded by an attempt, more bold than satisfactory, at a general bibliography of American music in 1876. To his *Dictionary of Musical Information* (Boston, 1876), John W. Moore added in small type, on pages 187–211, "A List of Modern Musical Works Published in the United States. (Giving the popular title of each publication, with the name of the author or compiler, when known, and the year in which many of the older works appeared, but not including periodicals. From 1640 to 1875.)"

As a matter of fact, a good many other things were excluded from the list. Only psalm-tune collections, instruction books, some cantatas, operas, and the like seem to have come under Moore's eyes. Yet the list should not be underestimated, as it contains a good many references otherwise unavailable. If John W. Moore possessed the power of application to issue, in 1854, a *Complete Encyclopedia of Music* that, in its day, certainly was the most conspicuous work of the kind in the English language, then the failure of such a born compiler to furnish more than a skeleton of a bibliography of American music proves how difficult, not to say impossible, the task must have been in those days. Had Moore cast but one glance at the three hundred bulky volumes in the Library of Congress that contain most, though by no means all, of the sheet music published in our country between 1820 and 1860, I believe he would have abandoned his attempt in despair.[5] I fear those not famil-

---

5. Though this paper was not published until 1906, it apparently was written in 1904, when Sonneck had been at the Library for only two years or so. He therefore had not yet learned what he speaks of in the next paper, written in 1908: Moore could not have examined the bulky volumes at the Library of Congress because they were not there. In 1854 they were stored in the Department of State, as specified by the copyright acts of 1790 and 1831. The act of 1859 ordered them and all other deposits transferred from State to the Department of the Interior, whence they came to the Library some decades later after it was firmly established as copyright headquarters by the act of 1870. (It is true that the act of 1846 *added* the Smithsonian Institution and the Library of Congress as places of deposit, but a reasonably workable system was not achieved until after the 1870 act.) — ED.

iar with the musical output of our country have no idea of the task that would have confronted him.

To further illustrate this problem, I take pleasure in referring to the fact that a "List of Southern Music, Published between 1860 and 1869," which Mr. Walter Rose Whittlesey of the Library of Congress is compiling, alone contains 6,000 titles, and this gentleman proposes, with a courage demanding our respect, to furnish as pendant a "List of Northern Music" published during that mighty decade, a list that will comprise at least 20,000 titles[!].

In speaking of unpublished musical bibliographies, perhaps I may be permitted to draw your attention to an effort of my own. When collecting material for a "History of Secular Music in the United States during the Eighteenth Century," I found it necessary, of course, first to form a bibliographical basis for the work. The result was a "Bibliography of Early Secular American Music," completed in 1902. By consulting histories, catalogues, and bibliographies, by personally examining certain public and private collections from Providence, R.I., to Charleston, S.C., and — above all — by extracting data from the scattered files of our early newspapers, I believe (without false modesty) I have given (on 550 pages manuscript, including a subject index with valuable biographical information) a fairly complete record of secular music and the literature of music as written, proposed for publication, and published in our country prior to the year 1800. In detail or in form the work may not quite be to the taste of bibliographers, but if even Mr. Warrington shares the prevalent, though absolutely incorrect, opinion that "early music in the United States . . . was entirely sacred"[6] I hope that the severest critic, should ever the work be published, will admit that it throws new light on our early musical life.[7]

Probably other authors are also engaged in smoothing the path of the future historian of American music, but the works mentioned represent the bibliographical literature of our musical life as far as I know. Incidental (and accidental) bibliographical information may be found in such books as F. O. Jones's *Handbook of American Music and Musi-*

---

6. See the preface to his *Short Titles*.

7. Since the above was written, the book has been printed for me by H. L. McQueen, Washington, D.C. . . . in a revised and condensed form. — O. S. [For a summary of the book's subsequent printing history see no. 45 in the Lowens bibliography and note 3 to the Kinkeldey article, both in Part 2 of this volume. — ED.]

cians (Canaseraga, N.Y.: Privately printed, 1886), Henry M. Brooks's *Olden-Time Music* (Boston: Ticknor, 1888), and Julius F. Sachse's *Music of the Ephrata Cloister* (Philadelphia, 1903), in the several histories of music in America, in musical and nonmusical American and foreign magazines, as also in compilations not limited to American conditions — foremost among these, perhaps, John W. Moore's *Complete Encyclopedia of Music* (Boston, 1854; appendix, 1885) and Arthur Low Bailey's noteworthy *Bibliography of Biography of Musicians in English* (1899).[8] However, until an effort is made to fit all these references into some sort of bibliography of bibliographies, or even a list of lists, the material will remain practically inaccessible except to students gifted with the rare bibliographical scent. These rare individuals will also soon discover that a mass of information awaits them at the sesame of bibliographies and histories, either bordering on music, or, for one reason or the other, including special branches of our art. Before a congregation of bibliographers it will be sufficient to mention at random in this connection names like Julian, Dunlap, Durang, Wegelin, Roden, Thomas, Brinley, Roorbach, Sabin, Hildeburn, and Evans.

Without underestimating what has been accomplished, it may safely be argued that the bibliography of American music is still in that stage of infancy when the future of the infant depends upon the care bestowed upon his proper development. Under the circumstances, and as this society intends not merely to record deeds but to promote bibliographical research, my paper would be one-sided should I not at least outline the main problems that, in my opinion, still confront us. My horoscope may not be substantiated in the near or far future, but that is a risk that all astrologers run.

The whole subject matter lies in three distinct, though overlapping, spheres:

I. Produced by Americans.   II. Published by Americans.
III. Owned by Americans.

To these may be added, as an appendix to the second sphere: produced by Americans, but published in Europe.

A further analysis points to the three main sections of musical literature:

a. Music,

---

8. Published (at Albany?) by the *New York State Library Bulletin* as no. 17 (1899) in its Bibliography [Series]. — ED.

b. Literature of music (history, biography, esthetics, etc.),

c. Instructive (theoretical or technical) books and music.

It is also clear that the subject matter may be approached on this principle:

Music —

a. Produced by Americans,

b. Published by Americans,

c. Owned by Americans,

and similarly the literature of music and the instructive material, or on this principle, i.e.:

Produced by Americans —

a. Music,

b. Literature of music,

c. Instructive literature.

Subordinate or superordinate, as required by the bibliographical theme, may become an investigation with reference to special

a. Periods,

b. States and places,

c. Individuals,

d. Kinds and forms.

Further subdivisions *ad libitum,* closely following the most minute classification imaginable, will show an almost unlimited number of special bibliographical problems. In fact, the possibilities become so kaleidoscopic that it is obviously impossible to trace them all. Certain problems, however, appear to be more important than others for the time being, and seem to call for the earliest possible solution in the interest of historians, librarians, collectors, dealers — in short, of all who are interested in American music.

It is, for instance, exceedingly to be regretted that we possess no compilation that would fulfill the same mission in our country as Hofmeister's *Handbuch* does in Germany.[9] In this work a splendid record is kept of all musical publications in very much the same manner as Hinrichs, Kayser, or Heinsius do for the book literature. That such a music

---

9. For order brought out of the bibliographical chaos, see Carl Friedrich Whistling and Friedrich Hofmeister, *Handbuch der musikalische Litteratur: A Reprint of the 1817 Edition. With a New Introduction by Neil Ratliff* (New York: Garland Publishing Co., 1975). — ED.

publishers' union catalogue is badly needed can hardly be doubted by
any person who handles music, and who is now compelled to wade
through any number of catalogues in order to find the publisher, the
date, and the price of a particular composition. It is plainly the duty of
the Music Publishers' Association to help to remedy a state of affairs
that has become embarrassing to those publishers and dealers who
stand above petty jealousies or shortsighted fear of competition. Why,
in a country world-famous for the spirit of enterprise, nobody has
summoned enough courage to become the American Hofmeister[10] is
difficult to understand.[11]

Indeed, we narrowly escaped the humiliation of seeing a union list of
American music embodied in the stupendous compilation of a Viennese
publisher, Franz Pazdírek. This gentleman conceived the bold idea of
issuing a *Universal Handbook of Musical Literature* covering all countries and periods. The first twenty volumes were to contain the music
still obtainable at first hand, and about ten further volumes, under the
editorship of prominent historians and bibliographers, were to be devoted to the literature of books on music and to music published or
unpublished before the nineteenth century. Unfortunately, this extraor-

---

10. "To become the American Hofmeister" has a sadly familiar ring to it.
Just since World War II a pair of serious efforts have been made: one by Virginia Cunningham, who as head of the new enlarged Music Cataloging Section
of the Copyright Office in 1946–57 expanded the music section of the *Catalog
of Copyright Entries* into something as close to an American Hofmeister as she
could make it on the basis of copyright deposits alone, and tried to persuade
music publishers to send her section copies of *everything* they issued. The other
effort was by Richard S. Hill, head of the Reference Section in the Music Division, Library of Congress (1939–61), who tried in the late 1950s to arrange for
R. R. Bowker and Company in New York to put out a musical companion to its
Publishers Weekly. The first attempt failed partly because an unsympathetic register of copyrights replaced the sympathetic one in midstream, but also both
failed partly because certain music publishers opposed a project that would ad-
vertise the produce of their competitors. — ED.

11. Mention should be made, however, of the complete catalog . . . published by the Board of Music Trade . . . 1870. This useful classified list of 575
pages has now become so exceedingly scarce that copies are said to bring about
$100. — O.S. [The original edition was entitled *Complete Catalogue of Sheet
Music and Musical Works Published by the Board of Music Trade of the United
States of America, 1870*, and appeared in 1871 with no place of publication
given. It was finally reprinted in 1973 by the Da Capo Press of New York in a
complete facsimile folio edition, with a splendidly informative and authoritative
introduction by Dena J. Epstein that reveals all sorts of esoteric data about
music publishing in this country during the latter half of the last century, a
world that was *terra incognita* even to Oscar Sonneck. — ED.]

dinary undertaking seems not to have been well managed financially, and since the first volume of the first section (covering the letter A) was published last year the work appears to have come to a standstill, though the entire first section is said to be ready for the printer.[12]

Having mentioned Hofmeister and Pazdírek, let me also recall to your memory the names of Eitner, Kade, Vogel, Schwartz, Friedlaender, Fétis, Wotquenne, Weckerlin, Torchi, Gaspari, Barclay Squire, and others, be it only to show the contrast between the interest taken in musical bibliography in Europe and America. Perhaps the allusions to the activity of these scholars, many of whom merely exploited the resources under their surveillance as librarians of particular institutions, will increase the number of those American librarians who pay to music the respectful attention that the art deserves as a factor of civilization. With particular reference to musical bibliography, it will be admitted that we have done very little so far to show the world what our music libraries really possess. To my knowledge, none of the American institutions that house valuable musical collections has issued an "up-to-date" catalogue of its music and literature of music.[13] In a country like ours, where the centers for musical research are very few and scattered, such catalogues would be hailed with relief by music students; for, after all is said, a card catalogue is of but local value.

---

12. In another footnote Sonneck adds, "Since the above was written, the publication of the *Universal Handbook* has been resumed and now covers letter C. I have tested the work and can only say that it is extraordinary both in its *fortes* and its shortcomings." By 1910 the letter Z of this remarkable *Universal-Handbuch der Musiklitteratur aller Zeiten and Völker* had been encompassed, the whole totaling (according to the Library of Congress card) thirty-three volumes in nine. Sonneck's characterization is still apt. While the work is weak in reporting publications outside Europe, it is a godsend for what it does report — especially in band music, operetta, and other popular fields poorly represented in more high-toned and specialized lists of works, and especially from Central Europe and its fringes (including Russia). — ED.

13. It goes without saying, I hope, that I am somewhat familiar with the fact that the lamented Mr. James Sumner Smith, of Yale University, compiled a remarkable catalogue of the Lowell Mason collection, that the printed card catalogue of the Allen Brown collection in Boston is nearing completion, that the New York Public and the Newberry libraries possess reference catalogues of their musical libraries. Nor do I forget the Peabody Institute (Baltimore) catalogues, or the bulletins of the New York Public and Boston Public libraries, and I know that the *Catalogue of Joseph W. Drexel's Musical Library* (Philadephia, 1869), was followed by the *Lenox Library Short Title List, No. XL ("Drexel Musical Library")* shortly after the Lenox Library had acquired the collection; but all this by no means weakens the statement made above.

If, as in the Library of Congress, such a printed catalogue — be it only a "short" or "medium" title catalogue — is a physical impossibility for years to come, or impossible for administrative reasons unless issued for class after class, then at least an effort should be made to list the musical literature published before 1800, inclusive of manuscripts. The Newberry Library,[14] the public libraries of Boston[15] and New York,[16] and the Library of Congress[17] individually and certainly combined possess a very considerable number of coveted early European, not to mention early American, works. If the respective librarians could be induced to issue a list of this early material by way of well-planned cooperation, they would not regret the step. The scientific historical study of bygone music would be facilitated immensely in our country; and, incidentally, these institutions would enhance their reputations in a Europe where at present they are greatly underestimated.[18]

In turning to music produced by Americans, Mr. Warrington's contemplated bibliography of psalmody and my bibliography of early music may be said to cover the eighteenth century for several years to come. Economical reasons would, therefore, forbid us to waste bibliographical energy on a duplication of these works when other and not less important themes have not yet found their Perseus. For instance, a bibliography of nineteenth-century operas, in continuation of the list given in my essay "Early American Operas" (*Sammelbände der IMG* 6 [1905]: 428–95) is badly needed, as are also bibliographies of American oratorios, cantatas, orchestral and chamber music. Though it may seem incredible, the fact is nevertheless true, owing to the lack of an American Hofmeister, that in compiling want lists for the Library of Congress I encountered more obstacles in tracing, for example, Ameri-

---

14. See Mr. George P. Upton's descriptive article "The Musical Department of the Newberry Library" in *Nation* 48 (1889): 361–62.

15. Mr. William Foster Apthorp's description was reprinted in the annual report for 1894.

16. See Hugo Botstiber's descriptive article with short titles of rarities, "Musicalia in der New York Public Library," *Sammelbände der Internationalen Musikgesellschaft* 4 (1903): 738–50.

17. See the cursory remarks in my article "Nordamerikanischen Musikbibliotheken," *Sammelbände der Internationalen Musikgesellschaft* 5 (1904): 329–35. The articles to be found in *Music* (1898, 1900) and in *Etude* (1900) are antiquated and amateurish.

18. Mr. H. E. Krehbiel's *Libraries in the United States of America* in the new edition of Grove (1906), largely based on material furnished by me, gives a good bird's-eye view of music collections in our country.

can orchestral music than European. Even when limiting myself to the most prominent contemporaneous American composers, I again and again had occasion to regret the nonexistence of reliable individual bibliographies. To illustrate this, you will find it by no means an easy task to compile an accurate and exhaustive list of MacDowell's works, inclusive of reprints, revisions, dates of composition, dates of first performance, and so forth. When preparing a lecture on MacDowell I had occasion to try it. Suspicious of omissions, I submitted the list to the composer, with the result that after Mr. MacDowell had very kindly obliged me with marginal notes, I knew less than before.

This experience, I hope, will prove how much we music librarians would appreciate it if somebody, perhaps a student in our library schools, would select as his graduation theme the compilation of a bibliographical list of works by representative contemporary American composers. By giving such themes the library schools would assist in supplying the demand for expert musical librarians, a demand that is gradually increasing and that, at present, it seems difficult to supply to our satisfaction. If we retrace our steps to earlier American composers, for instance to Benjamin Carr, I believe none but an experienced bibliographer will be able to cope with the difficulties of research.

Further interesting themes of varying difficulty and extension would be a list of American compositions published in Europe, a bibliography of American psalm and hymn tune collections published after 1820, and a bibliography of American national music. The latter has been undertaken, as I stated, for the Civil War period by Mr. W. R. Whittlesey, who has also collected much material for a list of compositions by our colored musicians. Finally, separate lists of music relating to the several presidents would certainly be of interest, revealing incidentally the greater or lesser popularity of the different presidents with us musicians, not to mention with the public in general.

The bibliography of the literature about music, written by or relating to Americans and American conditions, presents not only fewer problems but ones of decidedly less difficulty because much of the material has been embodied, in one form or the other, in general reference works, trade lists, and in the several accumulative periodical indices. Exactly for these reasons it is surprising that no bibliographers of a musical trend of mind should have paid Saint Cecilia the handsome tribute of collecting the embarrassingly scattered data. Of course, we Americans cannot boast, with the possible exception of Thayer, of such stars of first magnitude as Ambros, Chrysander, Spitta, Riemann, Kretzschmar, Gevaert, Fétis, Tiersot, Torchi, Florimo, Pedrell, Parry, Squire, Grove, Hadow, and Maitland, but our writers on music shine brilliantly enough in the historical firmament to deserve more attention than the bibliographical astronomers have paid them. For instance, Henry Edward Krehbiel, while prevented by unfortunate circumstances from giving full sway to his historical talents, has done an extraordinary amount of useful work.[19] A bibliographical record of his writings would show the versatility of this remarkable man, would make a vast amount of well-digested information accessible, and would encourage others to step forward as the champions of his critical colleagues, such as Dwight, Mathews, Upton, Apthorp, Elson, Hale, Henderson, and Finck.

To be sure, the work of these men has not frequently assumed the form of books. It is mostly stored away in the labyrinth of newspaper and magazine files; but, fortunately, the days are bygone when only voluminous books were considered worthy of bibliographical attention. One really cannot write a bulky volume on every interesting topic without watering the stock of information. As a matter of fact, in these days of special research, books that are entirely the fruit of independent research are becoming fewer and fewer, whereas the serious reviews devoted to any special branch of knowledge are becoming more and more the primary source of the most advanced information.

With these remarks I do not wish to convey the impression that I am advocating a bibliography of our entire literature of music, as printed in the magazines and newspapers that employ music editors, but I do believe that the time has come for a by far more nearly complete and, at the same time, better selected record of this literature than is to be found in the cumulative indices. The Anglo-Saxon, with all his vaunted progressiveness, is deep in his heart a conservative who will remain faithful to the tried good, though the untried better would be of more

---

19. What these "unfortunate circumstances" were is not apparent from various accounts of Krehbiel's life. Perhaps the single-minded Sonneck was perturbed by the fact that during the earlier part of Krehbiel's career, and even after he went to the *New York Tribune* about 1883, his duties were not confined to music but included other reporting and general editing as well. No doubt Sonneck was completely unimpressed, if he even knew, that Krehbiel is supposed to have played a major role in devising the baseball box score now in use by newspapers for over a century — this while he was a baseball reporter for a Cincinnati paper in the 1870s. — ED.

service to him.[20] Our reference indices to periodical literature are certainly good enough for the average reader interested in music, but music historians sorely need something better.

In speaking of music periodicals, those who have occasion to occupy themselves with American music magazines will agree with me that one of the first bibliographical problems that demand a solution, once bibliographers have shaken off their apparent indifference toward music, will be a more or less descriptive list of music periodicals issued in the United States. A step in the right direction was taken in the year 1899, when the New York Public Library issued a list of "Periodicals Relating to Music" in both it and the library of Columbia University. Though this list is not limited to American periodicals, it may even today be taken as the working basis for a compilation, as suggested. This compilation, I fear, will be unusually difficult, as most of our music periodicals enjoy but a short life, as they are in the habit of suddenly changing title or publisher, as their number is legion, and as comparatively few of them are to be found in our libraries.

But the blankest spot in the bibliography of American music has not yet been touched, and it is only with a keen sense of humiliation that I, as an American writer on the musical life of America, lead you for a moment into this "darkest Africa." What I mean is simply this: we do not even possess a bibliography of books and articles on the music history of our country. Still worse, with the exception of certain subjects mentioned above, not a single, separate branch of the literature relating to our own musical history has been accorded a conscientious bibliographical treatment. In vain you will look for a halfway complete list of contributions toward the history of American opera, American oratorio, American national music, American musical instruction, American musical societies; and the effort to locate a comprehensive or even fragmentary list of bio-bibliographical sketches of individual American musicians will be just as futile. Yet we continue to write histories of

---

20. Here Sonneck seems to be paraphrasing in reverse a German aphorism that says "The best is the enemy of the good" (see the translated article that follows). Here also, as in certain other passages in his writings, he clearly thinks of himself as a Teuton or German-American in a land dominated by Anglo-Saxons. Only in his last years, perhaps, did he think of himself as a distinct *homo Americanus.* — ED.

music in America, though we know, or at least should know, that bibliography is the backbone of history.

All these facts, I believe, justified me in calling the bibliography of
American music a deplorable vacuum. Perhaps it was not very patriotic
to thus cruelly expose our shortcomings, and I might have painted conditions more roseate, but in the world of science self-criticism is
infinitely more becoming than self-glorification. Fortunately, self-
criticism and pessimism are not synonymous, and I, for my part, feel
confident that in a few years it will be a by far more pleasant task than
now to speak of the bibliography of American music.

The Music Division
of the Library of Congress:
Methods, Policies, and Resources

⌣

The Library of Congress was founded in 1800 with an appropriation of a lump sum of $5,000 for the purchase of books. About 3,000 volumes had been accumulated by 1814, when the Library was destroyed during the British attack on Washington. Then Thomas Jefferson's collection of about 7,000 volumes was acquired by our government, and the collections had increased to 55,000 volumes when in 1851 the Library was again in part destroyed by fire in the Capitol. Not more than about 20,000 volumes were saved. Today, or rather at the end of the fiscal year 1908 (June 30), the Library of Congress contains about two million and a half of books, pamphlets, manuscripts, maps, prints, and pieces of music. More than four hundred and fifty persons are employed in this palace of books; the annual appropriations for the increase of the collections have grown from $1,000 in 1818 to more than $100,000, and the total appropriations for all purposes now reach the colossal sum of nearly $800,000.[1]

Reprinted from the *Papers and Proceedings of the Music Teachers' National Association at Its Thirtieth Annual Meeting, George Washington University, Washington, D.C., December 28 – 31, 1908,* Studies in Musical Education, History and Aesthetics, 3rd ser. (N.p.: Published by the Association, 1909), pp. 260 – 87.

1. Nearly three quarters of a century later, at the beginning of fiscal 1983 (Oct. 1, 1982), the corresponding figures were: total items accessioned in LC, 76,762,191; total LC employees (including 424 paid out of funds from other agencies and LC gift or other special funds such as printed catalog card sales or copyright fees), 5,246; the 1982 appropriations for "books general" (formerly

These figures bear a message. They imply a vast and complicated scale of operations, extraordinary problems for administrative genius, and opportunities for systematic development probably not equaled in any other national library. I say "national library," for though originally founded as a library for Congress and still fully maintaining this character, the Library of Congress has gradually become — if not in name, at least in fact, policy, and by circumstances — our national library. Historically considered, this tendency was made possible when, on August 10, 1846, an act of Congress directed that one copy of each copyrighted book, map, musical composition, etc., should be delivered to the Librarian of Congress. It is notorious that this far-reaching act could not be properly enforced until the passage of the copyright law of 1870 placed the copyright business under the Librarian of Congress, called for the deposit in the Library of two copies of each copyrighted article, and provided for the removal to the Library of Congress of existing copyright deposits from the U.S. Department of the Interior and from the United States district courts.

Thus the Library of Congress was enabled to exercise one main function of a national library: namely, in the words of Herbert Putnam, Librarian of Congress since 1899, "so far as possible, to preserve a continuous and unbroken exhibit of at least the important issues of the American press." Of great importance was further the international copyright act of March 3, 1891, which made it possible for foreign authors to obtain (under certain restrictions) copyright in the United States upon the same terms as native authors, except that the fee for entry in the case of foreigners is double that for the native author, $1.00 instead of fifty cents. Under the operation of this provision the privileges of copyright in the United States have been extended to the authors (including the composers, of course) of many European countries. The effect of this international copyright act was particularly far-reaching on the musical side of the Library of Congress, inasmuch as it allowed

---

"increase general"), including all types of material for the general collections including Music, but not including the Law Library, Congressional Research Service, Copyright Office, and a few other special units, $4,266,900; total LC appropriations for all purposes, in fiscal 1982, $206,450,204.23; funds transferred to LC from other U.S. government agencies, $11,491,333.24 (including receipts from catalog card sales and copyright fees, though a part of the latter go into the U.S. Treasury); plus fiscal 1982 receipts from gift and trust funds, $6,962,886.23. Grand total in fiscal 1982 of LC receipts from all sources for all purposes, $224,904,423.70. — ED.

European composers to deposit for purpose of copyright protection two copies of every musical composition *printed abroad,* whereas books proper (with certain modifications) cannot be copyrighted here unless printed in the United States.[2]

Not until the removal of the Library of Congress in 1897 from the Capitol to the new building was a special Music Division created, and I hasten to add that its present location and equipment are still temporary. The collection accumulated prior to 1897 was neither accessioned, classified, catalogued, nor made accessible. The labors of the Division during the four years after the removal were largely to reduce the material to order and make it available for use. But the current accessions, then numbering already more than 16,000 items a year, had also to be incorporated, and no one can appreciate better than I the task confronting my predecessor of infusing a semblance of life into a dead mass of several hundred thousand pieces of music. The present method of classification and cataloguing, the policy and manner of systematic development, the broader scope of usefulness date from the reorganization of the Music Division in 1902, when all the books on music and all music manuscripts — in short, everything of primarily musical interest — were put under the custody of this Division.

Aside from gifts, international exchanges through the Smithsonian

---

2. This sentence refers to what came to be known as the "manufacturing clause" demanded by the book-making industries (printers, binders, et al.) in order to prevent American publishers from having their books manufactured abroad where standards of living were lower and manufacturing costs comparably lower. Attached to the 1891 copyright act, when provision was first made for foreign printed matter to be copyrighted in the United States, it applied to all books printed in the English language, whether manufactured in Boston, London, or Hong Kong. Music, fortunately, even a song with English words or an opera with English libretto, was not similarly restricted.

Over the years various provisions of the manufacturing clause have been weakened, and in the copyright act of 1976 the Register of Copyrights was instructed to restudy the situation in 1982 and recommend to the Congress whether the remaining provisions should be kept or should be done away with entirely. The United States book-manufacturing industry may have been down but it was not out — with the result that in 1982 the Congress voted to continue the remaining provisions in force for at least another four years. President Reagan vetoed the bill, saying that in this matter his administration was in favor of free competition; but the Congress chose the bill as the first one on which to exercise its right to override the president's veto by more than a two-thirds majority. The manufacturing clause as set forth in the 1976 act is still with us. — ED.

Institution, and other minor sources, the accessions to our Music Division accrue mainly through copyright and purchase.[3] After the two copies of a musical composition deposited for copyright have been recorded in the Copyright Office, copy A is filed in the archives of that division and copy B is turned over to the Music Division.[4] Material that has been purchased comes to this Division from the Order Division, where all commercial accounts are kept. After receipt in the Music Division, the books on music and the music proper are accessioned as to source (copyright, purchase, gift, etc.) and are classified according to a scheme of classification that was devised and adopted after a critical examination of the schemes in force in the principal American and European libraries and with a view to the particular needs of the Library of Congress. There is nothing very startling about this scheme, which has been printed as a book of 112 pages, except its minuteness and general disposition.[5] We divide the collections into three large groups: music, represented by the letter M; literature of music (all biographical, bibliographical, historical, philosophical, etc., books and pamphlets on music), represented by the letters ML; and all theoretical or technical [pedagogical] material, represented by the letters MT. This last group includes not only books on harmony, counterpoint, pianoforte methods, etc., but also all purely instructive music such as etudes and instructive (teaching) editions, for instance of Beethoven's sonatas. Therein our classification differs materially from most schemes, which distinguish only between music and books on music of every description. This difference has led to a misunderstanding of our resources

---

3. In 1980 the Library distinguished ten sources, of which nine may benefit the Music Division. Copyright deposit and purchase were still the two most important sources, but gifts were then more numerous and exciting (the silver lining in the income tax cloud), there were occasional transfers from other government agencies (the Army, State Department, Smithsonian, et al.), and some foreign exchanges benefited the Music Division. Domestic exchanges were very few, because other libraries seldom have what LC wants and because the time consumed usually makes a "deal" unfeasible. The Special Foreign Currency act (which used to be known as the "wheat loan" bill or Public Law 480) profited the Music Division in certain soft-currency countries; and U.S. government publications came to the Music Division when pertinent, as did Cataloging-in-Publication copies. — ED.

4. Sonneck's statement as to the treatment of copyright deposits of music was an oversimplification even in 1908, and the procedures have varied greatly over the years since then. — ED.

5. For information as to the publishing history of the class book, see note 12 at the end of the Kinkeldey article, below. — ED.

when a comparison was made between our and other collections of books on music. If the customary distinction is made the basis for comparison, naturally a substantial part of our MT section would have to be added to the ML section, with the result that instead of possessing about 8,000 books on music, the Library of Congress really possesses about 12,000.[6]

The three main sections are systematically and logically subdivided, proceeding from general to special, by forms, instruments, subjects, periods, countries, as the grouping would suggest itself with slight differences of opinion to every musician and musical scholar. Each subdivision is represented by a numerical symbol, the sequence of numbers bearing, as far as possible, some logical relation to the subject matter to which they have been assigned. Thus, for instance, M1500 means full scores of operas, M1503 means vocal scores of operas, M2000 full scores of oratorios, M2003 vocal scores of oratorios. At first sight the minuteness of the scheme bewilders, but it is in keeping with the bewildering extent and variety of the collections and it is planned to provide for future as well as for present needs. Upon examination it will be found that this apparently rigid scheme is elastic, permits both contraction and expansion, and may therefore be used with convenient modifications in smaller or, if such exist, larger collections. For instance, a small library, instead of using our numerous subdivisions with the corresponding numerous class numbers for books on the history of opera, would keep all such books alphabetically arranged by author under our number ML1700, regardless of country, period, and so forth. We ourselves, I hasten to add, do not use more subdivisions than are convenient for our purposes; the others are simply provisional. While to a novice the scheme may look somewhat complicated on paper, we have found it to be comparatively simple in application; and while im-

---

6. About 1959 Library statistitions outside the Music Division protested that the MT classification (of which Sonneck had been duly proud) was neither fish nor fowl and did not fit into the Library's overall statistical structure. Since then the statistical distinction has been made only between pieces of music (M material, including bound scores and hymnbooks) and books (ML material, whether a 16-page pamphlet or multivolume sets of Grove). MT (music theory) materials go as either books or music, depending largely on whether they would be read or played. Phonorecords, with which Sonneck did not have to concern himself, are of course a world apart — and since August 1, 1978, that world is no longer situated in the Music Division, but rather in the newly created Motion Pictures, Broadcasting and Recorded Sound Division. — ED.

provements have suggested themselves from time to time, some too late for insertion, the scheme fortunately has, on the whole, stood the test of time and strain.

At any rate, it is not merely a theoretical scheme on paper, as some schemes are. It is really applied. That means, the books and the music are really filed on the shelves according to this scheme, regardless of size, bulk, or date of acquisition. In other words, all vocal scores of oratorios, all symphonies, all biographies, all books on harmony and so forth stand together on the shelves in the sequence of the scheme. The advantages of such a method for supplying a reader with as much material as possible in the shortest possible time would appear to be obvious, but as a matter of fact the method is not in use everywhere, and in some important institutions books and music are still shelved regardless of their contents merely by size or date of accession. Our method has some further advantages, but I shall mention only one that is more or less characteristic of the Library of Congress. Our policy is to give responsible, serious students access to the shelves. This privilege would be of no earthly use unless books on the subject in which a person is interested were kept together in one particular group. The applied scheme of classification together with this privilege will obviously save a student much time, and the satisfaction of thus having saved him much time more than outweighs the fact that he occasionally turns a book upside down or forgets to replace it at all.

After all is said, the opponents of a subject classification of music, which the Library of Congress champions, have only one argument to offer that deserves serious consideration. It is this. We do not keep all the works by one composer together, but we separate them according to form, instrumental combination, and so forth. Thus the works of Raff, for instance, will not be found in one place under Raff, but his operas are shelved under Raff with all other operas, his symphonies, songs, etc., with the symphonies, songs, etc., of other composers. I do not know but that the other scheme would work better in a small or medium-sized collection; but in a huge collection, like ours, it probably would not for certain physical and technical reasons. The whole matter is one of preference. It depends upon the answer to the hypothetical question: are musical readers more interested in studying chamber music, songs, oratorios by different masters, or in studying the chamber music, songs, oratorios [i.e., all the works of all types] by one master? The answer is just as problematic as the question is hypothetical.

After a book or composition is classified and before it is bound and placed on the shelves, it must be catalogued. All books on music are turned over for this purpose to the experts of the Catalogue Division. Their catalogue cards are then printed and supplied to us by the Card Distribution Section for author and subject entries; and, if a book is a collection of essays, it may happen that thirty or more cards are filed in the catalogue for one single book. After years of steady work the Catalogue Division has finished cataloguing all our books on music, but it must be noted that this catalogue exists in the form of printed cards only — not in book form, as some inquirers appear to think.

Music proper is catalogued not in the Catalogue Division but in the Music Division, and no cards are printed for music of any kind. This might seem to be an anomaly, yet the explanation is simple. Exactly because our catalogue experts are expected to work with precision and accuracy, the task of handling about 20,000 musical compositions yearly, in addition to many thousands of books, would be physically impossible. Consequently, we of the Music Division are forced to struggle with the problem as best our inadequate force of six persons can.[7] We have evolved a set of cataloguing rules that answer our needs and all practical purposes. In most cases two cards must suffice, one for the composer and the other for the form or combination. In the case of operas, songs, and other works with specific titles we also enter a shorter card under the title, so that generally no more than three cards are written. We abstain from analyzing the contents of collections, and we bestow analytical attention generally only on such volumes as those of the different *Denkmäler*.

Formerly the *Catalogue of Copyright Entries*, issued by the Copyright Office, was printed in such a form that to use it even as a current index to composers was impossible. Consequently we of the Music Division made desperate efforts to catalogue every copyrighted piece of music that came to us. Two years ago, however, the form of this monthly bulletin was changed so that any copyrighted piece may now be traced

---

7. The cataloging of music, as opposed to books about music, remained in general the responsibility of the Music Division until the Great Reorganization of 1943 when a number of jobs were taken away from the Music Division and put into the new Processing Department. The old arrangement had one definite advantage: those who cataloged music also spent part of their time helping readers and performing other functions that enlarged their vision when it came to cataloging. — ED.

under either composer or title; hence we now catalogue in the Music Division only such compositions, or rather classes of compositions, as in our judgment warrant the labor involved. And, of course, this rule applies to every piece of purchased music, inasmuch as we do not buy music that is not desirable.[8] The rest is filed on the shelves according to the classification scheme. For this material the copyright *Catalogue* is presumed to be a sufficient guide. Nor do we really need such a guide, because the scheme of classification in itself acts as a guide and allows us to find every piece of music whether catalogued by us or not.

This obliging feature of the classification scheme is our salvation and that of the public, because more than one-half of our music collections remains uncatalogued. The catalogue is complete only for the material received since 1897, and in its present form of entry only for the material received since 1902, including such arrears as we have been able to consider from time to time. Even for this material a complete catalogue by subject or form does not exist. We are bending all our efforts toward completing the subject catalogue at least for the most important classes (such as in orchestral and chamber music), but I fear that we have a Tantalus task before us.[9] Only for one class is our subject catalogue really complete: for our collection of full scores of operas. That is also the only branch of our collections of which so far the catalogue has been printed in book form.

One other part of our catalogue has aroused interest, in Europe perhaps more than in America. Every number of each musical magazine currently received is analyzed by me personally, and subject cards for every article thus analyzed are written by me (yearly about 4,000) and

8. One blushes for Sonneck that he should speak so assuredly of "music that is not desirable" — and later of "undesirable music" and "musical trash." The Music Division's clientele at that time was presumably narrower and more homogeneous than it came to be thirty years later, and Sonneck the librarian obviously still had to learn that what was trash to him might be a jewel to someone else. One would guess that by the time he spoke as a historian, in the passages referred to by Mr. Chase, below, he had broadened his viewpoint on musical esthetics as a librarian as well. — ED.

9. The M Subject Catalog did in time become a formidable and highly useful weapon — until, late in World War II, a non-service-oriented high official in the new Processing Department succumbed to the passing vogue for classed catalogs and had the lovely subject catalog literally rent asunder to provide the makings of a classed catalog (which itself became useful only after many years had passed and an elaborate word index to the class scheme was contrived to aid the user). — ED.

Samples of Sonneck-made cards for the Music Division's periodical index. The subject entry at the top he wrote off perhaps eight or nine years after the article was published in 1898, and it must certainly represent one of the earliest public uses of the word *musicology*. At the bottom is his author entry for his own MTNA paper, reprinted on pages 31-59 of this volume.

entered in a separate catalogue.[10] As we receive currently about ninety musical magazines, of which fifty are important ones from Europe, the Library of Congress possesses an index to current music periodical literature such as perhaps no other institution can boast of. Not only this, but back sets are gradually being taken up and the beginning has been made toward a catalogue of articles on music in the nonmusical American magazines in greater numbers than in *Poole's Index* and more systematic besides. The value of what has been done already is recognized by European scholars, as well as American, and it is realized that by sheer necessity some day this periodical index of the Library of Congress will become invaluable, indeed one of the principal assets of the Music Division.

After a book has gone through these and sundry other library processes it is at last ready for use, and "the purpose of the administration is the freest possible use of the books consistent with their safety; and the widest possible use consistent with the convenience of Congress." Regulations limiting use are adopted very sparingly and only as experience proves them to be necessary. For instance, there is no limit to the number of books a reader may draw for reference use in the Music Division itself, but a certain limit, of course, governs home use. The latter, inasmuch as the Library of Congress is in principle a reference and not a circulating library, is restricted to persons designated by law, such as members of both branches of Congress and of the diplomatic corps; but the Librarian has the power (and he is known to exercise this discretionary power with liberality) to extend the privilege to persons engaged in research that is likely to widen the boundaries of human knowledge. This power applies also to the Music Division, and he does not hesitate to include, upon proper and convincing application, heads of music schools, conductors of important musical organizations, prominent local musicians, and others who for special reasons and for a specified time need the home use of certain material that is to be had only at the Library of Congress or is too expensive for a musician's private library, or cannot be obtained at all at the music stores. Resident musicians are, of course, expected to consult very rare items at the Library,

10. It is not every library that has on its staff a periodical indexer of the stature of Oscar Sonneck, who in this discussion does not even mention the thousands of author cards he scribbled off along with the subject entries (see the samples reproduced here). — ED.

which is open to readers from 9 A.M. to 10 P.M. on weekdays and from 2 P.M. to 10 P.M. on Sundays and most legal holidays.

For the convenience of our music readers a pianoforte has been installed and is used frequently. Not, of course, for finger exercises, but for *prima vista* reading purposes. This distinction, by the way, could not at first be made clear to certain of our patrons, and some of the tricks invented by that imperishable class of people who will grab the whole hand when a finger is offered were really amusing. One ingenious future Paderewski, for instance, asked ostensibly for a Beethoven sonata, placed it on the piano, and gleefully practiced a Czerny etude.[11] Nonresident musicians engaged in such serious research as defined by the Librarian may occasionally avail themselves of our services through what is called the system of interlibrary loan. That is, they apply to their local library; it, in turn, applies to us and we send the material to that particular library for the applicant's use at his expense, but not to him personally. It goes without saying, of course, that we do not forward musical books or music such as it is the duty of his local library to supply. In this manner, we are glad to assist quite often some well-known scholars of Boston, New York, and other cities. Indeed, in the interlibrary loan we see one of the vital duties and functions of our national library.

As to types of use and users, it would be difficult to classify them, or to point out such as do not frequent other libraries in America. Here, as elsewhere, some seek information on points of musical technique, others on bibliography, history, or esthetics, on national songs, on the finer distinctions between the different editions of a master's works, on questions of copyright, on formation and management of libraries, on prices of rarities, on best methods for music in schools, etc., etc. In short, we meet a variety of subjects approached as the case may be from the standpoint and with the interest and methods of the businessman, the lawyer, the person desirous of musical culture, the critic, the scholar, the music teacher, the conductor, or the "mere" musician.

In addition to the bona fide reader, we also deal with a large number

---

11. This phenomenon has not changed since Sonneck's time. For years the Music Division had a frequent visitor to the piano room who was called "Beethoven": first because he would ask for the Beethoven sonatas (an edition was kept handy for such occasions) and then practice scales or anything else, and second because his physiognomy was reminiscent of Beethoven as usually pictured. — ED.

of persons who merely ask questions, either in person or by letter. As far as the Library may be expected to answer them at all, we do so promptly and to the best of our ability. Generally the inquiries pertain to good or best books on special subjects or, preferably, to biblio-graphical and historical facts.[12] If these do not require too elaborate research, every librarian who considers himself first a friend of the pub-lic and second a Cerberus of books will answer gladly all inquiries that reach him. We draw a diplomatic line, however, if we are asked to fur-nish articles ready made for club use, or to give a complete list, with prices, of all the works of Bach, or to trace the first composer guilty of consecutive fifths.

The extent of these legitimate and illegitimate inquiries has not been made a matter of statistics here, nor do we lay much stress on checking pedantically the number of real readers or the number and authors of books used. We hold that it is not the quantity of use that counts but the result, the effect of use. Still, it may be interesting, as a matter of comparison, for you to learn that we supply annually about 16,000 books, pamphlets, and compositions to some 3,500 readers.[13] Consider-ing that Washington, a city of about 350,000 inhabitants, is not yet one of our main musical centers and that for obvious reasons practically only two-thirds of the population really count, this use of our Music Division is considerable and gratifying.

Were the capital of the United States located at one of the main musi-cal centers of our country, possibly the Music Division would be used to a far greater extent. But since the Library of Congress is located at Washington, and since every American now looks to the Library of Congress as to our national library, this question of relative use cer-tainly does not enter into the problem of how far the musical collections of our national library should be developed. Logically, since a special

---

12. Here, on the other hand, there has been quite a change since Sonneck's day, a change due largely to the technological developments in photocopying and in sound recording. Not very many readers now are content with simple questions of historical fact or advice as to the best *book* on a subject. — ED.

13. Compared with Sonneck's reader statistics for fiscal 1908, the figures for fiscal 1982 show 32,107 volumes and other units served to 19,019 readers at the Library. If interlibrary loan requests, written reference inquiries, the ever-ringing telephone, photoduplication requests, and miscellaneous special searches are added to those figures, the total number of items involved in service to users both at and away from the Library was an estimated 45,339 used in serving 47,176 users (estimate of 4,000 items involved in 16,956 telephone services). — ED.

music division was created in our national library it should at least be made worthy of being a special division in a national library so that the musicians of our country will take a reasonable professional interest in the collections.

It was on this premise that a policy of systematic development was outlined in 1902. Even more important was the premise that in music, as in other fields, the Library of Congress as a national library exercises functions differing, at least in theory, from those of a state, municipal, or college library. This is true whether the functions pertain to ready reference or to deep research. Briefly stated, the aim of the Library of Congress is to provide a reasonably comprehensive collection of all material bearing in any way on music in America, and more particularly on American music. Beyond this goal, what the Library of Congress attempts to do is exactly the same thing as is attempted by any other large library that recognizes that the art of music is and always has been a very essential factor in, and feature of, civilization.

The starting point of our policy also clearly suggests the characteristic difference between the Library of Congress and the national libraries of Europe. Those libraries have only a slight interest in American music and music in America, except insofar as American composers, methods, or conditions have become or will become of international interest. We, on the other hand, have a dual responsibility. American music, as the product of American brains and American industry, is deemed to be of paramount importance in our national library; yet the peculiar development and status of music in America, being mainly a reflex of music in Europe, compel the Library of Congress to collect the musical product of European brains and industry very much in the same manner as European libraries do or would like to do. The difference in attitude is merely one of degree, and the boundary line of competition begins where the community of historical interests stops: roughly speaking, about the year 1700.

For this reason, the Library of Congress does not at present and as a rule enter into competition with European institutions with reference to music, published or manuscript, before 1700. Any such attempt would clearly tend to scatter the scarce and costly works of the old masters still further and give undue prominence to a selfish *museum of costly relics* policy over the best interests of the scholar. What sense would there be, for instance, in paying heavily for possibly unique copies of original editions of a few works by Palestrina, and thus possibly prevent some

European institution from putting before the Palestrina specialist a full set of his works? Such a set, or even a collection of the original editions representative enough to be of any practical use to the American scholar, the Library of Congress at this late date could never hope to acquire even if its entire appropriation were given to the Music Division. If such works are of great interest in some other direction, let us say as characteristic and sufficiently illustrative specimens of early music printing, it is part of our policy to make exceptions to our rule; and such exceptions are frequent, of course, as concerns early English music. Nor do we turn our back pedantically on recognized musical landmarks if their price is at all within the means of a public institution. Therefore we did not hesitate to buy a fine copy of Caccini's *Nuove Musiche*. But on the whole, the Library of Congress contents itself at present, so far as music before 1700 is concerned, with acquiring that music as reprinted principally in the splendid historical subscription publications undertaken by foreign governments, learned societies, and such firms as Breitkopf & Härtel of Leipzig.

It is different with the old printed books on music. In the interest of the American scholar, the Library acquires the originals extensively because extremely few of these books have been reprinted and because it is still entirely feasible to form a representative collection at a reasonable cost. Beginning with the eighteenth century, *the Library of Congress aims at a collection of music and books on music sufficiently comprehensive to ultimately relieve the American scholar of the necessity of consulting European libraries, except for research not bearing directly or indirectly on music in America as a reflex of music in Europe.* This policy involves the need to be inclusive rather than exclusive in collecting characteristic works of any form: first, by masters known at any time to the American public; second, by those not known here but having an evolutional relation to them; third, by all masters not affected by this distinction but who are essential for a proper historical perspective. We also hold it to be a sound principle of development that by generously considering the present, we prepare best for the usefulness of the collections to the future historians for whom our perhaps now commonplace present will be a fascinating past. Strange to say, this obviously correct attitude is not shared by all my European colleagues, but I believe I succeeded in driving the argument home when I had occasion to present my theories of methodical development of musical libraries before the congress of the IMG [International Music Society] at Basle in 1906.[14]

These are the main, one might say the philosophical, principles governing our policy of systematic development. But of course any number of minor theoretical and practical considerations enter into the problem. For instance, as the Library of Congress is a reference and research library, not a circulating or a conservatory library, scores have precedence over orchestral parts. The latter are acquired as a rule only if scores do not exist — as, for instance, with most symphonies of the early nineteenth century. Similar considerations govern the acquisition of arrangements, with the exception of vocal or pianoforte scores, which very frequently must take the place of full scores if such do not exist or are too expensive (in the case of works neither artistically nor historically very important). In addition, of course, the usefulness of piano-vocal scores in breeding familiarity with the great operas or oratorios is obvious. If important works are not to be had in good printed editions, we make it a point to acquire them in contemporary manuscript copies, transcripts made specially for the Library of Congress, or (if preferable) in photographic reproductions. Nor does this policy stop at older works, as we occasionally have important modern works transcribed that are not to be had in printed scores — as, for instance, Heinrich von Herzogenberg's beautiful *Erntefeier*. On the other hand, we feign to take no interest in musical autographs except of desirable works that exist in no other form, may be had at a price only slightly higher than that of a manuscript copy, or come our way (as has really happened) on the presumption that they were a copy and not the autograph.[15] After all, what help would a sincere interest in autographs of the great masters be to us if a letter of Wagner costs several hundred marks and a

---

14. Sonneck's successors have blessed him without ceasing for his foresightedness in making it standard policy to acquire items when they are new and the channels routine rather than forcing future librarians to go to more trouble and pay higher prices when the items are no longer "current." For an abstract of Sonneck's presentation at Basle, see No. 57 in the Lowens bibliography, below. — ED.

15. Over the past forty years or so the Music Division has been able to avoid feigning no interest in musical autographs from time to time through the beneficences of patrons such as Mrs. Gertrude Clarke Whittall and the Heineman Foundation. Yet the economic wheel goes round and round, and where it stops nobody knows. — ED.

Beethoven sonata fetches 40,000? You all know the fable of the fox and the grapes, and so do we.

In the matter of autographs the great European libraries — think of the stupendous collection of Bach autographs at the Berlin Royal Library — are so immeasurably far ahead of us that to wrest a few specimens from them on the open market would be folly. In this respect our professional policy is exactly the same as expressed above in regard to original editions of Palestrina. Yet, once the problems nearer us have been solved, we may perhaps afford to give expression to the dictates of sentiment and acquire such autograph specimens in the same spirit as an American patriot may acquire Washington or Lincoln souvenirs. It is entirely different with autographs of American masters. These should be saved from disappearance and destruction, and the logical place to preserve the manuscripts of great American musicians for future scientific or tributary reference is the Library of Congress, our national library. That goal, however, cannot be accomplished unless the American composers or their heirs or public-spirited citizens concur in this view, entrust such national treasures to our care, and follow the example set by Edward MacDowell, Dudley Buck, Professor and Mrs. John Knowles Paine.[16]

It is one thing to have a definite policy, another to carry it out effectively. We had the advantage of not being hampered by rigid traditions, and we therefore could adopt such constructive methods of systematic development as will always suggest themselves when a good collection is to be built from the ground up. The usual — one might almost say, the old-fashioned — method is to patiently wait for and check desirable items as offered in the catalogues of publishers and secondhand dealers. This method is probably the only feasible one for new books or new music. It is even a fairly sensible one if a collection is so far advanced that the problem merely is one of filling in gaps. Yet even then the objection is that during the patient reliance on one's good luck with secondhand catalogues the gaps may become too numerous for successful ultimate action, and that many years may pass before annoying gaps can be filled.

---

16. The goal envisioned by Sonneck has come closer in recent decades, thanks to the generosity of American composers and other public-spirited citizens, thanks to the campaigns waged by Harold Spivacke, Edward N. Waters, and Donald L. Leavitt, and — of course — thanks to the Internal Revenue Service, at least prior to the Tax Reform Act of 1969. — ED.

In the Library of Congress we, too, use this passive method where it may be applied with substantial results, but we go far beyond it by bringing also the specialist's constructive energies and abilities into play. He is supposed to know where his collections require strengthening and what books are needed to make the collections symmetric and of practical use to the general reader or scholar, and it is part of his business to compile systematic want lists covering the interests of his special division. This is not the work of a few months, of course; it takes years of careful work, such as only a specialist with adequate knowledge of his particular subject may be expected to undertake. Moreover, it is frequently a very monotonous task, and perhaps this is one of the reasons why specialists prefer the Pandora's box of secondhand catalogues.[17] Naturally they do not advance this monotony as their real argument against the constructive method, but they say that such want lists are of no practical use in view of the generally inadequate appropriation allotted to music divisions. This is a grave mistake. Not even in the Library of Congress are such long want lists acted upon at once; but when the Librarian of Congress does see his way clear to switch a substantial sum to the Music Division, we are ready for the campaign at a moment's notice. The lists are then placed into the hands of reliable and energetic dealers. It is to their advantage, of course, not only to ransack their own stock for report but also to keep a sharp lookout on the market for the things we want, particularly for rarities. Moreover, they can afford to supply us such large orders at a very much lower price than would otherwise be feasible, and the saving in clerical labor, correspondence, and therefore expense of time and money is also considerable.

After all, the test of any method is the result it produces, and this constructive method undoubtedly has brought speedier and more substantial results to our library than would have been possible by the catalogue-checking method alone. The results repay the specialist amply for his many months of tedious toil in compiling such want lists, which otherwise fail to give the personal satisfaction that the compilation of a catalogue or of a bibliography affords.

To give an adequate idea of the extent of this activity, I may mention that a fairly comprehensive list of all the books on music published before 1800 was compiled by me for our own administrative benefit,

---

17. Pandora and her box of evils seem oddly placed here. Perhaps Sonneck was thinking of a "grab bag" in some more elegant form. — ED.

plus a representative list of such books from 1800 to date, plus further systematic want lists of early English psalm-tune collections, orchestral and chamber music of all nations, early vocal scores of operas, etc., etc. Those of last year alone fill 350 typewritten pages, and many more are to come. Perhaps the most difficult and interesting, though one of the smallest, was that compiled in the interest of our collection of full scores of operas. Realizing the impossibility of buying many old opera scores on the open market — I mean scores of the seventeenth and eighteenth centuries that, with the exception of the French, generally exist in manuscript only — we embarked on the project of acquiring the historically important operas of olden times in transcripts made specially for the Library of Congress.[18] This project called for much painstaking and complicated preliminary work. The idea is not absolutely original with us, but the scale — we are reaching out in all directions for several hundred transcripts — was unprecedented. We had the satisfaction of seeing Professor A. F. H. Kretzschmar, to whom as the greatest living authority on the history of opera the list was submitted, advise but comparatively few modifications and additions.

All this may create the impression that the Music Division of the Library of Congress is working with unlimited means. It is not. We have a liberal but limited allowance that the Librarian stretches if he considers it to the advantage of the Library. At any rate, we are obliged to expend this allowance with discrimination and by a strategic concentration of our financial artillery on certain points. In other words, we are working along the lines of carefully laid plans of development in a chronologically backward direction, and we allow ourselves to be swayed from this path only in case of emergency. These plans carry into effect what I have elsewhere termed the theory of *concentric* development. This means that first the nucleus of a library of moderate size but complete in itself was formed, what one may call a good working collection. Then we drew a wider circle; and now the circle that we are

---

18. The hundreds of large and spaciously laid out green volumes in M1500 are another example of Sonneck's foresight. Today it very likely would cost almost as much to microfilm the scores from which they were copied as it cost in 1908 to have them copied by hand. A signature I recall as "Waldemar Kupfer" will be found at the end of a great many of these hand copies, and I have often tried to visualize Herr Kupfer working at a desk — I do hope he had his own desk — with ink bottle near and eyes and pen racing back and forth. — ED.

drawing, and that is so wide it will require years to perfect it, reflects the "duty of the National Library to aid the unusual need with the unusual book."

On July 1, 1908, the Music Division housed 481,568 volumes and pieces of music; 8,020 biographical, historical, and similar books and pamphlets on music; and 10,990 theoretical and technical works, of which possibly 4,000 would be classified at other libraries with books on music: in all, 500,578 volumes, pamphlets, and pieces.[19] Of this huge collection naturally the bulk came to us through copyright: during the last six years a total of 127,405 items, the fiscal year 1905–6 reaching the maximum of 25,086. For the past fiscal year [1907–8], however, only 13,609 items were reported, and our accessions through copyright will not exceed the last figure materially in the future. This calculation, however, does not permit the inference that suddenly the actual number of copyright deposits has fallen off. On the contrary, it is keeping pace with the development of the music-publishing business in our country; but the Music Division no longer accepts for its files every copyrighted article as it still did in 1905–6. We now weed out and leave in the archives of the Copyright Office all material that plainly has either no value whatever or only an ephemeral value — in short, what we or any other library would unhesitatingly describe as undesirable. This material, however, is not lost to posterity, since with the aid of the annually published *Catalogue of Copyright Entries* it may be traced and even placed before an insistent reader.

That other libraries would desire all the material we do accept for our files is doubtful; yet, given adequate appropriations, they surely would not object to at least one-half of what is now considered desirable for the Music Division. This material includes the majority of European copyright deposits; and although in the last several years European music publishers have sent in a much smaller proportion of their whole output than they did even six years ago (thus forcing us to buy extensively from desirable current European music), still the copyright act of 1891 tends to swell our collections every year with thousands of scores,

---

19. At the end of fiscal year 1982 the comparable figures were: accessioned volumes and pieces of music, 3,690,395; books and pamphlets on music, 528,315 (statistics on MT matter are no longer kept separate; if an MT item is a school songbook or a teaching edition of a sonata, it goes with the M figures, whereas if it is an MT 125, orchestra program book, or a book on how to sing, it goes with ML in the 528,315 figure above). — ED.

songs, piano pieces, and other material that libraries elsewhere, here and in Europe, are compelled to buy. And this advantage will be ours until the rules governing copyrights are radically changed. However, the 13,609 items that were selected this year by the Music Division from the mass of copyright deposits do not represent the actual number of our accessions for the year. These accessions amounted to 20,759 items.[20]

In other words, leaving aside gifts and exchanges, we purchased last year alone about 7,000 volumes of music and books on music; and in 1905 – 6, when we still accepted all copyright deposits of music, our total accessions reached the enormous figure of 28,977. Within the last six years we have bought more than 19,000 items, ranging in commercial value from twenty-five cents to the lustily climbing market price of Caccini's *Nuove Musiche* or Marco da Gagliano's *Dafne*. Keeping all this in mind and taking a bird's-eye view of the entire huge collection of more than half a million items, I should say that two-thirds of it are copyrighted trash from the standpoint of the musician. The other third is at least desirable, and we may safely estimate that at least one hundred thousand items merit preservation from the standpoint of the historian.

Until 1902 the Music Division depended for its resources almost exclusively upon the double-edged effects of the copyright deposit regulations. Leaving aside the several thousand items copyrighted by European music publishers between 1891 and 1902 — mostly music by present-day composers and therefore very little by the majority of noteworthy composers of the nineteenth century — the collections until 1902 represented in general only the product of American publishers, either as original compositions and books on music by Americans or as reprints of European publications. Furthermore, though music copyright in our country dates at least from 1783, the peculiar history of our copyright registration as it affects the Library of Congress, and to which I have already briefly alluded, accounts for the fact that our collections embrace, in the main, musical products of American publishers only from 1819 on. But within these limits, our collection of American music and books on music, while not absolutely complete, is by sheer force of circumstances unique and always will be. The output of the last sixty

---

20. Figures are no longer kept on items coming to the Music Division as to source (copyright, gift, purchase, et al.) — ED.

years is distributed on the shelves according to our system of classification, but that for the thirty years previous is preserved in 300 substantial volumes that have been assigned a place of honor. These 300 volumes elicited what is to my knowledge the first newspaper article on our
collection. It appeared in the Washington *Globe*, November 3, 1854,
and was from there reprinted in part in Dwight's *Journal of Music*,
November 11, 1854, under the heading "Extraordinary Collection of
American Music." "Recently arranged and neatly and substantially
bound," it was termed "the most extraordinary collection of music, we
suppose ever beheld in this country or perhaps in any other."

This compliment applies, of course, with still greater force to the sixty
years following.[21] As to American music or music printed in America
previous to 1819, it must suffice to remark that our collection of sacred
music, principally the psalm-tune collections, is good, but probably not
as good as the Hubert Main collection in the Newberry Library in
Chicago, or the James Warrington collection now under Professor
Waldo Selden Pratt's care; and not better than those at Yale, Worcester,
and elsewhere. Nor have we much reason to boast of our early secular
American music. Our only consolation is that no really comprehensive
collection of that kind exists anywhere, and probably cannot be formed
at this late date because, through negligence, ignorance, and natural
forces of destruction, most of this music has entirely disappeared.[22] It is

------

21. Sonneck's figures here are hard to comprehend and hard to square with
his own classification scheme and long practice. The "300 bulky volumes" of
copyright deposits relate to the period defined in the class book as 1820–60.
But those volumes in M1A.12 are the lesser part, statistically speaking, of the
Music Division's holdings in American music of that period. The year 1819 has
no discernible significance in American music publishing history; 1831 would
have made more sense, since only then was music per se accepted for copyright,
and it was only in the 1840s that the number of deposits increased sharply with
the appearance of lithographed sheet music covers. No doubt Sonneck was
thinking of the Copyright Act of 1819, which gave to the U.S. district courts the
responsibility for hearing all actions involving the exclusive rights of authors
and inventors to "their respective writings, inventions, and discoveries" — in
equity as well as at law. He apparently viewed this as the first recognition of
music under the copyright law, and began keeping a box in which he placed the
occasional deposit of music. This 1819 act no doubt influenced him in setting
up the period 1820–60 as a separate class for music copyrights in his
classification scheme. But music had been accepted for copyright as early as
1794 under the appellation "book." — ED.

22. Sonneck would today be both astounded and gratified to see how unduly
pessimistic he was in 1908 about the survival of American music prints whether
before or after 1800. Sonneck-Upton and Wolfe (see the preceding article) to-

easier to find medieval codices than the compositions of Francis Hopkinson or Alexander Reinagle and other American worthies of the eighteenth century. True, the latter arouse only a largely patriotic antiquarian interest, but it is exactly this purely American point of view that
defines their importance in our national library. Thus, when the late
Mr. Lewis J. Davis presented some autograph keyboard sonatas of his
ancestor Reinagle to us, we rejoiced more than if they had been autographs of such composers as Hasse or Galuppi. Similarly, the autograph
scores of MacDowell's *Indian Suite*, Dudley Buck's opera *Serapis*,
Paine's unfinished symphonic poem *Lincoln* — these autographs appeal
to us quite as fully as would important autograph scores by Tchaikovsky, Brahms, or César Franck to a European librarian. And, again,
the musical by-products of the Civil War would hardly be deemed attractive abroad, yet in our country their patriotic associations give them
a distinct value regardless of the question of musical merit. For instance,
the first edition of "Dixie," by dint of its scarcity and the spell its stir-
ring melody casts over all good Americans, is a treasure from our point
of view immeasurably more precious than the first edition, let me say, of
"Die Wacht am Rhein" or the Garibaldi "Hymn." Of these by-products
of the Civil War period, we possess probably by far the most important
collection in existence. And if we have succeeded in rescuing much of
the Southern musical ammunition, which was not copyrighted in the
Union and for this and other reasons has become very rare, this success
is due largely to the familiarity with this type of publication on the part
of my assistant, Mr. Walter Rose Whittlesey.

Before 1902 the Library of Congress possessed ludicrously few European publications, whether music or books on music. European music
copyrighted since 1891, some old English song collections, a few odds
and ends of mysterious provenience including a pitifully lonesome edition of Beethoven's symphonies — that was about all. It would have
been absolutely impossible to study here with profit the music of even
the greatest masters. A vast desert extended wherever one looked beyond the comparatively narrow confines of the American publishing industry. We have had but six years to remedy this frightful state of affairs. It
is, therefore, only fair that our efforts be judged in the light of this fact. We

---

gether offer handsome testimony that literally thousands of prints, both songs
and piano pieces, have survived but were hidden beneath the debris of time
from his pioneering eyes. — ED.

are not given to megalomania. Neither are we victims of the equally obnoxious habit of micromania. We know better than any casual observer possibly could know where the shoe pinches us. On the other hand, we no longer discourage comparison with the most famous institutions of the Old World.

Remarkable, in some respects unsurpassed, as our resources have become almost overnight, they are not yet what our plans of development are bound to make them within a few years. Hence the expert will find a certain lack of symmetry in the branches of the collection. Some are fully developed, others not yet so. To judge the merits and defects of our present collections therefore calls for the same attitude of mind as would viewing a half-finished monumental building. For instance, our collection of national songs and their literature, while substantial enough for a good working library, is not what we expect to make it.[23] Similarly, our collection of vocal scores of oratorios, cantatas, even operas, our organ music and so forth will be strengthened so considerably in the near future as to be in keeping with our fully developed sections. Then again, only during the last two or three years have we found it convenient to turn our ambition to eighteenth-century music. Though probably we already have more of the latter than may be found in other American libraries, the collection could not bear a moment's comparison with, for example, that at the Royal Library in Berlin. Still, it is growing rapidly into something really useful to the historian, and we already possess quite a few things — particularly in manuscript or of English imprint — that are not frequently found. We appear to have, for instance, some symphonies by that master of strange epicurean tastes, Anton Filtz, not mentioned in Hugo Riemann's bibliography. We have about thirty of the forty-five cembalo concertos of C. P. E. Bach, and we were able to supply some of Haydn's unpublished divertimenti to the editors of the complete edition of his works now in process of publication.

On the other hand, our collection of old opera and oratorio librettos is painfully weak, and yet without these the student of early opera and

---

23. "National songs" was a blanket term defined by Sonneck in the classification schedule as encompassing "folk, patriotic, political, typical, traditional, etc., music" — in other words, songs that in some way have a direct association with a particular nation. Such a term may have been valid in 1904; but the trouble is that the various categories have gone on their separate and burgeoning ways since the time of World War I. — Ed.

oratorio will always find himself handicapped.[24] Furthermore, our collection of music either printed or in manuscript from before 1700 does not deserve to be called a collection. In fact, we have little music of this kind unless it is printed in English or has been reprinted. For the reasons stated, we do not waste our energy and funds in that direction, nor on autographs [signatures] of great musicians of which we possess mostly only such ones as come incidentally in dedication [inscribed] copies. Finally, not even the original editions of the works of Bach, Mozart, Beethoven, et al., so important for text-critical and editorial purposes, are numerous on our shelves. Until recently we contented ourselves with their works in the *Gesamtausgaben* [collected editions], but we are now gradually going back to the original editions. In this connection, it is significant that not a single library exists that can boast of complete sets of our classics in the original editions.

These, and others, are our defects and weaknesses, temporary or intentional, if the single branches of our collection are compared with each other or if our collection, as a whole, is compared with other collections of corresponding magnitude and scope. Fortunately we have our strong points, too, and strong not only in plan but in fact.

The figures for our books on music speak for themselves, yet it may be added that we are particularly strong in biographical and general historical literature and in current periodicals. With the orders already placed, it is only a question of weeks or months until the Library of Congress may point to a collection of books on music surpassed only in a very few categories. Unprecedented has been the accumulation of books on music printed before 1800. When Mr. Henry Edward Krehbiel compiled his valuable article on American libraries for the new Grove, we still had reason to send him conservative information. The volume was published in 1906, and already the information concerning us is entirely out of date. Mr. Krehbiel, when dealing with the Lenox Library, took occasion to remark that their moderately trustworthy catalogue of 1869 contains twelve volumes of sixteenth-century musical

---

24. [Sonneck speaking:] It is characteristic of the speed of our development that these words, written in October [1908], are now absolutely incorrect. Not only did the acquisition of the Longe Collection of old English plays enrich us by several hundred early English opera librettos, but the Library of Congress has also since acquired the famous Albert Schatz collection of more than 11,000 librettos — presumably the largest collection of its kind. — O.S. [The number actually was about 12,200. — ED.]

publications, forty-eight of the seventeenth, and 483 of the eighteenth. He does not make it clear whether or no he alludes to books on music or music *and* books. Nor does it appear that this collection has been very materially increased since then.

The Library of Congress, however, now possesses eleven hundred books on music alone — not volumes but different books — and of these about 70 belong to the fifteenth and sixteenth centuries, 200 to the seventeenth, and 800 to the eighteenth century. According to my estimate this is about one-third of all the books on music printed before 1800, not counting different editions or translations into languages other than English.[25] If it is considered that many of the books or pamphlets, such as most of the queer Latin dissertations and orations on music, are not worth having, and that many others have entirely disappeared, our collection will be conceded to be already quite extraordinary — indeed equal to those at Bologna, London, Brussels, Berlin, or elsewhere. Otherwise the bibliographical committee of the IMG for the revision of Eitner's *Quellen-Lexikon* would hardly have agreed to accept our printed cards as the practical basis for their work. Our exhibit in honor of your meeting in Washington at this time fortunately relieves me of the necessity of letting special works by Tovar, Aaron, Gaffurius, Cerone, Glarean, Ornithoparchus, Luscinius, Koswick, Guerson, Jumilhac, de Caus, Lord North, Tapia, Mersenne, Simpson, Locke, and many other early theoreticians pass in review here by title.

These old-timers will always interest the theoretician and the antiquarian more than the practitioner, to whom they generally appeal not as sources of historical information but as curiosities. Yet the practitioner too may now venture on a *Studienreise* [research mission] to Washington without being disappointed. By practitioner I mean the performer, the conductor, the critic whose interests are centered in the present and last centuries. This modern music may now be found in the Library of Congress, regardless of country and school, in a more exhaustive representation than in any other institution, American or European, except possibly one. As I am familiar with the resources of the most important collections here and abroad, this statement is not an

---

25. By 1945, following publication of Hazel Bartlett's supplement to the 1913 *Catalogue of Early Books on Music (before 1800)*, the accepted estimate around the Music Division was that by that time the Division had copies of probably two-thirds of all the books on music printed before 1800 in the European languages. — ED.

idle boast. It is a fact. The exception made refers to the Deutsche Musiksammlung [Collection of German Music] at Berlin, the result of a very clever idea of Professor Dr. Wilhelm Altmann, who has actually succeeded in persuading a large number of music publishers of all countries to deposit at Berlin, free of charge, the issues of their firms, some running back a hundred years or more. How far this appeal to the generosity of the music publishers has carried Professor Altmann is not yet fully known, but that it has placed the Deutsche Musiksammlung, an annex to the Royal Library collections, *hors de concours* in many respects, particularly with reference to modern German music, cannot be doubted.

We have found ourselves able to rely on the generosity of the European music publishers only insofar as they were willing to grant a substantial reduction of price on wholesale orders. This arrangement has enabled us to acquire a collection of modern music, whether German, Russian, French, English, Italian, Bohemian, Scandinavian, or some other nationality, that is sufficiently comprehensive for all practical purposes. The more important a composer, the more numerous, of course, are his compositions here represented; and we have not permitted personal predilections to interfere in the least with the application of this principle. The American student who desires to study or write on the art of prominent composers of the nineteenth century no longer need paraphrase what he finds in articles or books, and certainly need not travel to Europe. The fullest opportunity is given him here to base his observations on the works themselves, thereby facilitating original comment. To mention names might not be necessary before a congress of musicians, but just as an illustration of the variety of our resources in this respect it may interest you to know that we possess all or the majority of the printed works of such major and minor masters as Brahms, Raff, Rubinstein, Draeseke, Kiel, Rheinberger, von Herzogenberg, Jensen, Kirchner, Bruckner, Wolf, Richard Strauss, Reger, Liszt, Volkmann, Smetana, Dvořák, Fibich, Gounod, Saint-Saëns, Franck, Lalo, Massenet, Lefebvre, Boisdeffre, d'Indy, Debussy, Benoit, Lekeu, Glinka, Balakirev, Tchaikovsky, Rimsky-Korsakov, Arensky, Scriabin, Rachmaninoff, Musorgsky, J. P. E. and Emil Hartmann, Gade, Grieg, Sinding, Sjoegren, Stenhammar, Peterson-Berger, Nielsen, Sibelius, Parry, Mackenzie, Stanford, Coleridge-Taylor, Elgar, Bantock, Delius, etc., etc. These and other masters form the pillar of our collection of what may be called current music. Around these pillars we have, of course, built up a sufficient representation of the art of such composers as have not visibly influenced the current of music but who in their best and ripest work approach the level of real merit, at least from the standpoint of the historian. In certain directions we have not quite perfected the scheme; but as concerns, for instance, orchestral music in score we have now practically reached our goal.

The best I have reserved for the last. It is our collection of full scores of dramatic music: the best, though it by no means yet exhausts our ambitions. In the prefatory note to the printed catalogue I recorded the chief difficulties that confront every collector of this type of material. One of these difficulties is the great and sometimes prohibitive cost of opera scores; another is the fact that many important old operas were never printed, are preserved only in a few libraries in autograph or contemporary manuscript copies that rarely if every appear on the market. A third difficulty is the stubborn refusal of certain publishers to sell their opera scores to libraries, and a fourth is the still more stubborn refusal of certain libraries owning unique copies of old opera scores to permit the copying of those scores.[26]

This last difficulty interferes annoyingly with our project described above, to acquire old operas in special transcripts. Still, we are beginning to see daylight. The transcripts made at the libraries that treat us in a spirit of professional courtesy are accumulating rapidly, and it is merely a question of a few years until our collection of old, unprinted opera scores will represent in good proportion the art of composing operas in the seventeenth and eighteenth centuries. The acquisition of the comparatively few printed operas of the seventeenth century depends on a combination of funds, luck, and circumstances. One may aspire to Peri's *Eurydice* in the original print, but its possession depends entirely on these three factors; and it is even a question whether a public institution like ours may not prefer relatively cheap photographic reproductions to the very costly originals.

The third difficulty enumerated above explains why we do not yet possess such full scores as that of Lalo's *Roi d'Ys,* Nessler's *Trompeter von Säckingen,* Pfitzner's *Rose vom Liebesgarten,* or Mascagni's *Cavalleria Rusticana.* In almost every instance of this kind we have made heroic efforts to place the scores before the American musician

---

26. This problem is still met with where certain countries are concerned.
— ED.

but we have failed; and we certainly were warranted in breaking off negotiations when the offer was accompanied by restrictive conditions that the Library of Congress could not with dignity accept. Finally, we are powerless in situations where the scores of well-known modern operas have never been published and the manuscripts have either disappeared entirely or are known to be in private hands.

Viewed in the light of these difficulties and obstacles, our collection of dramatic music scores is — as every impartial expert will admit — a unique collection, at least in the realm of modern opera, and it bids fair to become the most evenly developed center of research known in this field. You may not find at present, for instance, more than six operas by Alessandro Scarlatti instead of thirty or forty, but on the other hand you will find thirty or forty and more composers represented by their best works who do not figure in other libraries at all. Furthermore, the collection is not restricted to a few nations but is international to an unprecedented extent, as a comparison of our catalogue with other catalogues will prove. On this fact we of the Library of Congress lay greater stress by far than on our possession of single rarities such as, for instance, Marco da Gagliano's *Dafne*, Vitali's *Aretusa*, Rinaldo da Capua's *La Bohèmienne*, Dargomyzschky's *Rusalka*, Verdi's *Falstaff*, Dukas's *Ariane et Barbe-Bleue*, Musorgsky's *Boris Godunov*, the "new" *Rienzi* of Wagner, César Franck's *Hulda*, Debussy's *Pelleas et Mélisande*, Schillings's *Pfeifertag*, Strauss's *Salome*, or the autograph score of Cyrill Kistler's *Kunihild*.[27] All this may be more or less my private opinion; but it surely signifies something in support of it that Dr. Alfred V. Heuss in a review of our printed catalogue intimates that at some future date the historian of opera may more profitably undertake a journey to Washington than gather his information from all corners of Europe. It is, furthermore, a fact that Mr. J. E. Matthew, certainly an authority among collectors, claims that already only one collection — that at the Royal Conservatory in Brussels — compares with ours; and that another authority, Mr. Henry de Curzon, does not even

---

27. By "the new *Rienzi*" Sonneck apparently referred to the *Neue Ausgabe nach der Original Partitur* of Wagner's *Rienzi* issued in 1903 by Adolph Fürstner in Berlin. The LC copy is signed by Fürstner following an ink inscription that warns (in translation): "This copy of the score, No. 9, is intended solely for the 'Library of Congress' in Washington, D.C." — indicating one of those little arrangements referred to by Dr. Kinkeldey (see note 9 to his article, below). — ED.

extend this courtesy to Brussels. Possibly these compliments are a trifle exaggerated; but they were based on our catalogue printed early in 1908, and since then we have acquired about three hundred additional scores. The American musician is thus enabled to study at the Library of Congress about sixteen hundred operas in score.

Such, then, is a candid statement of our relative strengths and weaknesses. Even in our best developed sections gaps will be found — I find them every week and not always such as could not have been avoided — yet the critical visitor may in fairness be expected to re-member that we accomplished what has been accomplished in six years, and that this is too short a period for the display of dainty filigree work.

Another parting remark! If ever the musical profession comes to a full appreciation of what is being done in the Library of Congress, may it not forget that the efforts of the specialist would have been wholly futile without the liberal, broad-minded attitude toward our art of the chief of the chiefs, Mr. Herbert Putnam. And, finally, though the Library of Congress may be predestined to stand in a class by itself, we should not forget that there exist other fine collections in America. Not nearly as large as ours and no longer so important, the collections at the Lenox Library in New York, the Newberry in Chicago, and the Boston Public Library (with which Mr. Allen A. Brown's name is so indelibly associ-ated) would nevertheless hold an honorable place in any country. Each of these institutions, by the way, may point to treasures that now and for all time will help the Library of Congress to remember that spiteful little fable of the fox and the grapes.

German Influence
on the Musical Life of America

In German-American circles one often confronts the mistaken notion that the musical life of our country is of real worth only insofar as it has been influenced by German music and German musicians. Not that this influence is overestimated — to do that would be to fly in the face of the historical facts — but what is underestimated is the extent to which our distinctive musical life is non-Germanic. There are some who tend to disapprove of the quest for musical independence on the part of those who have come to feel themselves truly American. Such an attitude of disapproval does the German cause in America no good. That cause in fact is harmed if many Germans, who themselves have not yet developed a feeling for American attitudes and customs, still yearn in speaking and writing for the musical fleshpots of Germany and turn up their noses at musical life in America whenever it departs from German norms. In doing so they forget that in German musical life, too, not everything is neat and tidy. There, too, music nowadays is often pursued as a means of making a living rather than as an art. There, too, the musical horizon of a large part of the population does not extend any farther than beer-garden concerts, military bands, and the often dubious worth of the singing society sort of thing. It is not every German, by any

Translated from "Deutscher Einfluss auf das Musikleben Amerikas," in *Das Buch der Deutschen in Amerika,* ed. Max Heinrici (Philadelphia: Walther's Buchdruckerei, 1909), pp. 355 – 67. Translation by the volume editor, with help from colleagues.

means, who can appreciate the masterworks of genius that have made Germany the nation of philosophers, poets, and musicians.[1]

It happens also in German-American circles (or, more properly, in American-German circles) that often no sufficiently sharp distinction is made between the direct effects and the merely indirect effects that the musical activities of the Germans in America have had and continue to have on the general musical life of our country. Furthermore, one must not overlook the fact that on the whole the educational level of the German immigrants of recent decades has not been as high as that of a Carl Schurz generation, insofar as these immigrants have figured at all in serious musical matters. At any rate, it appears to me no accident, at least, that the sometimes overwhelming dominance of German music and German musicians in this country first achieved its full impact around the year 1850.

It goes without saying that the Germans of the seventeenth century brought with them across the ocean their folksongs, their chorales, their love of music in general. They had little influence worthy of the name on musical life over here, nevertheless, for strictly speaking no such musical life existed here as a general thing until toward the middle of the eighteenth century. After that it evolved rapidly, but — and this fact is important to an understanding of later developments — the evolution was along entirely English lines. This is not the place to document this perfectly self-evident fact. Suffice it to say that from the introduction of public concerts and of opera (in the form of the so-called ballad operas) around 1730, our musical life bore a predominantly English imprint until well into the nineteenth century; and that this English imprint has by no means disappeared despite the vast German admixture, itself now diminishing. That we had, however, a real musical life (at least in certain branches of the art) as early as the eighteenth century has become known and been soundly documented only in recent years. Previously just the opposite was thought, and America "of the olden time" was considered to have been a land of the most primitive psalmody. One can understand, therefore, how a false historical perspective took hold. The German share in the development of an American musical life was viewed on the one hand, so to speak, only in foreshortened guise; yet on

---

1. To the old Germanic saying that the Germans are a nation of "Denker und Dichter," Sonneck has added "und Musiker." — ED.

the other hand it was seen as unnaturally magnified, since one is apt to place beginnings too close in the foreground of time.

Instead of deploring this correction of the historical perspective, we German-Americans should rejoice inasmuch as it can be shown that our part — even if at first in only a very modest way — reaches back to the very roots of American musical life. Not, to be sure, in the sense that Conrad Beissel and his curious Ephrata Cloister had any musical influence, nor dare we exaggerate the influence exerted by the Moravian Brethren at Bethlehem or in their other settlements near and far. We know that Benjamin Franklin, Samuel Adams, George Washington, and other intellectually significant Americans of the colonial period were deeply impressed by the musical life of these thoroughly German [Moravian] communities. We know, too, that this musical life truly blossomed in home, church, and field, and in a more artistic sense in the Collegium Musicum (by which was meant not a music school but a musical society) that was founded in good German fashion about 1750 at Bethlehem, the Moravians' chief settlement. Yet anyone who knows even a little about the history of this industrious brotherhood, austere but full of the joy of living, is aware of why — save through certain individual members — its influence even in musical affairs did not extend far beyond the bounds of its settlements and only later, through the zealous Bach cult under Fred Wolle, caused a stir in wider circles. The German influence must be sought elsewhere, in another direction.

How does such an influence assert itself? First of all through the music that is constantly played, then through the musicians who play it, and above all through the musical establishment, its practices, and so on. If one applies this analysis to the statement made above, that in the eighteenth century American musical life developed along entirely English lines, then we German-Americans paradoxically but inevitably arrive at our historical right: to be named joint godfathers of American musical life. It is well known what an enormous impression Handel made on England (and perhaps not entirely to the advantage of English music); how he was virtually the first German to serve as a counterweight to the Italians — though he did it not as a German but as a quasi-Italian composer. Therefore it is significant that his *Messiah* was performed for the first time outside England (with possibly one exception) in America, at New York in 1770. The same close relationship between the motherland and the colonies may be seen in the case of other German masters who had taken a deep root in England.

Sonneck as he appeared in the early 1900s

These masters were also heard in America, along with the English, Italian, and French composers. This was true not so much with their vocal works (for conditions in this field were and remained for a long time primitive, or were naturally confined, especially in opera, to English productions) as with their instrumental music. Johann and "Carlo" Stamitz and other composers of the Mannheim school found here a rousing reception, and it was not long before Haydn took the place of honor on programs. At a proper distance from him were many other German composers such as Abel, the "London Bach," Pleyel, Steibelt, Wranitzky, Pichl, Andre, Dittersdorf, Hofmeister, and others. Indeed, even Gluck and Mozart were far from unknown in eighteenth-century America.

Of the musicians who contributed to the musical cultivation of the Americans, it was naturally the Britons who predominated. In the first half of the century one encounters only a few isolated Germans, such as for example the travel-loving Carl Theodor Pachelbel, who was perhaps a kinsman of his illustrious namesake.[2] The latter, Johann Pachelbel, was born at Nuremberg in 1653. He was outstanding as organist and composer, a pupil of Heinrich Schwemmer; he studied in Altdorf, Regensburg, and Vienna; and at his death in 1706 he was organist of the St. Sebaldus Church in Nuremberg. He was an effective proponent of church music and he introduced into Germany a kind of overture for keyboard instruments.

More and more German names crop up, and significantly not only in Pennsylvania. To be sure, one must be alert and not jump to the conclusion that behind every German-sounding name was a German musician. A case in point is that of Jacob Leonard, who in the 1760s in New York founded, together with one colleague, a kind of music school. The same doubt does not arise with Hermann von Zedwitz, an original genius who was a one-time Prussian lieutenant, a master of chimney sweeps, a musician, a lieutenant-colonel in the Revolutionary War, and finally a despicable traitor to the American cause. To this same period and later belongs Philip Roth, a German bandmaster in the service of the English, who deserves mention here because he is one of the two contenders for recognition as composer of the "President's March" that

---

2. Since Sonneck's time it has been established that C. T. Pachelbel was indeed a son of Johann. See Virginia Larkin Redway, "Charles Theodore Pachelbel, Musical Emigrant," *Journal of the American Musicological Society* 5, no. 1 (Spring 1952): 32–36. —ED.

Joseph Hopkinson used in 1798 as the musical basis for his patriotic song, "Hail Columbia."[3] During the war the German music element here was increased by defections from the ranks by such Hessians as forsook their native land for our own country; and following the war German musicians soon began coming here by the dozens — without, however, challenging the primary role played by the English. We dare claim, for example, the most important American musician of that time, Alexander Reinagle, only by the roundabout means of his Austrian ancestors. In contrast with him are such noteworthy musicians as the church choir director Heim at Philadelphia, Hupfeld, the Van Hagens, Johann Christoph Moller, Hans Gram, the Gilferts, and others of undoubted German origin.

When it comes to the "rank and file" of the orchestras, we have contemporary evidence that these ranks and and files were already strongly German in makeup. If one leafs through the pages of the old directories he is downright surprised to meet with so many Germans listed under "musicians" and "music teachers." One such artist deserves mention because his influence reached well into the nineteenth century: Gottlieb Graupner. A one-time oboist in a Hannover regiment, he came to America in 1795 and established himself in Boston, where he became unquestionably one of the most important pioneers of the German musical art in America: as virtuoso, music teacher, and co-founder of a Philharmonic Society (1810 or 1811 to 1824). Graupner also was intermittently a music publisher, and this fact leads me directly to observe what a leading role the Germans played from the beginning in the development of the music trades in general and of American instrument making in particular. It is even a matter of record that as early as 1799 or 1800 the German firm of Breitkopf & Härtel, later world-wide in its activities, entered into a business relationship with one Hutter of Lancaster, Pennsylvania.

It is of especial interest with regard to instrument making that there can be no mistake in pointing to a German, Henry Neering (with whom the vestry of Trinity Church at New York negotiated as early as 1703 regarding an organ), as the earliest American organ builder. Those negotiations were broken off, so the honor of having built the first

---

3. It has long been known, from Sonneck-Upton and other sources, that the composer of the music to which Joseph Hopkinson put his "Hail Columbia" words was the other Philip, Philip Phile. — ED.

organ (1739 – 40) for Trinity Church goes to another German-American, Johann Gottlob Klemm. He apparently was preceded by a certain Matthias Zimmermann in Philadelphia who built an organ, and he was succeeded by a whole series of German organ builders among whom I shall mention only David Tannenberg. In the field of American piano making it appears that the pioneer was Johann Behrend, who is known to have made a piano as early as 1775; but it is not impossible that he could be strongly challenged for this place of honor by David Wolhaupter of New York, another German. Be that as it may, these two are far exceeded in importance for this industry by a third German, Charles Albrecht of Philadelphia.[4] As a curiosity, finally, it may be remarked upon that John Jacob Astor founded his fortune in America on a dealership in the piano business.[5]

Such was the stamp of the eighteenth century. I have intentionally dwelt so long upon this period because it is only thus that the pattern of the steady and eventually overwhelming influence of the Germans on American musical life can be made clear. To the historian the nineteenth century, therefore, is of interest only as it offers new points of view, when favorable circumstances allowed us to transplant German seedlings into ground that hitherto had lain fallow for us. The tag end of the eighteenth century and the first quarter of the nineteenth marched under the banner of Handel and Haydn, a banner memorialized in 1815 by

---

4. Our twentieth-century Philadelphian, Otto Albrecht, long an officer of the American Musicological Society, has told the editor that he can claim no blood relationship with the piano-making Charles Albrecht of eighteenth-century Philadelphia. — ED.

5. Astor in fact founded his fortune on flutes; the pianos came later. At age sixteen in 1779 he wanted to escape his father's butcher shop and make his fortune in North America; but the Revolutionary War was on, so instead he left his native town of Waldorf, in Germany near Heidelberg, and went to London, where he worked in the music shop and instrument manufactory of his older brother George. In 1783, the Revolution ended, he put five of the guineas he had saved into seven flutes (which he may or may not have had a hand in making) and took ship for America. After some four months on the ship (half of them in the ice-bound Chesapeake Bay) he managed to get to Baltimore and thence to his brother Henry in New York. The flutes were sold, music dealerships set up (in cooperation, needless to say, with the firm of Astor and Broadwood of London), and soon John Jacob began wheeling and dealing in the fur trade and later in real estate. See, e.g., Kenneth W. Porter, *John Jacob Astor: Business Man* (Cambridge: Harvard University Press, 1931), *passim.* William Arms Fisher reports (in *One Hundred and Fifty Years of Music Publishing in the United States*) [Boston, 1933], p. 10) that as late as 1789 the sign over Astor's shop in Maiden Lane read "John Jacob Astor / Furs and Pianos." — ED.

the founding (with Gottlieb Graupner's expert assistance) of the famous and epoch-making Handel and Haydn Society. As time went on, Haydn was succeeded by Mozart, Beethoven, Weber, Mendelssohn, Schumann, Brahms, Wagner, Bach (the eternal "modern"), and the other German masters who made German music supreme in the New World as in the Old. So obvious is this pattern that it really does not bear description.

Yet it would be worth a detailed study to show how the German influence in America sprang from more sources than it did elsewhere: not only from those born in America and those who immigrated, but — just as in earlier times — from those who came by way of England. When, for instance, Mozart's *Figaro* (1823) and *Magic Flute* (1832), Weber's *Freischütz* (1825) and *Oberon* (1827), and Beethoven's *Fidelio* (1839) were heard over here at the dates given, those were not German productions in either language or spirit but rather English "para-phrases," one might almost say. The historical facts clearly indicate that in the realm of opera the Germans still had a long way to go before they drove English opera from the field and took their place as equals alongside the Italians and French. It was first in 1855, if I am not mis-taken, that German opera in German had a short season at Niblo's Theater in New York. Hence it must be counted one of the greatest milestones in the history of German music on American soil when *Fidelio* was performed at the New York Academy of Music on Decem-ber 29, 1856, under Carl Bergmann. The same true German artist, whose service to American music in America has lain too long in the shadow of Theodore Thomas, directed Richard Wagner's *Tannhäuser* at its first triumph in America in the year 1859. Eleven years later he made a further effort to create a home for German opera over here in the old Bowery City Theater. Also worthy of note are similar attempts by Carl Anschütz in 1862, by Madame Rosa Pappenheim in 1878, Adolf Neuendorf's "*Walküre* experiment," G. Carlberg's first performance of *The Flying Dutchman* in Philadelphia, and, finally, the presentations (sometimes staged but more often in concert) of German opera by the German singing societies, especially in the Middle West.

Still, these efforts had little effect beyond purely German circles; and as usual the perversity of the impresarios allowed German masterworks to be sung to Americans in Italian, at times by German artists. In the end it was the daring of Leopold Damrosch, near the end of his fruitful career, that did away with this atrocious practice. When he took over the Metropolitan Opera House in 1884, German opera entered a new era — in which the gifted Anton Seidl's feat of presenting in 1888 – 89 the entire Nibelungen trilogy, despite all attendant difficulties, will always remain a milestone.

When it came to choral works with instrumental accompaniment, the situation was simpler. Since the days of Frederick Amelung's Apollonian Society (Pittsburgh, 1807) Americans of German and English heritage [*Zunge*] had supported and complemented each other in the cultivation of German music. It was in the very nature of things that in the realm of choral music the classics of the oratorio repertory should be sung almost universally in the language of the country — for instance, Haydn's *Creation* as early as 1816, Mendelssohn's *St. Paul* already in 1838 (only two years after the Düsseldorf baptism of the work), and Schumann's *Paradise and Peri* in 1848 (under H. C. Timm at New York). Indeed, the question arises whether the cultural role of German opera in America would not have been better served if English, the language of the country, had been made the standard language of the operatic stage — as it is everywhere else in the world except London. This was one of the lifelong dreams of Theodore Thomas (whose American National Opera Company of 1886 was, to be sure, a failure). Hundreds of thousands of Germans would admittedly have suffered the loss of a certain artistic pleasure and their sense of racial brotherhood; but millions of Americans who knew only English would have profited thereby.

This language problem is one of the reasons why the peculiarly German institution of the male singing society has had only an indirect influence upon musical life here. The Germans themselves, whether natives or immigrants, have found in this branch of art one of the very strongest means of nurturing the German character and of maintaining a sense of community. From this standpoint the moist and merry male chorus [*feucht-fröhliche Männergesang*] holds a powerful place in the history of German life in America and in governmental politics, one with which politicians will have to reckon — even those who have little taste for song but an enormous hunger for votes. It was only in the middle of the nineteenth century that the male choral union [*Männergesangverein*] came into its own even in the fatherland; the fact that the Germans transplanted it into this country and spread it around with uncanny speed shows how important they considered this blending of the pleasant with the profitable on American soil. Think what it means that in the Far West, in St. Louis, a German *Männergesangverein* was founded as early as 1838;[6] that Philadelphia and Baltimore could by 1846 contemplate a joint venture; and that by 1849 — only four years after the first singers' festival in Germany — conditions in America were such that, through a union of singers from Cincinnati, Louisville, and Madison (Ind.), the first Festival of Singers [*Sängerfest*] of the North American Federation of Singers [*Sängerbund*] could take place at Cincinnati. Sometime it would be interesting as well as worthwhile to write a comprehensive history of the German male singing society in America; but on this occasion it is beyond my goal even to mention the most important dates.

To say that this German institution had and has in the broader sense only an indirect influence on American musical life, and one even smaller than that of the less numerous glee clubs and similar male singing groups patterned after the English, would meet with lively opposition. At any rate, I am by no means the only one holding that opinion. But that the German *Männergesangvereine* have also had a remarkable direct influence no reasonable person can deny. This influence is evident not so much from the purely German groups as from those that, like the Washington *Sängerbund,* bear a strongly Anglo-Saxon or Irish cast, and more especially from the song festivals. By the enlistment of huge masses of singers, by their very size, these festivals lure many thousands and put them under the spell of German song and German *Gemütlichkeit.* These multitudes never take an interest in the "Dutchman" except when they can put him to political advantage, and they would never even think of attending even the most ambitious and finest concerts of the individual societies. At any rate, whether the influence of this institution is direct or indirect, it is plainly evident. It seeps through society and reaches even the universities, where a great many of the favorite songs are borrowed from the treasuries of German folk and student songs.

In the realm of instrumental music, no problem of language or of anything else could interfere with the unrestrained cultivation of the German art. Without any difficulty and — be it freely admitted — apart from the occasional noticeable and understandable rebellions by the Anglo-Saxons against Teutonic hegemony, the German influence here

---

6. No Sonneckian exclamation mark here (see Mr. Hitchcock's article); in 1838 St. Louis was indeed "far west." — ED.

could be described as a great flood. It is noteworthy that, for instance, in chamber music — which did not emerge from the "chamber" into the public concert hall until toward the middle of the nineteenth century — the German "Dr. Kuhn" is mentioned as early as 1750 at Philadelphia, along with Francis Hopkinson and Lt. Governor John Penn, as a cultivator of this branch of music. Later, too, Germans were among the trailblazers in chamber music: for instance, Daniel Schlesinger, who died (1838) all too young, and men such as Kirchhoefer, Rakemann, Schmidt, and Koelker. From them it was only a short step to the propagation of this most intimate but also "most difficult" of the musical arts by Theodore Eisfeld (1851), Theodore Thomas, Carl Bergmann and his colleagues (1855), and by the constantly touring and preponderantly German Mendelssohn Quintet Club (1849). Since then, what with the Spiering Quartet in the West and the Kneisel Quartet in the East, to name only two of the most important German musical groups, their contribution to America's musical life really does not need to be spelled out.

   In the field of orchestral music exactly the same situation prevails. Orchestras came and went, blossomed and faded, in the East and in the West. In all probability Beethoven and the other grand masters of the symphony would have made their way to the top just as surely even without the German conductors and German orchestras, but it would not have come about with the lightning-like rapidity as it actually did. There is astonishment not only in Europe but even among newer generations of German-Americans when it is reported that Beethoven's First Symphony was performed as early as 1821 by the Musical Fund Society of Philadelphia and that even this was probably not the first performance over here; that Schmidt at Boston in 1841 gave Beethoven's First and Fifth, Mozart's *Jupiter,* and Mendelssohn's *Scottish;* that there was a presentation of the Ninth Symphony as early as 1846 by the epoch-making New York Philharmonic Society. And it would be easy to show that not only this co-operative [*sic*] orchestra, founded in 1842, but also other well-known and predominantly German orchestras (whether in Chicago, Cincinnati, St. Louis, Milwaukee, Boston, Pittsburgh, or Philadelphia) led the way in publicizing new works by German and foreign [*sic*] masters — often before many, sometimes before the majority, and on occasion before all of the famous orchestras of the fatherland. It may be that this state of affairs was due in part to the Americans' urge to be "up to date" and to the fact that our country has behind it a much older musical life than is usually supposed. At any rate, it is significant that since about 1850 it has been almost exclusively German conductors and German orchestra musicians who have satisfied this urge.

At all events, the development in the West would not have come so unprecedentedly fast had it not been for the pioneer work of such touring orchestras as Carl Eckardt's Saxonia, August Fries's Lombardi, and Carl Bergmann's even more important Germania Orchestra. They paved the way for such Westerners as Hans Balatka, who possessed not only the will power to achieve great heights but also the necessary artistry. In saying that I in no way belittle the contributions of the original pioneers such as Julius Dyrenfurth, Henry Ahner, Julius Unger (Chicago), Frederick Amelung (Pittsburgh), Wilhelm Feltow (Cincinnati), Wilhelm Robyn, Johann Georg Wesselhoeft, Egmont Fröhlich, R. Fuchs (St. Louis), and many others.

If, as I said, it is obvious that German music found in America a second home (which it would have done here, as in Russia, even without the millions of German immigrants), it is not quite so easy to understand why it was the Germans who gathered unto themselves such power as conductors and orchestra musicians, even beyond the proportions to be expected from the very considerable German element making up the American people. It is most understandable in the West, where the Germans themselves had to lay their own foundations and could not — as in the East — build on a broad Anglo-Saxon base. Nothing parallel can be found in music history except for the domination of the Italians in eighteenth-century Europe. There is, however, one fundamental difference: Italians outside of Italy are still Italians, still foreigners, whereas the Germans here could and did become good Americans. Their sons (one has to think only of Walter and Frank Damrosch) are no different from full-blooded Americans except in name.[7] This capacity to assimilate has been one reason why Americans have borne the German music yoke [*sic: Musik-Joch*] without much grumbling.

Another reason springs from natural feelings of gratitude. Let one only ask Americans who do not themselves move in German circles, and who have rubbed shoulders a bit with music history, to whom the musi-

---

7. Are second-generation German-Americans any less "full-blooded Americans" than second-generation Italians or Japanese? — ED.

cal life of their country in the nineteenth century owed the most. Apart from men such as Uriah C. Hill, John Knowles Paine, John Sullivan Dwight, Benjamin C. Lang, Albert A. Stanley, William Lawrence Tomlins, William C. Woodbridge, and Lowell Mason (the latter two having eventually based their services to school music on the principles of Pestalozzi and Nägel), I believe the Americans would name Henry C. Timm, Hans Balatka, Carl Bergmann, Leopold Damrosch, Carl Wolf-Zerrahn, Anton Seidl, Fritz Scheel, Theodore Thomas. The last-named, in particular, whether really rated in the proper proportion to the others or not, lives in the memories of the American people as does no other German musician; for the impression made on our people by Bülow, Rubinstein, and the gifted German singers of both sexes has proven to be only transitory in nature. We younger people, who perhaps heard Theodore Thomas at the end, at the extremity of his career, can scarcely appreciate the legacy he bequeathed us. Only when the memory of him loosens the tongues of our musical veterans shall we be able to measure what America gratefully owes this great prophet of German art.

Preoccupation with this hero worship, however, must not allow us to overlook the part played by countless German music teachers in the musical education of American youth. Their methods, when well learned, have been reasonable and suited to the character of the American people; when not well learned, as has too often been the case, German thoroughness and German conscientiousness have been sacrificed, out of concern for making a living, on the altar of "Humbug." In another direction, we German-Americans may point with pride to the fact that among the most prestigious music schools of the country those founded by Germans assume a place of honor, and that, for instance, Dr. Florenz Ziegfeld's Chicago Musical College can be placed side by side with the New England Conservatory of Music, inasmuch as both have been in operation since 1867.

Even if all this were not the case, there would still be the German music "Professor" who has marked us Americans with his indelible stamp: *Made in Germany*. With a few isolated exceptions, for instance, the most significant American composers have learned a good part of their craft at German conservatories. This circumstance most certainly had its drawbacks for the development of an American musical style in the sense that we speak of a Norwegian, Russian, French, German, or other national style; but nevertheless the fact remains that techniques of composition stemming for the most part from Germany are a part of

Dudley Buck, John Knowles Paine, George W. Chadwick, Edward MacDowell, Ethelbert Nevin, Frederick S. Converse, and others. And it is not the technique alone but the blood as well that is German when we speak of such significant American composers as Henry Schoenefeld, Johann H. Beck, Ernest Richard Kroeger, Adolph M. Foerster, Bruno Oskar Klein. And we can also point to hundreds, even thousands, of capable American instrumentalists who acquired their artistry in Germany — though if they had looked closely into the matter they would have found they could learn the very same things by studying with the virtuosos and theoreticians resident in America.

By "music teacher" one ordinarily means only him who instructs by the ear-splitting torture of blasting, pounding, scraping [*Tonansatz, Anschlag, Strich*]. It is often forgotten that serious music critics and writers on music — not the ones whose pens serve the most shamelessly blatant or cleverly disguised promotion efforts — can also lay claim to being music teachers of the populace at large. If one thinks along these lines it is at once apparent that in this field, too, the German influence has not been unimportant. Consider how salutary, enlightening, and instructive to the American people has been the work of such men as Carl Mertz, Emil Liebling, Gustav Kobbe, Philip H. Goepp, Louis C. Elson, Henry T. Finck, and Henry Edward Krehbiel alongside that of a Dwight, Hale, Henderson, Apthorp, Aldrich. One could almost count in this phalanx one of the pioneers of American music history, the noteworthy composer and conductor Frederic L. Ritter, were it not for the technicality that he was born in Strassburg during the time it was under the French flag. On the other hand we must not make too much of the numerous German-language music magazines published in America. They have never exerted any notable influence on American affairs; doubtless an August Spanuth, for example, of the *New Yorker Staatszeitung,* has been of greater educational service to our country than all these German music journals put together.

Earlier in this article reference was made to the important part played by Germans at the very beginning in the music trades and instrument making. With the passage of time this part has grown not smaller but larger. In an article wherein the extent of the German influence can only be sketched, it is enough to say that a disproportionately large part of the American music industry remains in German hands. Let the American music publishers pass in review, and if English names such as John Church and Oliver Ditson are put on one of the balance pans then such

other names as Schirmer, Schmidt, and Fischer weigh just as heavily on
the other.[8]

Likewise, if ingenious piano makers of English origin such as Jonas
Chickering are paid well-deserved tribute, then the German-American
may point with pride to equally old and honorable names such as
Steinway and Knabe, names perhaps even more widely known in the
world at large, names that have brought honor on American soil to
German business sense and skill at invention.

America's musical topography is still in bad shape.[9] Little has been
done toward a thorough and accurate description of the music histories
of the more important cities, especially those in the West. That job is
much too vast for it to be undertaken by any single individual who
might set himself up as a history-writing authority on the entire country — although useful and well-meaning attempts in that direction have
been made. Only when objective local histories have come into being
can the methodically schooled universal historian hope to render an
accurate account of all that has passed. Then it can be expected that
many adjustments will be made in our current viewpoints, that certain
personalities will recede into the background and others will come to
the fore; and it will probably happen that the part played by the
Anglo-Saxons, especially in the West, will have to be given more prominence. A complete reversal of the relative values, however, is scarcely
conceivable, and the part played by the Germans will assuredly never
lose its luster [Klang]. No matter what conclusions the historians finally
come to, we Americans of German origin will never lose our place of
honor in the musical history of the country. We therefore have respon-
sibilities. They should inspire us to put to use in the realm of music such
German cultural achievements and cultural levers as we still lack here.

One of these undertakings should be to create in our colleges and
universities a place for musicology, in the German sense and along
German lines, a place that is now utterly lacking. Another should be to
make the political gentlemen for once understand that music is more

---

8. Two decades later, Sonneck could have observed (no doubt with mixed
feelings) that the firms of Church and Ditson had been bought out by Theodore
Presser of German heritage. — ED.

9. See note 1 to the following article on Sonneck's use of "musical topography." Here it clearly means "the literature descriptive of musical life" (not "of
music," a shallower term that Sonneck always carefully avoided in such
circumstances). — ED.

than an aid to digestion and a pastime. That the Germans are a people dedicated to music they well know; what they do not understand is that the Germans would not have become such a people without governmental subvention of music. And if the esthetic or cultural argument does not work, then the Americans of German origin should change the politicians' minds by pointing to the economic and business advantages that would accrue to the country in fullest measure with the establishment of state and municipal operas and conservatories — and, as the ultimate goal, a national opera and a national conservatory.

The Musical Life
of America from the Standpoint
of Musical Topography

The aim of this report is not to stress the obvious similarities between the musical life of America and that of Europe.[1] Whoever regularly reads the music journals knows that we in America make music in general just as the Europeans do. We too have mixed choruses, male choruses (whether of the English glee-club type or the German *Liedertafel*),[2] women's choruses, military bands, symphony orchestras, chamber music groups, church music, school music, opera houses, music libraries, instrument collections. We too have our composers, virtuosos, critics, publishers, concert managers. In short, all the paraphernalia of a highly ramified musical life are also to be found in America. There are still some strange characters who deny this, especially those

---

Translated from "Das Musikleben Amerikas vom Standpunkte der musikalischen Länderkunde," in *III. Kongress der Internationalen Musikgesellschaft, Wien, 25. bis 29. Mai 1909. Bericht vorgelegt vom Wiener Kongressausschuss* (Vienna: Artaria & Co.; Leipzig: Breitkopf & Härtel, 1909), pp. 446–58. As with the preceding article, the volume editor made the translation with help from colleagues.

1. Sonneck apparently was fond of the somewhat exotic term *musikalische Länderkunde,* which he himself translated as "musical topography." In the preceding article (see its note 9) he clearly used it to mean "the literature descriptive of musical life." In the title of this article it clearly refers not to the literature so much as to the features, the musical landscape, all the elements of musical life. Elsewhere in the article it suggests something like "historiography" — or, better still, "historiology." — ED.

2. The "songs-table" is a quasi-musical, semi-social German institution said to have been founded at Berlin in 1809 by Carl Friedrich Zelter, satisfying at once two human thirsts: for song and for liquid refreshment. — ED.

who gather their musical impressions between express train and dinner party and serve them up to their European readers in the form of *feuilletons*. We no longer excite ourselves about these European specimens of "bucking bronco,"[3] knowing very well that many works (witness the Tchaikovsky piano concerto and Strauss's *Symphonia Domestica*) have begun their triumphant careers in America. Taken one by one, these instantaneous impressions often are correct; but they lack either the proper perspective or any perspective at all — a perspective, moreover, that we Americans ourselves can scarcely claim to possess.

One has to remember that the United States range over half a continent; that the population numbers only about ninety million; that the populating has been the work of all possible nationalities and races, including ten million Negroes; that in the East many of the cities are hundreds of years old, whereas in the West, where large and flourishing cities now stand, it was only forty years ago that the prairie wolves still howled. Does it not stand to reason that in such a country the musical life will inevitably be primitive here, highly developed there? That here everything is well established and well ordered while there the smack of musical exoticism is still in the air? Is it not likewise clear that one cannot speak in terms of any generally applicable norm, of any single applicable point of view; that, in short, our musical landscape has a motley appearance such as surely is found nowhere in Europe? In addition, this motley itself is not stable but — especially in the West — changes like a kaleidoscope from year to year as conditions vary. To draw from this motley of appearances any similarities with conditions in Europe, more or less superficial and at any rate obvious, would be a completely superfluous and at best statistically useful task — and one, moreover, of purely ephemeral value that in particular would shed little light on the actual circumstances of musical life in America. It is not the similarities that are instructive but the dissimilarities; and — contrariwise in American musical life itself — the similarities among the dissimilarities. Thus the problem is to reveal, in the motley, basic patterns that may have general applicability — and I know perfectly well that many of my countrymen will say that my observations, for obvious reasons, constitute nothing more than personal opinions.

The distinctive characteristic of American musical life is and always has been private enterprise. The European who overlooks this funda-

---

3. "Arizona kicker" is the exact term Sonneck used. — ED.

mental fact will never be able to understand the situation with its weaknesses and its strong points, and if an American makes the same mistake he will understand only up to a point. The United States constitute a federation of more than forty republics in which the republics [or states] do next to nothing for music and the federal government does even less, if that were possible. What is more, even the individual cities — apart from occasional minor contributions for public band concerts and other likewise mostly unimportant efforts — take no official interest in musical life. All is left to private enterprise. How different it is in Europe, where the princes further musical life in their realms out of their private coffers, where republics carry on these monarchial traditions, where central government and city officially devote large sums to the same end and then as a matter of course have a word to say about the disposition of those sums — in other words, about the control of musical life. The concept in Europe of the government as a paternalistic institution ensures that art will not be allowed to grow unattended. Whether for better or worse, it sees in art an important and necessary— because natural — branch of popular culture; and it feels the obligation, in the interest of the people, to give the garden of the arts the necessary means of keeping it beautiful and in good order — just as if it were a botanical or zoological garden.

Such institutions as the latter by no means lack official support in America, too; but, as I have said, for the garden of the arts there is virtually nothing. There is a contradiction not at all easy to eliminate if one views, as we [Americans] do, the cultivation of the natural sciences and of esthetics as two fundamentally different concepts relating to the cultural well-being of the people. Now, the American concept of government, in contrast to the European, has never viewed the government as paternalistic. On the contrary, the average American cannot conceive of the government as a solicitous father, or at least he has no taste for such a concept. He sees in the government, or rather in a particular governing body, merely some officials elected and paid by the majority whose duty, among other things, is to interfere as little as possible in the private affairs of the individual. The American representative of the people thus regards himself, generally speaking, not as a leader of the people but as an instrument, their servant, who represents their (that is, the voters') desires and opinions rather than his own. He stands, furthermore, between the administration and the people and watches to see that the administration indulges in no paternalistic endeavors that are contrary to the clear wishes of the people.

So long, then, as the people themselves do not press for some kind of governmental support for music, just so long will the elected representatives of the people take not a single step in that direction. What is more, should the administration itself make a move in that direction these representatives would allow the move to sink into the legislative swamp without any ado. In addition, many jurists have convinced themselves and others that our Constitution does not allow under any circumstances a subvention of music on the part of the federal government. For all that, I suspect that if the people really wanted it, the Constitution could be made suddenly to change its mind, so to speak. But why, the European will ask, do the people not insist on something so obviously beneficial in the cultural sphere? The answer to that is very simple: one must never forget, if he wants to understand American affairs, that our country grew out of an English colony. Since then the two peoples admittedly have gone their separate ways, and we have grown with our English heritage in our own particular way; and furthermore the English have never been so paternalistically inclined [toward government subvention of music] as the peoples on the Continent. In short, the idea of municipal or higher subsidy of music has always been foreign to the nature of most Americans. It seems to them therefore neither necessary nor advisable. Indeed, the very idea of such a thing would seldom enter their minds if they did not run upon it in articles about Europe. The thought of such governmental subsidy of music therefore comes down in the end to one word: un-American.

What is the consequence of this dependence on private enterprise? In such fields as choral music, the *Männergesang*, and others that in Europe also are based on nongovernmental support, we follow naturally enough the same paths that are customary in Europe. Orchestral music, however, is quite another matter. Not a single American orchestra, to my knowledge, enjoys any support from a city. Hence the financial risk rests entirely on the shoulders of such private individuals as have the necessary local pride, feeling for the art, and financial means to carry the burden. And a large symphony orchestra in America is a very costly undertaking: the orchestra musicians and conductors receive much higher pay than in Europe, our virtuosos reckon in dollars rather than marks, even the hall rental fees and other expenses smack of

America. Indeed, and despite the much higher cost of tickets, there probably is not a single orchestra that breaks even, and a deficit of $30,000 or more is the rule with our large orchestras. Under these circumstances it goes without saying that really good and at the same time financially sound orchestras are not exactly numerous in America. There are good orchestras, some of them quite excellent, in Philadelphia, New York (there, e.g., the Philharmonic, the New York Symphony, the Russian Symphony), Pittsburgh, St. Paul, Minneapolis, St. Louis, San Francisco, Seattle, New Haven, Los Angeles, Milwaukee. Once past those names really notable orchestras are few — and this in a land of ninety million people. Probably the two most distinguished orchestras in the country are the Theodore Thomas Orchestra in Chicago and the Boston Symphony Orchestra, and these have achieved exceptional stature: the first, thanks to the energy and popularity of Theodore Thomas, has been established on a sound basis of widespread popular support rather than on support from wealthy patrons; and the wonderful Boston Symphony Orchestra is the creation of a single Maecenas, Mr. Henry L. Higginson.

Other cities have from time to time made efforts to possess orchestras of their own. But the efforts have run aground mostly, as in Washington, on the lack of proportion between proportionately normal receipts and disproportionately high expenses; for after a while a chronic deficit dampens the pleasure that even an American millionaire derives from making fine concerts available to his fellow townsmen. And to this pattern has to be added still another consequence of cause and effect. Since almost everywhere there is a gratifying desire for symphony concerts, nearly all our great orchestras are touring orchestras, following far-flung circuits on which they provide other cities with symphony concerts. Since, however, these touring orchestras enjoy a more-or-less secure financial footing and are well above average in artistic quality, the old adage about the better being the enemy of the good proves true to the detriment of American musical life as a whole. Meritorious as is their part in raising the level of musical understanding in the cities visited, and of the music lovers in those cities, these orchestras make it virtually impossible for the cities to satisfy the need for orchestra music with establishments of their own. This is a basic deficiency in our system that is more and more understood but can only gradually be eliminated.

Let us turn to opera. It is the sorest spot in our musical anatomy.

From what has already been said it can be taken for granted that it will nowhere get any help whatsoever so far as municipalities are concerned. Yet an opera house with all its inhabitants is a much more expensive undertaking than an orchestra. Understandably enough, the millionaires — still more the theatrical producers — have shrunk from its attendant risks except in New York and, just recently, in Boston. The operetta, to be sure, blossoms in all shades. But apart from it, and from sporadic itinerant opera troupes that by European standards are no better than third-rate, with repertories that are usually very limited, our opera life amounts to no more than the famous Metropolitan Opera Company and Oscar Hammerstein's likewise currently famous Manhattan Opera Company, both with establishments [*Hauptquartier*] in New York. In New York, therefore, there obviously is no dearth of opera during the winter; but outside New York, opera is a poor relation. What can it possibly mean for the musical life of the whole of America if both these mighty enterprises shower operatic productions during the winter on a wealthy city of a million like Philadelphia? In these circumstances Philadelphia is and remains nothing but a satellite of New York. And what does it matter if the Metropolitan Opera closes its season in New York and wanders off to California and gives my compatriots in the cities it visits a stopover of the "stars" for half a week, or one week, or even three weeks, under the high-sounding name of "season"? Well, in place of further remarks it is enough to say *sapienti sat.*

No matter how proud one is of his country he must admit that this is a backward state of affairs, a downright sick situation made even more so by the fact that the really worthwhile opera companies sing their repertories in all conceivable languages except that of the country. Opera in America is for that reason still an exotic flower of art, and it follows that the appreciation of opera as music drama is still at a minimum. Where the operatic life is so primitive and exotic, any talk of a flourishing indigenous opera establishment naturally is out of the question. In other fields we have competent composers, even some excellent ones; and without hesitation I count MacDowell among the most original and gifted composers of the nineteenth century.[4] But when it comes to opera we have little to show because there is so little oppor-

---

4. Elsewhere Sonneck makes it clear, by equating MacDowell with Bizet, that he is speaking here only of composers in the United States and does not equate MacDowell, say, with Beethoven, Schubert, or Brahms. — ED.

tunity to practice writing for the stage. How curious our opera situation must seem to a European, in that such a furor could have been aroused in musical circles by the decision of the Metropolitan Opera Company to venture the production of an opera by an American, in the English language — namely *The Pipe of Desire,* the first operatic effort by the very gifted Frederick S. Converse!

The relationship between the principle of exclusively private enterprise and our musical life has still other ramifications that produce concomitant phenomena on the musical landscape whose consequences become evident only in the light of this principle. In our country, as I have said, there are relatively few permanent symphony orchestras and less than a handful of opera orchestras. All of these orchestras, moreover, are made up largely of European musicians. One wonders, why so? It could not happen if our conservatories turned out enough well-rounded orchestra musicians, and the young people then had sufficient opportunities to win their spurs. What happens, however, is that the latter possibility is precluded by the existing state of affairs, and that our conservatories (with isolated exceptions such as the gigantic New England Conservatory, which has long since outgrown its financial birth pangs) can place relatively little emphasis on this branch of the profession, perhaps the most important of all for a modern music school. They cannot do it because they all are based on the principle of private enterprise, which prevents them from devoting sizable sums (unless they are willing to upset the entire business applecart) to training for a profession so little profitable because its doors are closed.

Exactly the same situation confronts those Americans who are vocally and temperamentally equipped for the operatic stage. Opportunities for employment simply do not exist. That is one of the reasons why so many rising American stage artists (some with fictitious names redolent of Italian or other nationalities) find themselves in Europe. Another is that unfortunately an American very seldom finds favor with our impresarios until he has made a name for himself in Europe. So each situation feeds upon the other. But is there not, you will ask, in America a national conservatory that could work along artistic-educational lines for the whole of musical life without paying attention to the material aspect [*nervus rerum*], and that could sow far and wide the seeds that are inherently necessary for indigenous concert and opera life? No: this idea would be opposed as un-American in principle not only by the members of Congress but also by musicians, private music schools, music dealers, and so on because it would put them in direct competition with the national institution. So extensive is this opposition to a federally supported conservatory that the article of a well-known writer who expounded on the advantages — artistic, educational, economic on a national level — of such an institution was rejected by our most serious music periodical, not because it was badly written but because to print it would have been a waste of paper!

In one area of music my countrymen are finally beginning to investigate not only the surface aspects of the situation but its deeper-rooted causes as well — all of which derive (whether they will admit it now or not) directly or indirectly from the system of private enterprise. In one area they are beginning to weigh the advantages and disadvantages of the system according to their merits. That is in music education [*Schulmusik*]. In Europe too this field certainly is often a source of grief, but in few other places is it so disorganized [*ungeregelt*] as in America. Just as in Germany, it falls within the jurisdiction of the states of the Union; but in the states themselves sheer chaos reigns, with the exception of a few progressive states such as Massachusetts. School officials in the cities, to be sure, often pay it commendable attention and in certain cities achieve superior results; but almost everywhere there is a decided lack of purpose and of generally valid methods.

This situation can be seen in the fact that until recently not one bit of official, statistically useful information on music education in America was to be had. One of the greatest contributions to the basic development of our musical life is by the Music Teachers' National Association (founded in 1876): its survey of the situation, undertaken in cooperation with the U.S. Bureau of Education (something like what in Europe would be called a ministry of education) with the aim of solving this problem, so vital to the future musical life of the country. The well-known musical pedagogue, Mr. Arthur L. Manchester, to whom this worthy but extremely difficult task was handed, summed up his conclusions on the chaos in music education to the effect that individual opinions prevail too much everywhere. In other words, the authorities do not cooperate enough among themselves in their capacity as authorities, but rather leave the weal and woe of music education too much to the personal methods of individual school music teachers. Similar, even if not quite so chaotic, is the situation in our colleges; and here too the

Music Teachers' National Association is making headway. Its *Year-books* must be especially recommended to those who are interested in the serious currents in American education.

At the same time there is one thing that one must bear in mind from the outset: that in our colleges it is the music faculty that deals with musicology. Apart from musical esthetics, psychology, and ethnography (which really do not require a specifically musical faculty), musicology in the narrower sense does in fact have a place in America, even though there is as yet no real need for it. This latter truth is immediately apparent in the lack of scholarly music journals. Even the best of our music magazines are in the popular-scholarly, pedagogical, or general-interest veins, or else they provide picture-studded news. Our best writers on music are, moreover, too busy with their main job as music critics to be able to devote themselves to deep-probing, time-consuming, musicological researches and source studies. As critics, however, they are — I want to emphasize — fully on a par with their finest European colleagues. Even our best music histories, such as that by Professor Waldo Selden Pratt, are not so much the fruit of independent musicological research as the assiduous, judicious piecing together of scholarly findings for educational purposes.

But where there is no demand for musicologists, it goes without saying, their unprofitable field lies fallow; so here again the one situation gives rise to the other: our colleges and universities do not bother to train professional musicologists and altogether lack the necessary staff. That at least is the general situation, though here and there are professors not only intelligent but also learned enough to teach the discipline. In contrast with Europe, the profession as practiced by our music faculties is for two reasons at once narrower and broader: first and primarily they are concerned with the training of composers and musicians [*Komponisten und Tonkünstlern*]; second, they are responsible for the musical education and stimulation of the entire student body. In the one sense, therefore, these institutions are conservatories in the musical sense, while in the other they are greenhouses of that musical culture that is a necessary attribute of every well-bred person. The president of our section [at the IMG Third Congress], for example, is Professor Albert A. Stanley of the University of Michigan at Ann Arbor; the fortunate and far-reaching influence he has exerted on the college youth of the Middle West has and can have no parallel in Europe. Another by-product of this peculiar musical phenomenon has had an effect on our colleges that must be of uncommon interest to Europeans: that is the strong movement to make musical subjects equal in value and academic qualification to other subjects in the humanities through the "credit system" (a remark that of course presupposes a knowledge of the difference in general between European and American universities). The leaders of this movement, by the way, are almost all members of the International Music Society.

Finally, I should like to express my personal belief that the anemic condition of our concert and opera life, due in large part to the system of exclusively private enterprise, has led the people to insist on a substitute in the guise of church music, that many of our churches have, so to speak, been turned into concert halls and our church music secularized and reduced to the level of an entertainment. And with that remark I conclude what I hope is an outline of the weightiest problems in the musical topography confronting American musical life. All of these problems are more or less economic in nature. To complete the picture, however, there must be added a psychological problem.

The American views music as a business — not, of course, as a trade that like the butcher's caters to the body, but rather one that caters to the esthetic sense. In America, therefore, the musical artist as such holds no special place in social life in the sense that Schiller had in mind. He pursues an art, or at least so the people suppose, not as an apostle of art but because his artistic ability serves him through art as a natural and effective weapon in the struggle for existence. Of course one cannot interpret the concept of business in the derogatory sense of the word. The heart of the matter is that the American musician views the business side of musical activity not as a necessary evil but, on the contrary, as the artist's only healthy and artistically appropriate means of changing cause into effect. He is therefore not what one can see so often in Europe: the victim of a hypocrisy that blushingly with one hand pretends to ignore Mammon as unimportant to the artist, while invoking the purest ideals, even as with the other hand it greedily grabs and counts up every penny.

From another standpoint it is clear that this practical (shall we say) concept of art as a means of making a living easily and often leads innately weak characters to turn business into a "racket" [*aus dem Geschäft ein "Geschäftchen" zu machen*]. In Europe such characters are often saved from the fall at the moment of temptation by the time-honored concept of art as an idealistic mission. Now, it must be categorically denied that the excesses of the American system exhibit their most repugnant aspects in native Americans; on the contrary, most of those who fall victim to this system are European musicians who emigrate to America in the hope of making "big money" and, once there, imitate not the idealists but only the "businessmen." How could it be expected that those who, with very minor exceptions, emigrated to America without any thought of idealism, who live by the European axiom that business and art are mutually exclusive, should all at once come to understand the apparent paradox that business and art can share a mutually beneficial relationship? They, as do most Europeans, see American musical life only as mirrored by certain musical magazines that to a degree engage in unabashed puffery and only in puffery. These magazines, however, do not give a true picture of American musical life and of Americans as musicians, insofar as the latter think of themselves as artists and not merely as artisans. The American artist regards these magazines with scorn and uses them, when he does use them at all, just as he uses the respectable ones — for puffery after all plays a natural part in every business. Thus he does not even notice the evil influence that systematic, garish, often childish, and sometimes dishonest advertising gradually exerts on his artistic conscience. Those who are not involved, on the other hand, can see very well the danger in this aspect of the concept of art as a business and in no way deny the harm that has already been done. They console themselves instead with the thought that in the end it is better if the darker aspects are exposed to view rather than being glossed over, only to serve as hiding places for hypocritical idealism.

In everyday life the distinction between the prosaic view of art as a business and the romantic view of art as a selfless mission narrows down to a precise point. From this crossing point on, the two views separate again. The question thus arises as to which of the two is the more deeply rooted so as to grow tall and strong despite the dead weight of daily life. If only the profile of American musical life depended solely on the artists, then perhaps they would be able through the power of their idealism to control satisfactorily the threats posed by the problem of art as a business. Such, however, is not the case, nor can it be. Even if in the end art exists only for artists (artists naturally in both passive and active senses) the fact remains that in everyday life art and artists rub shoulders constantly with the masses, the people. But now if the artists themselves see art as a business, not as something higher and finer that has acquired a commercial connotation merely from the unfavorable circumstances of the way musical life is conducted, then the masses, the people themselves, cannot be inoculated with the latter idealistic concept against their will, as in Europe. The people take the artist strictly at his word and compel him, in his dealings with them, to draw the conclusions from his premise. These people are indeed democratic, and insist in theory all the more on the principle of the Declaration of Independence, that all men are born free and equal, the more it is contradicted in the practices of everyday life.

The American people love music and have loved it openly from the beginning. They are, however, more musical than artistic. By that I mean that they do not intrinsically love art as art, or even art for art's sake. Indeed, how could they, for that would presuppose as axiomatic Liszt's concept of *Tonkunst* [musical art] as an aristocratic art. In a democracy, moreover, that has had no openly admitted need of an aristocracy since the beginning of the nineteenth century, an aristocratic art would have a difficult position to maintain even if artists as a body held an entirely esthetic view of art. But, as it happens, everything is aimed at a gratification of the masses; and the musician with his regard for music as a business (not in itself unwholesome) becomes simply a "Citizen Carmagnole" who has sunk to the level of the masses and has to accommodate himself to them. They see in the artist perhaps a music teacher, but not an educator in the art of music, a guide to the higher esthetic spheres that are inaccessible to them. They want art as amusement, as a "show." Art as a *Gradus ad Parnassum* is to them a wholly incomprehensible and unpalatable concept.

In this somewhat questionable relationship between artist and public there are those who play the role of seducer with the slogan "Art as Speculation." Here, finally, we come to the leading theme of private enterprise in its inevitable claim. Where neither the artist himself, nor through him the people, where neither the officials nor the state (in the name of and on behalf of the people) throw up obstacles against Art as Speculation with their motto *do ut des* ("I give in order that you may give") — in short, where all is left to private enterprise, there reigns unchecked the music speculator — who must be distinguished from the true businessman dealing in music. To the music speculator, despite the best of intentions, the artist is only a device to satisfy the craving of the multitude to see and hear; and the multitude is only a device to fill his pockets. The business competition between the speculators forces them to vie for the best showmen and box-office "draws" with offers of completely outrageous fees; it forces them to blunt the hunger of the multitude for the good and to overstimulate its hunger for the best; it forces them to beat the drums of publicity in a manner unworthy of art; it forces them, to be plain about it, to prostitute art, the artist, the people, and themselves. Hence the dollar has become the symbol of our musical life; the concept of art as an esthetic Grail is a seemingly dead concept. Year in and year out we hear the best music and the best artists, but our musical life nevertheless is throughly unsound because at bottom it is inartistic.

"A seemingly dead concept," I said above. Why only "seemingly"? Because the democratic masses are not in a position to bury the artistic ideals of an (in the Lisztian sense) aristocratic minority. In this minority the idealism of the Americans celebrates its resurrection. This growing minority sees in true art a cultural necessity, and it knows just as well as the minority anywhere that music should serve higher ends than merely to fill the purses of certain persons or to pass as nothing more than entertainment. The government, as has been said, will not help as a matter of principle; so help will come from private individuals. Only if we divide our musical life into its abstract components, only if we comprehend the obstacles in the way of a purely musical culture in America, will we then know how to honor the idealism of those who, as patrons, as teachers, as artists, as writers are leading a magnificent battle against evil powers in order to save America's musical life from the fate of Rome. In this exercise of a selfless, clear-sighted, tough-minded idealism on the part of individuals lies the strength of an exclusively private enterprise system. One will understand, then, why many Americans, aware of the astounding achievements of private enterprise, shy away from attempts to experiment with a mixture of private and government enterprise.

One result of the American system, finally, deserves to be especially pointed out. We can think what we want to about art as a business and exclusively private enterprise; the assumption and at the same time the result of this approach is that from a purely economic standpoint the system has worked, so that the average musician in America lives better and in more regular circumstances than he would in Europe. For that circumstance he can in the main thank the union activities of the American Federation of Musicians. It is true that any one of us would like it better if there were less dictatorial activity in that quarter and less downright hostility to art, since for them the art of music is merely a means of earning bread, and art for art's sake is dead as a doornail.

These are my views on the economic and psychological bases of American musical life. That these conditions did not develop overnight is sufficiently clear. What is there now by which one can gauge their historical evolution? In the narrow sense of specific sources the answer is: very little. The literature on music in America is fairly voluminous and is constantly growing, but the books and articles deal more with the history of music and musicians in America than with the history of America's musical life. For example, the scientific historical study and comparison of the German, English, Italian [and other] influences would immediately be paralyzed from a lack of such literature as can be taken seriously. Opportunities are not much better for reading up on a scientific, useful treatment of the historical vicissitudes of single masters in America (such as Haydn, or Wagner), or of the development of music in the various states and cities, of church music, chamber music, orchestral music, choral music, opera, music in our colleges, the music trades, the manufacture of instruments, the music-publishing industry, musical societies and organizations, municipal and government interest in and subvention of music, folk music, and a host of other subjects. Even exhaustive biographical and bibliographical literature is not impressive in quantity. Whoever seeks scientific information in any of the fields enumerated must laboriously dig it out from books and sporadic articles in magazines innumerable, not to mention newspapers, in which often our best writers on music have buried their investigations alive. Moreover, a good part of this literature does not possess the character of original research.[5]

What is more, it is almost all based on false historical hypotheses. Writers have overlooked the fact that Americans have constituted a nation since 1776, but that at the same time as a people they are much older — exactly as old, in fact, as the people who colonized the land. Until recently, paying no attention to the psychology of peoples, our historians assumed that in the eighteenth century secular music was not

---

5. The translation of the foregoing paragraph is Sonneck's own from the beginning of the fifth sentence ("The literature . . .") on. It comes from his 1916 paper, "The History of Music in America: A Few Suggestions," read to the Music Teachers' National Association and printed in its *Papers and Proceedings* 11 (1916): 50–68; this paper was reprinted in Sonneck's *Miscellaneous Studies* (New York: Macmillan, 1921), pp. 324–44. — ED.

only very primitive but was even scorned, and moreover that our entire musical life more or less found expression in antediluvian psalmody (a kind of choral song). In view of such absurdities, this reporter naturally found no difficulty in creating to some extent a firm foundation at least for America's secular music of the eighteenth century with his books *Francis Hopkinson and James Lyon* (1905), *Bibliography of Early Secular American Music* (1905), and *Early Concert-Life in America* (1907). A history of America's opera life in the eighteenth century has remained in manuscript these many years simply because your reporter has not yet found the desperate courage to offer a publisher a work so forbidding to the multitude. Fortunately the contents are to be found, much abridged, in the *New Music Review*.[6]

Through these works the previous opening chapters in a general history of American music have been consigned to the scrap heap in one job lot. These works have further shown that New England's role in the historical development has not been overestimated but that the roles of the Middle Atlantic states and the South have been greatly underestimated. From the latter fact comes the grievous lack of sympathy for his adoptive land shown by Frederic L. Ritter in his pioneering *Music in America* (1883; 2nd ed., 1890). This lack, at least, cannot be charged to Louis C. Elson's fresh and smooth-flowing *History of American Music* (1904), although in some respects it does not surpass Ritter's work; it puts Boston much too firmly at the center of the universe and misses the opportunity to do justice to music's swing around to the West.

The *One Hundred Years of Music in America* (1889) by G. L. Howe and W. S. B. Mathews should also be mentioned as an assiduous collection of historical (chiefly biographical) sketches. A capable but somewhat uncritical compilation is the volume *History of American Music* (1908) in the multivolume *American History and Encyclopedia of Music*.[7] Henry E. Krehbiel contributed some worthwhile articles to the new edition of Grove and to certain other encyclopedic works, although his greatest contribution lies in the field of New York local music history. It is him we have to thank in regard to *The Philharmonic Society of New York* (1892), *Notes on the Cultivation of Choral Music in New York* (1893), and most especially for his *Chapters of Opera* (1908). This

---

6. The entire book finally was published in 1915 by Schirmer in New York. — ED.

7. The volume on American music was prepared by G. W. Chadwick and Frank Damrosch. — ED.

book is valuable as a concise history of opera life in New York, but in particular it makes uncommonly interesting reading as the fruit of Krehbiel's more than thirty years of experience as a reviewer of opera. To Krehbiel add Arthur H. Messiter's *History of the Choir and Music of Trinity Church* (1906), and the list of useful studies on local music history in New York is just about complete. On Boston there would be even less were it not for the affectionate way that this Munich of America has been treated in general histories. Apart from Henry Mason Brooks's *Olden-Time Music* (1888), a collection worthy of mention only as a curiosity, and from the conscientious and informative *History of the Handel and Haydn Society* (vol. 1, 1883–93) by Charles C. Perkins and John Sullivan Dwight, there is almost nothing in book form that is useful and — above all — accessible to Europeans.

Certainly it would hardly occur to a European music librarian to procure the fat-volumed *Memorial History of Boston* for the sake of Dwight's assiduous contribution on music; or, turning to Philadelphia, to get a copy of the history of that city by J. Thomas Scharf and Thompson Westcott (1884) that contains much, though uncritical, material on music in the city of Francis Hopkinson's birth. After those general works one could point out the superficial and moreover obsolete book by W. G. Armstrong, *Record of the Opera in Philadelphia* (1884), and Louis C. Madeira's *Annals of Music in Philadelphia and History of the Musical Fund Society* (1896). Recently a young historian named Robert R. Drummond has published articles on local music history in Philadelphia in newspapers, articles that one hopes will be expanded into a broader and methodically developed presentation. One treasured but seldom seen pamphlet is Rufus A. Grider's *Historical Notes on Music in Bethlehem* (1873, a product of the Moravian Brethren). Great circumspection is required in using Leopold Sachse's *The Music of the Ephrata Cloister* (1903), in which he treats the musical activities of Conrad Beissel's union of mystics with great diligence but with a wholly unsatisfactory grasp of the musical rudiments.

Chicago has to some degree found a champion in George P. Upton with his *Musical Memories* (1908), and smaller works exist on other cities — Cincinnati, for example. Yet apart from the works mentioned, the field of local music histories in America is almost completely barren. This field must be thoroughly plowed before any sensible person can even think of writing a new history of music in America or anything of that kind that is fully proportioned and satisfies a genuine need.

Local histories alone, however, will not suffice. We lack, for instance, any generally useful study of American church music. George Hood's *History of Music in New England* (1856) concerns itself only with psalmody, is entirely out of date, and would become utterly useless if Mr. James Warrington could secure enough subscribers (at $45) to his monumental history and bibliography of this topic in America.[8] With that work a narrow branch of church music will have found its historian, but not the whole of American church music with its many terrifying problems. The history of opera in America has fared even worse. With the exception of Mr. Henry C. Lahee's superficial little book, *Grand Opera in America* (1902), we have nothing on this subject. Likewise with our literature on national song and folksong: we cannot claim much honor so far as material in book form is concerned. The best is still Elson's *National Music of America* (1900); although it fills a need it must be used with care because of its many errors.

On the interesting subject of the music of the Negro in America, what is found in books and pamphlets is totally unsuitable. Some worthwhile little articles are to be found in newspapers, but the time has come when finally, and for once with scholarly methods, the songs and dances of the Negro should be collected, winnowed, and examined in the light of their "white" impact. If that is not done soon it will be too late; and it can be said in this connection that for understandable reasons such an undertaking could be carried out only by a superior person, perhaps only by a Negro of American birth trained in scholarship and music. Much more attention has been paid to the music of the Indians. Not only do we have the books by Alice C. Fletcher and Natalie Curtis published by the Bureau of American Ethnology, but also close to two hundred more or less useful articles on the subject. It cannot truthfully be said, however, that there is any treatise on the subject that deals exhaustively with it, taking into account all the problems peculiar to it and all of the Indian tribes.

Our biographical and bibliographical literature is, as has already been said, not abundant. Lawrence Gilman's biography *MacDowell* (1908), Upton's two-volume biography of Theodore Thomas, the biographies and autobiographies of John Sullivan Dwight, Morris Steinert, Thomas Ryan, William Mason, Stephen C. Foster, my *Francis Hopkinson and*

---

8. See note 4 to Sonneck's "The Bibliography of American Music," above. — ED.

James Lyon, and some few others — that pretty much includes a majority of the most important books. Perhaps overenthusiastic but very useful is Rupert Hughes's *Contemporary American Composers* (1900). Bibliographical works in the narrower sense so far amount to virtually nothing. In the border areas between bibliography and catalogue moves my own book previously named. In place of further remarks let me refer, regarding problems in American music bibliography, to my study "The Bibliography of American Music" in the *Proceedings of the Bibliographical Society of America* (1904–5).[9] That study of course does not list the *Catalogue of Dramatic Music* (1908) of the Library of Congress, to which it is hoped other such catalogues may be added; nor the book catalogue, unique in form, of the Allen A. Brown Collection at the Boston Public Library, expected from the press at any moment. If, finally, we mention such books as Daniel Spillane's *History of the American Pianoforte* (1890), then we have brought into consideration a fairly good review of the literature so far as it applies to the more obvious features of musical life in America. At the least we have commented upon or cited by far the major share of the books that should not be lacking in any large European library that considers the musical life of America within its sphere of interest. To us Americans ourselves, on the other hand, it should at length become evident that the musical historiography of our country is still in bad shape, and that it is therefore mostly our own fault that there prevails in Europe such a confusion of ideas about our musical life.

---

9. Reprinted above. — ED.

A Contemporary Account
of Music in Charleston, S.C.,
of the Year 1783

My book *Early Concert-Life in America* is supposed to have buried beyond resurrection certain historical blunders about music in America in the eighteenth century. But nonsense dies hard, and some of our "historians" continue to revel in the same old tales of the exclusive cultivation of psalmody, etc., during the colonial period. Facts and their inevitable interpretation do not fascinate such scribes. Indeed, one of them asked me: "Why destroy the romance of history, if the people do not care for facts?" A question to which politeness forbade the proper answer.

In my book I insisted it would be foolish and unfair to look for a real musical life in the colonies outside of the comparatively few prominent cities. In those days, Charleston, S.C., was musically the Queen of the South and rivaled New York, Boston, and Philadelphia. Today only the venerable St. Cecilia Society, to which the contemporary article about to be quoted refers, testifies to the glorious musical past of Charleston, and that only by name. For many years now this aristocratic society, once musically so active, has been a still more aristocratic but purely social society. Membership in the St. Cecilia Society guarantees the stamp of

Reprinted from the *New Music Review and Church Music Review* 11, no. 129 (August 1912): 373–76. The letter there is printed in the original German with the title "Ueber der Zustand der Musik in Amerika, besonders in Charles Town in South Carolina, in den Jaren [sic] 1776 bis 1783," as taken from Hans Adolf Freiherr von Eschstruth, *Musikalische Bibliothek* 1 (1784): 113–16.

absolute approval by Charleston society; and this membership, so I have been told, is largely hereditary. These considerations of ancestry, of family, would seem to go so far that the history of the St. Cecilia Society is deemed to be of no legitimate interest to an inquisitive but noneligible historian. In my own case, at least, inquiries found a ready response only through the kind intervention of a lady of the bluest Southern blood.

Unfortunately the answers were negative, as the records of the Society do not appear to have been preserved. Perhaps they, too, fell victims to the late unpleasantness between the North and the South. For this reason, the historian, after exhausting the Society's necessarily very meager old news in the public press and elsewhere, finds himself dependent on the accidental discovery of contemporary accounts in other sources. Not until after the publication of my book, for instance, did I run across a description of the very elegant ceremonial surrounding the concerts and entertainments of the St. Cecilia Society. And now another accidental find has brought to light a contemporary account that throws interesting light on the activities of the St. Cecilia Society as the center of Charleston's musical life in the last quarter of the eighteenth century. But who could possibly have suspected the existence of such an account in the rare and fairly insignificant *Musikalische Bibliothek* edited by Hans Adolf Freiherr von Eschstruth? It appears there in the first volume, published in 1784, under the heading *Auszüge von Briefen* [Excerpts from letters] on pages 113–16.

The account is dated: "St. G. 20 Dec. 1783." It is very improbable that the "St. G." stands for the abbreviation of a name — such as, for instance, that of the violin virtuoso and composer Chevalier de Saint-Georges (1745–99), whose compositions were not unknown in America. Even if this eccentric hero of a novel by Roger de Beauvoir had come to America, he would not have been acceptable to white society and he certainly would have been excluded from the functions of the St. Cecilia Society since he was the son of a Negress. Probably the "St. G." stands for the name of some city, possibly Sankt Gallen or Sankt Goar. At any rate, our anonymous historian seems to have been a German, since his "Ladies and Gentlemens" (instead of "Gentlemen") is a typically German grammatical error. The words "in the years 1776 to 1783" perhaps point to some German or Swiss officer in the colonial or British army, and I am all the more inclined to this hypothesis because the years of his sojourn in America coincide so remarkably with the years of the War of the Revolution.[1] That our historian did not write from hearsay but from actual observation is proved conclusively by comparison with the chapter on Charleston in my book. If he seems to have expected to find a more lively interest in music, he shares this fault with other foreign visitors who did not take into consideration that a people fighting for their liberty are not likely to devote much thought and leisure to symphonies and sonatas.

Exceedingly interesting is his remark on the ability of Americans to distinguish between good and bad singing. This critical faculty, *cum grano salis* of course, we seem to have preserved intact, as many a foreign "star" has found to his or her dismay; but we have also learned — unless that, too, is merely a survival from colonial times — to rate properly the composers and instrumentalists. If, finally, the European notion that "music supports her masters handsomely in America and one can speedily make one's fortune" there dates at least from 1783, this belief would explain why, after the war, European musicians flocked to our shores in such rapidly increasing numbers. In our country, as elsewhere, I believe, music supports many of her votaries handsomely; but I fear that only a very few of her masters have speedily accumulated a fortune here.

[Editor's note: At this point Sonneck prints the letter in its original German, which he says "has all the flavor of olden times" and employs Von Eschstruth's "cranky orthography . . . which is a treat in itself and which reminds one vividly of the excesses of some of our own beloved reform-spellers." Following the German he proceeds with his own English translation of the letter, here reprinted without editing:]

ON MUSIC IN AMERICA, PRINCIPALLY AT CHARLESTON
IN SOUTH CAROLINA, IN THE YEARS 1776 TO 1783.

St. G. 20 Dec. 1783.

Music is not cultivated in America as much as in Germany. In Rhode Island we found music upon our arrival there in 1776 almost unknown. Therefore the dancing at balls was done to the music of two negro violins. In Charleston there were concerts twice

---

1. If "we" arrived in Rhode Island in 1776 and were later transferred to the Charleston area, with all the appurtenances of society, the writer could well have been an officer in one of the regiments from Hesse-Cassel that King George III hired as mercenaries at a price of something over three million pounds. — ED.

Sonneck on the porch of his Washington home, ca. 1913

a month, by four first and three second violins, two violas, two violoncellos, two bassoons, one harpsichord, two clarinets or oboes, two flutes and two horns, [by no means a primitive orchestra, but a typical, provincial orchestra in those days. The transl.] The price of the ticket was half a guinea. We met there the following musical artists: *Franciskini* [Franceschini] an Italian and good violinist, *Ebercromby* [Abercromby] a Scotchman, also a violinist, *Walton,* a harpsichordist, born in Charleston; [Peter Valton, advertised himself as of London.] Compositions by [Joh. Christian], *Bach, Abel, Toesky* [Toeschi], *Stamiz* [Stamitz], *Kammel, Haydn, Lord Kelly, Fischer,* Joseph *Schmidt, Möller* and *Pichl.* However, *Haendel* and even *Corelli* are still loved there.

The Englishman knows very well how to distinguish between a great composer and instrumental virtuoso and a poor one, but the accurate verdict of an American is restricted to vocalists. Ladies and Gentlemens [!] sing according to the usage of this country at social functions, particularly after the midday dinner, a song, one person after the other [presumably he means catches]. Of instruments, the clavecin, violin and viol d'amour are esteemed most. In England besides these, good oboists and flutists are appreciated. An oboist of the third regiment, by name of *Smith,* was a particularly powerful performer. Great singers or songstresses were not known in America during my sojourn there. The arias, which several aristocratic ladies sang at public concerts as *dilettanti* were written in the English language and were composed by *Arnold, Dibdin, Pinto, Weichsell* and others. Silence and attention during the music, however, one does not find in America as it really should be.[2]

Church-song consists in a chorale, which the organist first plays for the congregation in plain chords without any variations; then the chorale is sung by the congregation, the organist accompanying more fully with one or two additional "voices" [stops?], but pausing after each verse only until the congregation commences the next. Everybody sings so softly that one can hear the leader plainly among two or three hundred persons. The most powerful organ I saw in America had thirty-six stops, but like all organs there, it had no pedal. Most of them have two, even three manuals, but of the upper only one-half can be used because it is "blind" from contra F to C, or because the keys are there only for the sake of appearance and are "unbroken." At the same time, most of the organs have powerful sixteen foot basses.

---

2. [Footnote by von Eschstruth, in Sonneck's translation:]

Tout comme chez nous! but with this remark we do not mean to step too closely to the esteemed *perpetuum mobile* of our beautiful, respectively, not beautiful ladies. Our sweet gentlemen, too, often attend to this matter so well as not to require a so seductive example.

"Music supports her master handsomely in America and one may speedily make a fortune through her."[3]

Of course, the historian could easily challenge a few of these statements. However, the object is not to criticise our anonymous historian, but to save his account from further oblivion. To this account von Eschstruth added the note: "Im naechsten Stuek noch etwas hir von." This volume of 1785 is not in the Library of Congress, nor am I aware of its existence elsewhere in the United States. An inquiry about the promised continuation addressed to my colleague, Dr. Rudolf Schwartz, of the fine Musikbibliothek Peters in Leipzig, brought the reply that it does not appear to have been published. It would seem that von Eschstruth reserved it together with other matter for a third volume, but as his *Musikalische Bibliothek* ceased to exist with 1785, unfortunately the "noch etwas hir von" is lost to posterity.

---

3. Von Eschstruth would be amazed (Sonneck, with his historian's awareness of historical change, merely pleased) that the blue blood of Charleston now mixes with the robust bloods of Italy and — mirabile dictu! — of New York to help produce "Spoleta, U.S.A." On the matter of the "beautiful, respectively, not beautiful ladies" and the "sweet gentlemen" I have no recent information. — ED.

Sonneck Person-to-Person:
Three Informal Communications

I. Suggestions on Research into Music in Early America

It might seem a little strange to you that someone whose family has been in this country for less than fifty years should be addressing you, whose families settled here more than one hundred and fifty years ago, on a subject so close to your hearts. Perhaps if I tell you how my interest was aroused in the study of American music it may help to suggest to you how such work should be done.

It is now about sixteen years ago that I still held the belief (to exaggerate a little) that the history of musical art in America begins with the year 1860. I had read books by Ritter, Mathews, and others.[1] Nevertheless, I felt a little suspicious. In the first place, the history of music in this country was treated in those books as if the writer was sitting back

---

Here printed for the first time is a transcript of "excerpts from the informal address made by Mr. Sonneck . . . to the members of the Historical Research Committee [of the Pennsylvania Society of the Colonial Dames of America] regarding the contemplated work of the Committee on the music and musical life of Pennsylvania during the 18th century." The unsigned transcript, no doubt made by one of the ladies of the committee, came to the Library of Congress with other materials inherited (ultimately from Mrs. Alvin A. Parker, Chairman of the Committee on Historical Research) by the editor of the last volume in the set that resulted from "the contemplated work," who happens to be editor of this volume. Mrs. Parker had asked Mr. Sonneck what she and her committee could do about music in pre-1800 Pennsylvania and how they should set about it. This answer was given in person at Philadelphia on November 12 or 13, 1919.

1. Frederic L. Ritter, *Music in America* (New York: Charles Scribner's Sons, 1883; rev. ed., 1890); W. S. B. Mathews, *A Hundred Years of Music in America* (Chicago: G. L. Howe, 1889). — ED.

of a New England church window. Pennsylvania and other states did not seem to figure in the picture at all. That aroused my suspicions. I began to study the matter for myself by traveling from Maine to South Carolina, and spent more than two years of my life looking up old records and working ten hours a day trying to get at the sources. After that was done I put my researches into shape in the form of my books. What I found was this. The musical interest in our country started from the very time your forefathers came here. It is nonsense to suppose that people in England and France and Germany who were musical should lose their interest in music because they came to our country. Their life in this country of course did not have the same atmosphere as in the old country, but it is natural to suppose that their interest was kept alive. Down in Charleston, South Carolina, they were giving public concerts as early as they were in Vienna. In Charleston, Boston, Philadelphia, and so forth life was primitive, colonial, provincial — but it was there. As soon as we have the newspapers to work with we can trace these things. Previous to the establishment of newspapers we have to rely on other kinds of records. But to argue that if there are no records people had no interest in music is nonsense.

The first American composer was not William Billings of Boston, tanner; it was Francis Hopkinson, member of Congress, statesman, and a very cultured man.[2] Francis Hopkinson, like Thomas Jefferson, knew

---

2. The idea of Francis Hopkinson as "America's first poet-composer" seems to have been an *idée fixe* with Sonneck for at least twenty years. In the Lowens bibliography in Part 2, items 32, 47, 126, 127, and 134 are devoted to the matter. Part of the reason surely was the fact that when he undertook his researches along the eastern seaboard in 1900–1902 little was known about pre-1800 music in America and William Billings of Boston was highly touted; Sonneck was obviously delighted to be able to point the finger farther south and west, to Hopkinson in Philadelphia. As his crowning proof of Hopkinson's priority he further pointed to a sentence in Hopkinson's dedication of his *Seven Songs* (Philadelphia, 1788) to George Washington, a sentence that ended (see the facsimile reproduced here) " . . . I cannot, I believe, be refused the Credit of being the first Native of the United States who has produced a Musical Composition." Sonneck (in no. 127 of the Lowens bibliography, 3/2, p. 439) proudly asserts that "from all we know of Francis Hopkinson's character, I doubt not that he investigated the correctness of his claim and found his earliest compositions to antedate those of James Lyon. . . . so we may say that all available evidence points indeed to Francis Hopkinson as the first American composer." (James Lyon was a Philadelphian contemporary with Hopkinson.) As editor now, my reading of the evidence is just as it was in 1947 (see the dedication):
A. The compositions of Hopkinson and Lyon were antedated many years by the hymn tunes of Conrad Beissel, by the works of Moravian and other Penn-

a good deal about European music. If you study the programs you will find that colonial music lovers knew works of Handel, Corelli, and even Gluck. They had access to the music of the masters, through performances by musicians who had studied in Great Britain, France, and Germany. People have the idea that the only kind of music in the colonies was psalm singing. It is not true. I tried to cover the subject of secular music. I have written a book on the early concert life in America. I have also written a book on the early opera in America, up to the year 1800. Opera when it came here was mostly English opera. (The musical life in this country in fact does not rest on German models, but on English with German and other ingredients.) It is different with the church music. There too I have had the impression that the picture drawn by earlier writers of early church music life was not correct. If you study

---

sylvania composers, certainly by works both sacred and secular in New England, the South, and probably the Spanish Southwest, not to mention the French to the North. Even if Hopkinson had not come in contact with specific works, he certainly would have realized that even a pioneer civilization cannot exist for a century and a half without "producing a musical composition," no matter how crude or naive.

B. The language of the sentence in question obviously refers not to Hopkinson's works of thirty years earlier but to "this Work," the *Seven Songs* just "produced"; any other interpretation is grammatically as well as logically unsound.

C. In all his writings Sonneck almost invariably refers to his native land as "America," not as "the United States"; when he does use the latter he uses also a plural verb. It seems quite possible that the cultural and geographical concept of "America" was so fixed in his mind from his childhood and later influences in Germany that he was quite unaware of the newness of the concept and the name of "the United States" and of the very special significance "the United States" had for Hopkinson and his countrymen at the time Hopkinson's dedication was dated, November 20, 1788. Technically, the United States existed from June 21, 1788, when New Hampshire became the ninth state to ratify the Constitution; but only on July 26, following ratification by Virginia and New York, did the new country effectively begin its existence as the United States of America. No doubt Hopkinson's *Songs* and his new country were born almost simultaneously, and his claim changes from nonsensical grandiloquence to sweet reasonableness.

D. Finally, it seems possible that in his ardor to identify *the* first composer in British North America Sonneck completely forgot the sage advice he had given the Colonial Dames in the very sentence preceding: that lack of known evidence does not prove certain music did not exist in the past. Sonneck the sage and thoughtful historian was pushed aside by Sonneck the enthusiastic detective with an aversion to New England church windows and weakness — let it gently be admitted — for an attractive personage, a member so-to-speak of the Philadelphia aristocracy, self-profess'd (see his dedication) musical amateur though he was. — ED.

The dedication of Hopkinson's *Seven Songs*, from the copy in the Library of Congress

the books of Ritter and such men you will find that when anything has
been unearthed in the musical life, they do not take into consideration
that the same things happened in Great Britain. I have already suggested
what for you not to touch, suggested that you leave the secular music of
the eighteenth century alone.

It is different with the churches. As far as church music is concerned,
Pennsylvania is more interesting than New England. In Pennsylvania
you have the people from Great Britain, France, Germany, Sweden, and
so on, and all have kept more or less apart. Pennsylvania has not only a
larger field but a more varied field for that kind of work.

What I have said also suggests never to lose sight of where the church
music of these various denominations comes from. If you detach it and
treat it as purely American without European ancestry it would be up in
the air later on. If you pursue a systematic method of study, first you have
investigation, secondly the codification of these researches, and finally the
publication of your data. How should you go about it in the way of
research? I think very largely in the way I approached the secular side.

You have the newspapers, the diaries, and writings of those like
Washington and many others. You have the parish records. From these
records you will be able to glean references to the music of the period
and what use was made of it. It is not going to be an easy matter to do
this work. It has to be done, however, in order to offset that wrong
picture that has been painted. Every reference to music that is to be
found in the writings of Washington, Franklin, and other colonial men
in the historical magazines and other sources: get it together as far as
your subject is concerned.

I think it is just as important to know how to do it as to know what
to do. Suppose you have established what I might call a laboratory of
historical research, where under the supervision of someone trained in
this matter the ladies take up the study of the different subjects. Certain
ladies will undertake to investigate all the data in the Episcopal
churches. (By the history of music, I hasten to add, I do not mean the
history of the music and the composers alone, but of the musical life in
general.)

Dr. Benson's book treats the different denominations, all from the
standpoint of hymnology — from the literary side, with frequent allusions to music.[3] His book will help you to avoid a lot of mistakes. But

---

3. Louis F. Benson, *The English Hymn* (New York: Hodder and Stoughton,
George H. Doran, 1915). — ED.

you will have to go far beyond that if you want to reconstruct the *musical life* in Pennsylvania. It will be best to investigate up to the end of the eighteenth century and find out all you can about the musical life in the churches, and this you will have to get from the parish records.

It will be best to separate into different localities or branches; encourage everyone's ambition to get all the material out of all of the old records so it can be used later in a comprehensive and systematic way. Then, to repeat it, you want to go through the writings of the men of the colonial times, through the old newspapers, books, etc., that have been printed in America, and all the available literature, and extract all that is helpful to your purpose; and then reassemble the matter.

The first thing is to get the material out of the old sources, and it cannot be done by any other method than the laboratory method. What you want to do is to hunt up the sources well and then distribute the work, and then have someone keep her finger on the situation. I realize perfectly well that simply to dig does not appeal to anyone as a fascinating piece of work but it is the only way to do this work. Take for an instance the Gregorian chant. It has taken the monks of Solesmes fifty years and they have made 25,000 photographs of manuscripts of medieval times in order to reconstruct the old chant. They are not through yet, but they did succeed in restoring it. They felt the fascination of doing things in the interest of the result which they would probably not live to see. They did not do these things for the ambition of reading their own results in print — they wanted to get their material together and work along disciplined lines. That is what you will have to do.

As to what not to do, my suggestion is to avoid frittering away your energy. Get the material together by a corps of workers. Get it together in a form that will be useful to all of you. Get your notes together in a systematic form. Otherwise, the lady who is ultimately to put in form all of your work will have a lovely time. Why not start the thing in a uniform way in the beginning. It will save you a lot of trouble. I selected a certain size pad and did not make but one entry on a page so I could shift it afterwards where I wanted to. I had systematic headings that served as a card index.

Go to work and get together a list of such records as I have spoken of in the churches, have an index to the localities where you find something of use. Make this collection of data and then you can do whatever you wish to do in the way of publication.

I am perfectly aware that my remarks are informal, just a few rambling remarks. Still, they may be useful.

If you have made up your minds what you wish to do, if you go to Dr. Benson he will be of great service as to what to do and what not to do. Please keep in mind that Dr. Benson is largely interested in the literary side of hymns, and that what you want to do is to reconstruct the musical life. You must also approach everything connected with the Roman Catholic church. Monsignor H. T. Henry of the Overbrook Seminary is the best authority on this line and will be of great assistance.

You can spoil a good thing by approaching it from the wrong point of view. Too much of that kind of spoiling has been done. If you go to work in a direct scientific way and sacrifice your personal hobbies for the time being, the result will be that after a while you will have an accumulation of material, easily accessible, which some trained historian could use who would give you the credit of having put at his disposal the "bricks" upon which he builds his edifice. The method would be to have someone go to every church and find out if records exist, and if so it should be reported; if not, that also ought to be reported. Then copy out every reference to music. Then you only have a lot of material—but you have it in your possession! You must start by localities, find out what records exist. You must include in your search the religious concert music and the religious music in general. Concert programs could be copied out, etc., etc.

Previous to all this you have to make a survey of the historical literature that exists and then make cross-references to and from that. It will not do to excavate one grave, but you must dig up the whole graveyard—it will be much more satisfactory.

You will find that while Dr. Benson's book is very important for the study of early hymns of colonial times, he hardly touches on early organs. That was not his sphere of interest; there you have something to get which he does not speak of. The same is true of the personnel of the church choirs, the churchgoers and the families that listened to the music. It should not be restricted merely to hymns. That would leave out the sacred concerts and singing schools. It would leave out any number of things. Under able generalship I am sure the individual ladies will take a certain pride in doing this "stupid" work of digging interestingly. Without this "stupid" digging I am sure nothing will come of your project. If you can find out that certain families were musical through all their generations, it will be a neat little find. There is ample opportunity for the "historical short story" in that kind of work.

The itinerary [itinerant?] music teacher would be a good subject to dwell on. Information on this could be gleaned from the records in the possession of the families. You might be able to find the price paid to the teacher, what music was taught and by whom it was taught. Indeed, any number of interesting little historical things — if you go to the sources. The individual little stone signifies nothing; only the totality of such stones forms the mosaic.

Question from Mrs. Parker: Mr. Sonneck, do you believe it is worthwhile for us to undertake this subject?

Mr. Sonneck: Mrs. Parker, in all my experience I have found that there is nothing worthwhile — unless you make it so. If we succeed in making life easier for *one* genius or great scholar then we may take pride in having done our duty.[4]

---

4. Thus suitably inspired, Mrs. Parker and her committee got out two handsome volumes in 1926 and 1927 entitled *Church Music and Musical Life in Pennsylvania in the Eighteenth Century.* The fieldwork had not been quite what Sonneck urged, but the volumes contain much useful material on music among the Schwenkfelders, at the Ephrata Cloister, with the Moravians, and about various other groups, even including the Indians of Pennsylvania. The facsimiles and pictorial illustrations are numerous and valuable.

The third and final volume, however, proved to be a Jonah. It was unfinished when Mrs. Parker died, *aet.* 79, in 1931 (but not before she had accepted the invitation of Carl Engel, Sonneck's successor at the Library of Congress, to join with three other individuals in giving some thousands of dollars to found the Archive of American Folk Song in the Library of Congress). Her assistant died at a great age in 1943, having in 1938 issued a very slender part 1 of volume 3.

In early May of 1944 Carl Engel (by now Sonneck's successor with the music publishing firm of G. Schirmer in New York) was bearded in his lair by one Brooks Parker, accompanied by porters bearing some fourteen cartons of "Pennsylvania project" materials. Parker — a fencer on the American Olympic team of 1912 — was a businessman, a pioneer in aviation insurance; he had no great interest in music, early or otherwise. But he was also Annie Brooks Bloodgood Parker's son, and he had promised his mother on her deathbed that he would see her project concluded in decent fashion. He left the fourteen cartons with Engel, admonishing him (as he told the story in February, 1946) that "it was your predecessor, Sonneck, who got my mother — and thereby me — into this predicament, and it's up to you to publish this thing and get me out." On the following Saturday, May 6, 1944, Carl Engel was found dead in his home.

That circumstance gave Brooks Parker pause only until the war was over and he came — with his fourteen cartons — to the Library of Congress for help. Part 2 of the final volume was published in April, 1947, and Parker could finally rewrite his will and live in peace. It is a strange roster of names that were in one way or another involved with the Parkers and the "project" over a period of

II. Reader's Report on a Music Book Manuscript

This book taxes the patience and conscientiousness of the reviewer.

The style of utterance is unattractive and curiously ingrown. The English is often clumsy or slovenly. If the book be accepted for publication, much editorial work would have to be put into it in order to give to the author's ideas more fluency. The book is not so much tiresome as tiring.

The thirty chapters forming the book are uneven in interest, as might be expected of so many short articles — and they only a miscellaneous selection — serially published during the course of five or more years.

The title of the book leads one to expect a stimulating insight into what the future of music may be. The author was modest and honest enough to qualify the title by saying "some hints." That is about all one may credit the book with, so far as the future of music is concerned. The book had to have a title. So the author, as it were, picked up a piece of string and tied his articles together.

He appears to be a man who has thought earnestly about music and with considerable effort has arrived at opinions that unfortunately partake too much of the character of preconceived theories. On these he insists in a rather tiresome manner. The whole method of presentation is too centripetal, too dogmatic, too much of the *quod erat demonstrandum* type. This would not be a defect, if the book presented a real philosophy of music of the future, perhaps faulty but consistent and reasonably new.

Consistent the book is only in a somewhat wholesale condemnation of our present musical life and the practices that govern it. Consistent

---

This report, here printed for the first time from the carbon copy among the Sonneck papers at the Library of Congress, is dated "October 1921" and is addressed to one of the country's leading book publishers, who had asked for Mr. Sonneck's opinion of a book manuscript submitted for possible publication, the title being "Some Hints on the Future of Music."

---

thirty years (for the last editor had to continue "mopping up" operations until 1950). The roster included poor James Warrington, R. N. Williams II (also a 1912 Olympics contestant, a survivor of the *Titanic* disaster, and long director of the Historical Society of Pennsylvania), Irving Lowens, Harold Spivacke (who became involved with Brooks Parker's imported steeplechaser, Wunderprinz, who won his first race at Belmont), President Franklin D. Roosevelt, and a professor of American history at Stanford University. — ED.

also in this, that the remedy is seen (to quote the first lines of the book) in the necessity of incorporating with the practice of art that which is known to science of the laws governing sound.

In his introduction the author apologizes for many seemingly dogmatic statements but contends that through experiment he has had sufficient proof to lead him to hope that scientific principles may eventually replace personal theories in the training of future musicians. That is also the hope of a man like Carl Seashore — with this slight difference, that the latter writes with the authority of a scientist whereas the author of this book writes as so many other pseudoscientists have done before him.

His *idée fixe* may be the solution of all our troubles, whether real or only imagined by him, but it is not enough to insist on it like the advertiser of some cure-all patent medicine. To be convincing the author should not have limited himself to an apodictic flourishing of his pet notion, but should have demonstrated its soundness by detailed analysis and argument. To find fault with existing conditions, then to claim that the remedy is *science* (of an acoustical kind) and to leave the searcher after truth in suspense with a few commonplace, vague remarks about the purity of tone depending on a conscious study of fundamental tones and overtones is really not enough. The unwary reader will receive the impression that practically only the author has ever busied himself with the scientific principles underlying music and that he holds the magical key in some secret shrine. As a matter of fact even singers and instrumentalists, if to be taken seriously as musicians, know a good deal more about the scientific basis of their art than the author admits.

The author is opinionated but he is also observant. There are many remarks in the book to indicate that and often these remarks assume the quality of tersely worded aperçus. One would enjoy reading them more, if they were more frequently original than they really are. Their effect is weakened by juxtaposition of truisms of the stalest kind.

The author is at his best in the articles dealing more particularly with his speciality, namely the voice and singing. Indeed, the articles not devoted to these subjects could well be spared, except the general introductory article of faith in science as a panacea for us ignorant artists. The concentration of these articles would improve the book and give it more of a raison d'être as a book than it now has.

If published the book will find readers, of course, as does every book published, but the reviewer believes that the articles served their purpose sufficiently when published in the *Musical Courier*. They did most of the good they could do in that form and cannot have done much harm. In form of a book, their usefulness would probably not be increased very much, whereas the number of pseudoscientific cranks might be unduly increased to the detriment of art.

III. Letter to Carl Engel

Oct. 21, 1921

My dear Engel:

Rotten pen, rotten letter.

Well, I brought you two together at last. There remains nothing for me except to answer your letter without fear or favor and to tell you that the meeting between you and Mr. Putnam was polished off in Pittsfield, where I arranged even for the presence of Mr. Loeffler, if necessary.[5] Ha, he, hi, ho, hu — ha, ha!

But now to the serious business of answering your letter.

First let me give you the history of my resignation.

I had grown a little stale from fifteen years' excessive work at Washington. Not only did I build up the collection there to its present preeminent position in the worruld, but I devised all the technical machinery, bibliographical tricks, etc., trained the force as far as it could be trained, compiled catalogues published and unpublished with my own hand, wrote books, devised and designed practically everything you see there, edited the Quarterly, lectured, composed a little and did I remember not what. It was too much for one man, besides running the show in an administrative capacity.

Then came the war. I have never been able to join the anti-German hysteria. My studies in history taught me that "guilt" is not such a one-sided affair. The propaganda maneuvres of the other side were too clumsy to fool me. Living the life of a hermit at Washington, I meditated

---

This unedited handwritten letter, not only self-explanatory but explanatory of many other persons and things, is among the papers of Carl Engel at the Library of Congress.

5. Charles Martin Loeffler, composer and one-time violinist in the Boston Symphony Orchestra, was a great friend of Engel's and — like Sonneck — of Mrs. Elizabeth Sprague Coolidge, who began Berkshire music festivals at her summer home in Pittsfield, Mass., as early as 1917. — ED.

conviction, which I still have, that with all of Germany's sins committed by her evil genius, Arthur Zimmermann, America's entry into the war would ultimately be found to have been the most colossal blunder in American history. In my whole attitude I was inspired by patriotism in the best sense of the word and I suffered terribly, when I saw the whole country steeped in hypocrisy and bamboozled from within and from without. I was strictly Pro-American in my views and pro-German not even in the current popular sense, except that my blood would out, when it came to a preference during our period of neutrality. After that, I bowed to events, regretting them as an American deeply. I suffered the agonies of hell, like all native Americans who prided themselves on being "German-Americans" and were being treated more and more like outcasts and lepers by the Anglo-Saxon element in our population. That treatment I shall not forget and shall not forgive, conscious as I was, in my own case, of what I had done in my own little way for America. For fifteen years I had given myself up to my country — and they opened my private letters down there even before we entered the war! You have no idea how the discovery of that affected me, who had never said a disloyal word or done a disloyal thing but, as an American, claimed the right of interpreting world events for himself as his understanding of them impelled him to do. True, my views were decidedly unpopular, but I did not air them in public and my record coupled with my discreet behaviour during those agonizing years should have kept me out of the range

A page from Sonneck's letter to Engel

on the stupidity of it all and of all of them and reached the conviction, which I still have, that with all of Germany's sins committed by her evil genius, Arthur Zimmermann,[6] America's entry into the war would ultimately be found to have been the most colossal blunder in American history. In my whole attitude I was inspired by patriotism in the best sense of the word and I suffered terribly, when I saw the whole country steeped in hypocrisy and bamboozled from within and from without. I was strictly Pro-American in my views and pro-German not even in the current popular sense, except that my blood would out, when it came to a preference during our period of neutrality. After that, I bowed to events, regretting them *as an American* deeply. I suffered the agonies of hell, like all native Americans who prided themselves on being "German-Americans" and were being treated more and more like outcasts and lepers by the Anglo-Saxon element in our population.

That treatment I shall not forget and shall not forgive, conscious as I was, in my own case, of what I had done in my own little way for America. For fifteen years I had given myself up to my country — and they opened my private letters down there even before we entered the war! You have no idea how the discovery of that affected me, who had never said a disloyal word or done a disloyal thing but, as an American, claimed the right of interpreting world events for himself as his understanding of them impelled him to do. True, my views were decidedly unpopular, but I did not air them in public and my record coupled with my discreet behaviour during those agonizing years should have kept me out of the range of spying insults. I did not mind the occasional insult by hysterical idiots and I did not mind a bit that the government adopted methods of surveillance, which were necessary in many cases, but I was deeply offended by the discovery of lack of confidence in me personally, precisely because they might have known that I was above suspicion or ought to have been.

Add to that state of mind in 1917 the memories, ever fresh, of a

---

6. Arthur Zimmermann was the German secretary of state for foreign affairs in 1916–17 when the decision was made to engage in unrestricted submarine warfare with the Allies. Not being aware that his messages were routinely being intercepted and read by British cryptanalysts, Zimmermann in January, 1917, sent a message to Mexico offering that country a large part of the southwestern United States provided Mexico would join the Central Powers if the United States entered the war against them. It was this "Zimmermann telegram" — which the British of course showed to President Wilson — that finally tipped the scales away from neutrality and brought alliance with France and Britain. — ED.

personal experience of several years' standing that cast a shadow over my life in Washington and you will understand that Mr. Rudolph Schirmer's offer to join him found me in a receptive mood. The offer was tempting because it seemed to open a way for me to make both ends meet better and to counteract the unfortunate fact that I was always in financial difficulties though not spending money foolishly.

Somehow my instinct warned me against acceptance, but appearances won me over, especially when Mrs. Sonneck took the affirmative side and Mr. Putnam told me that he could not see how I could let the opportunity of such an increase in my income slip by. I accepted Mr. Schirmer's offer and have regretted it many a time since, not only because my rapidly increasing income did *not* put me on easy street — we seem to be *"Pechvögel"* ["hard-luck Charlies"] in that respect — but because I had jumped from the frying pan into the fire, or rather from a fairly clean atmosphere into the foul air of an out-house. I need not tell you what I went through at Schirmers during these years. You know enough of my life here to appreciate my confident belief that I need not go through Purgatory. I had it amply at 3 East 43.[7] Washington, even from 1914 to 1917 was Paradise in comparison. It can all be summed up in the one remark: what a difference between Mr. Herbert Putnam and Gustave Schirmer and his satellites! What a difference even to-day between Herbert Putnam and the Dioscures[8] who control things with me as a kind of "also ran."

It was an awful come-down for a man like me, powerless as I was and still am to do the grand thing in the grand manner and that is in the only manner which will permit Schirmers to remain Schirmers with corresponding benefit to the stockholders. Rudolph Schirmer had the necessary vision to see that, though unfortunately he did things that came pretty near wrecking the institution, even without the able assistance of Gustave Schirmer, your present boss. However, I shall not entertain you with old chest-nuts. We are agreed on that subject and it is not the purpose of this letter to unfold to you a history of my trials and tribulations at 3 East 43[d] nor my opinions of what the activity of a first-class music publisher in this country should be in his own interest,

---

7. For many years the music publishing firm of G. Schirmer, Inc., was located at 3 East 43rd Street in New York. — ED.

8. In Greek and Roman mythology the Dioscuri ("sons of Zeus") were the gemini Castor and Pollux. Insiders may conjecture as to who the Dioscuri were at Schirmer's. — ED.

in that of music and that of the public. It is a curious fact, however and
to return to the "theme," that when I left the Library of Congress I did
not receive one letter of congratulation but only letters of regret, some
of them even accusing me of being a deserter. Well, I was, in a certain
respect, since I had calculated that it would require ten more years to
complete the job that I had begun.

I might also consider myself a deserter, because my resignation put
Mr. Putnam into a bad hole. He could not fill the place properly, because it required a man who at the same time was a musician, a historian, a bibliographer, an executive, a business man and a librarian, or
rather a man endowed by Nature to develop what training and experience had not yet given him in all of these capacities. Mr. Whittlesey
obviously could not be more than the "acting" chief during the vacancy,
because his knowledge is merely a superficial routine knowledge.

Mr. Putnam practically kept the place open for the prodigal son to
return, should the Schirmer experiment turn out unbearable for him.
Repeatedly the deserter was on the verge of return. Mr. Putnam knew
that and he also knew and knows why I am sticking to my present job,
instead of sailing into my haven of refuge. I have to think of my mother
and of my wife. She and I live a very retired life, yet we do not seem to
be able to make that kind of a showing as many others with my salary
would manage to do. To drop back to a $3000 salary, would be to
invite disaster. We should not know how to get along on that, since my
talents for outside work are very limited and since the War has cut me
off from an extra income. Also, I must be in a position, where I can
come to the rescue of my mother.[9]

There is a further reason. Rudolph Schirmer looked to me to carry on
the business in the spirit of himself and his brother as publishers. I can't
desert that trust and I can't desert his two widows, while there is danger
of G. Schirmer Inc being turned into a purely "commercial" house.
Should I leave, furthermore, the American composers of serious music
would have no friend left there. I can't, in other words, desert the cause,
while there is still the punch of fight in me. And a fight it is that has
been undermining my strength. As long as there is a chance of my win-

---

9. Before World War I, Mrs. Julia Sonneck, Oscar's widowed mother, had
lived in comfortable circumstances as head of the household for a retired and
well-to-do banker in Frankfurt-am-Main. No doubt the war had affected her
situation drastically, so that by 1921 with the great trouble for the German
mark Oscar Sonneck felt responsible for her. — ED.

ning out, I feel that I ought to stay, though I should much rather work for a livelihood in more congenial surroundings.

Here is a dilemma, or was. For my worldly safety it was better that the haven of refuge be kept open for me indefinitely, but on the other hand the longer it was kept open, the sooner what I built up was likely to dilapidate. I came to the conclusion, though occasionally still casting anxious eyes at the Library, that it was more important to fill the place properly and see my work continued and possibly improved than to consider my personal bread and butter problems. So from time to time I urged Mr. Putnam to approach either Kinkeldey or you, the only two men in America whom I considered worthy of being my successors. Kinkeldey is out of the running, at least at present; you are the only candidate left. Kinkeldey has the advantage over you of having managed a library and of having been more continuously than you in the field of history and bibliography, but you have that advantage over him of being more conversant with the latest developments in music and of possessing a wider commercial experience, which is a rather important desideratum, since you would have to do a lot of buying, first hand and second hand.

What would await you in Washington?

First of all a "boss," who never lets you feel that he is boss. A man who will back you up every time, if you by your ability and industry and judgment have gained his confidence. It would be a relief and a pleasure, as it was for me, to work under an administrative genius, a diplomat, a gentleman of culture like Herbert Putnam.

Secondly you would find a musical library which in many respects is marvelous, in other respects not yet sufficiently developed and in some respects needs repairs. Its administrative machinery is not perfect, but it is as good as I could make it or dared try make [it] with the number and kind of assistants I had at my disposal. Not one of them was "wissenschaftlich ausgebildet" [trained as a scholar], with the exception of Bruno Hirzel who was with me for two years and later on the strength of that was made head librarian of the Zurich library! Their chief asset was their willingness to work and learn and their loyalty to me. Much had to be left undone, because our limited force was physically unable to do it and because it also was unfit by previous training, or lack of it. My two most intelligent assistants are no longer there and I understand from Mr. Whittlesey that not much may be expected of those assigned since to positions in the Music Division. If he says that, it must be pretty bad. You would still find there Mrs. Girard, a German by birth, fleissig [industrious] and faithful and Quiller, the colored messenger who used to make me quite as angry as Mr. Gus later.[10] Quiller is a capable fellow, but pompous and terribly conceited. He would soon get on your nerves, but he is capable, though erratic. Mr. Whittlesey I have already summed up, but it is only fair to add that he is a persistent worker and has a great experience in a routine way and a fair amount of executive ability.

If you accepted the job, the weakness of the force would soon become apparent to you. But you would be a new broom and I doubt not that Mr. Putnam would try to improve your staff within his legal limits. As he puts it, the Music Division is holding its own in a routine way. Perhaps, but I doubt it. At any rate it is not going ahead, except in a routine way. I have remained in touch with affairs to a certain extent; since my departure no important purchases have been made without my advice, except in one or two cases which were injudicious. Mr. Putnam would undoubtedly acquaint you with the Memorandum I drew up on the present and future status of the Music Division before I left for New York. In addition, my articles on the Music Division, sundry memoranda, and my annual reports (summarised more or less in extenso in the Librarian's annual report) would be of considerable help to you as guides.

Third, Washington is not Boston, artistically or musically. When I came to Washington I tried to improve its musical life which was rather too provincial for my taste. I gave up the job when I came into contact with too many musicians for whom I had no respect and retired into my shell. I believe, however, that Washington improved musically as time went on and most probably the difference in its musical life and interests between 1902, 1910, 1917 and now is pronounced.

There were even in my days a number of musically cultured persons there, with whom contact would be a pleasure. I do not believe that you would find it difficult to make friends there, though they might be interesting for talents and knowledge other than musical. The climate I found not ideal, whereas Mr. Putnam — diplomat that he is — always without a smile claimed that it was ideal. He spent his summers mostly in his little yacht off the coast of Maine, whereas we spent them in the

---

10. "Mr. Gus" was Gustave Schirmer III, grandson of the founder of the firm. — ED.

oppressive atmosphere of the District of Columbia! Spring and Fall are lovely, the winter is indifferent and the summer is trying. On the whole, I found the climate enervating. Life is decidedly cheaper than in New York, whether or no cheaper than in Boston I do not know. One advantage that the position carries with it is the opportunity to attend important conventions and to descend on New York, possibly on Boston, on Library business. Of that opportunity I did not make the most, though Mr. Putnam constantly urged me to brush up on new works, etc. in New York. He realized better than I did that an artist would have to get out of Washington now and then to fill his lungs with esthetic ozone. A still more important advantage that the position implies is the chance to go to Europe on Library business for a couple of months. I went to Europe every two years and it did me, and the Library, a lot of good.

The salary is still, I believe, $3000, but there is an effort on foot to increase corresponding salaries (which are comparatively few in the government service) to about $4000. To those of us who move in the commercial world, such a salary will appear as rather stingy. Indeed it is, for the knowledge required and the responsibility attached. However, the U. S. government in such matters is stingy and pays specialists salaries that are much too low. If you could not increase your income by outside work, it would be very difficult for you to live on your salary and you should not attempt it. Ten years ago it was feasible and easily so in a city like Washington where the standing of persons is not measured by their stocks and bonds; to-day it is not, especially if one has become accustomed to a more expensive living-standard.

If you could increase your income to about $5000, you ought to be able to live modestly but comfortably. That you could increase it to at least $4000, I am convinced. In the first place, you are lucky enough to be able to count on royalties. Then you may safely count on $200 from the Musical Quarterly, if we agree on the proposition I am making you in a separate letter, provided of course that the powers that be do not dish [*sic*] the magazine. At any rate on about $120, if you contribute two articles a year.

Next comes the fair opportunity to secure a few pupils among the well-to-do of Washington as victims of harmonic and contrapuntal longings. I never went into that kind of thing, though I had the chance. Furthermore, there is no reason why you should not be able to build up a little business as lecturer in and out of Washington. I did it in a modest way, without any special effort. My final fee was $100 per lecture, but it would pay you to be a little more modest in order to get regular engagements. Don't forget that there are several colleges or universities in Washington and any number of fashionable lady seminaries. Had I returned to Washington, it would have been precisely in that direction that I should have tried to add to my income. Don't forget that the position carries with it a lot of prestige and that may and can be exploited in a perfectly dignified manner. Don't forget, further, that the routine work as librarian of such a collection inevitably will exercise your mental muscles and somehow you would feel impelled to show your fitness in public. The stuff that you would investigate and crowd into your cranium, would want to get out somehow. And you would need such a relief from the daily, monotonous grind that is inseparable from bibliothecal work!

Summing up, I should say that with just a little ability for private business you ought to be able to add about $1000 a year to your salary, not counting your royalties.

I can't make the decision for you. Yours is the chance and yours the responsibility. I must step aside, after having made it possible for you to take my place and make a name for yourself in a more lasting way than any commercial job possibly can. You are no more sick of business and business men than I am, but such a change has to be considered from all angles and while bookworms may thrive on dusty, musty treatises, homo sapiens cannot. He needs the filthy lucre.

This long letter, I hope, will help to set you thinking still further on the subject. Come to New York and let me answer any searching questions you may think of. If you decide to accept Mr. Putnam's offer, you can count, that goes without saying really, on me for any advice that you may need professionally. I am quite sure that you would want to ask many questions, until you have found your bearings. I shall answer them to the best of my ability and it may tickle my vanity just a bit but pardonably, if you make the acquaintance of O'Gloom[11] from a side fairly unknown to you and utterly unknown to my associates at 3 East 43. The four years at Schirmers can't have driven my accumulated knowledge as a librarian out of my head completely. I had a lot to learn yet in that capacity, but I could and still can teach others a lot as Chief and Ex-Chief.

---

11. Mr. Hitchcock (see "After 100[!] Years," below) is right: Sonneck cannot have been all that gloomy if he himself joined in the jibes. — ED.

Should you go to Washington as my successor, no doubt you would do good work and in this or that way probably better work than I, but after a study of the history of the Music Division you would be, as others before you, utterly flabbergasted by what I accomplished in those fifteen years without the kind of assistance I really needed for the more scholarly aspects of the job and presumably you would stand in awe of me. Then would come my little joke: I should show you wherein I failed and I should delight in undermining a too good opinion of me.

All good wishes, my dear Carl,

Your

Oscar

99 Pacific Avenue
Or, In Search of a Birthplace

I was born on October 6, 1873, in Jersey City at what A.D. 1922 was No. 446 Pacific Avenue. And thereby hangs a tale.

My birth certificate duly and officially records the date of my birth, the names of my parents, George C. Sonneck and Julia Sonneck, either Jersey City or Lafayette (then still a suburb of Jersey City) — and, as the place of my birth, 99 Pacific Avenue.

In the spring of 1922 I suddenly conceived the notion to visit the spot where I was born. Partly out of curiosity, partly because my sense of humor (queer at times, I admit) pictured to me the possibility of renting or purchasing the house with the prospect of dying where I was born — completing the circle. So my wife, a friend of hers from Jersey City (who knew something about the topography of that beauty-forsaken place), and I made the pilgrimage one Sunday afternoon, reaching Pacific Avenue by trolley. It was strange, as afterevents proved, that we first took what seemed to be the wrong direction, toward the higher house numbers of Pacific Avenue. We then went in the opposite direction as far as the streetcar permitted and walked the remaining

Reprinted, with very minor editing, from *The Musical Quarterly* 19, no. 4 (October 1933): 456–62. Carl Engel, Sonneck's successor as editor of *The Musical Quarterly*, prefaced Sonneck's story with an introductory note that reads, in part: "On October 6th Oscar Sonneck would have been sixty years old; on October 30th it will be five years since he died. . . . We have thought of commemorating his sixtieth birthday by offering to our readers an amusing little skit of his — written in 1922 and hitherto unpublished — that reveals all the methodical exactness of the scholar and at the same time has the light touch of the ironist, an unusual combination, but quite characteristic of Oscar Sonneck. . . ."

distance. At first that lower part of Pacific Avenue presented itself as quite a respectable, habitable street of typically American red-brick two-story houses with basement, but gradually the "elegance" faded, and at No. 146 it vanished altogether. That is, the world came to an end. Unpaved, unkempt Pacific Avenue continued between railroad embankments, a few factories, and a vast dump of broken this and that, ashes, decaying fish, and similar dainties. Of houses, except a solitary saloon, half a mile farther, no trace. However, I proceeded to the hypothetical location of No. 99, and viewed the void with mixed feelings. Especially, when I saw the Statue of Liberty greeting me from the distance over the railroad embankment in front of me. The odor of my birthplace was too much for me, and I returned to the poorish end of inhabited Pacific Avenue, my vanity somewhat hurt, and my imagination painfully stirred by the apparent discovery that no admirer of mine, nor a grateful posterity could nail a memorial tablet to the house in which one Oscar George Theodore Sonneck was born.

The conclusion, of course, was that the house in which I was born must have been demolished or must have tumbled down under the weight of inoccupancy — for who but a poor, struggling civil engineer could have thought fifty years ago of living in such repulsive surroundings, in what at that time must practically have been a swamp?

In that light I reported the episode to my mother, though already suspicious of the success of the expedition and the accuracy of my findings. It seemed doubtful that houses could disappear so utterly in a street inhabited fifty years ago. It was more plausible to suppose that perhaps in later years the houses had been renumbered so that No. 99 had now perhaps become 199. At any rate, I reported to my mother the failure of the man seeking his birthplace, as good-humoredly as I knew how. Her answer was a mild rebuke for my belief that I was given the dignity of birth in such a poorish district and on the spot of a future, hideous, though colossal, dump-heap.

My mother's tenacious memory brought back to her the scene of my birthplace: No. 99 Pacific Ave. was in 1873 in the "better" part of the street, not far from Grand Street. It was a two-story red-brick house with basement, only about four or five years old, and the house was owned by a friend of my parents, "Uncle Graeven."

Well, the physical description fitted dozens of houses along Pacific Avenue, but that description with the reference to Grand St. and Uncle

Graeven furnished convincing clues that the ill-fated expedition had indeed been *"fehl am Ort."*[1] Since 1873, something had evidently happened to the house numbers. That something I was determined to run down during my next vacation, relying on my former technique of research.

In August I made my second expedition to Jersey City and betook myself to the Jersey City Public Library. There, with the help of an intelligent woman librarian in charge of city directories, I went through all the directories of Jersey City from 1873 on upward and downward. And this is what we found: none of them contained the name of Sonneck — another blow to vanity — and that of 1878–79 was the first with a street directory, informing the reader that Pacific Ave. (Lafayette) ran north from Greenville to Grand St. It began with No. 91 at the corner of Ash, and the block between Ash and the next street, Walnut Ave., began with Nos. 122–124. In 1895–96 the directory showed the change from Walnut to Johnson Ave., the numbering remaining the same for Pacific Ave. It so continued until the end of the century, but in the directory of 1900–1901 suddenly the first number mentioned for Pacific Ave. became 456, and the block between Ash St. and Johnson Ave. was numbered 456–414. This state of affairs we compared with the official Jersey City map and it agreed.

The conclusion was obvious: at the time of the consolidation of Lafayette with Jersey City, about 22 years ago, the city fathers decided to reverse the numbering of Pacific Ave. Where the high numbers had been, they now put the low numbers — those below 146 theoretically into that evil-looking, evil-smelling dump-heap — and where the low numbers had been they put the high numbers, so that Pacific Ave. now runs north from Greenville to Grand completely reversed as to the sequence of the numbers.

That was obvious; but it was also clear that No. 99, where I was officially born, must now be sought, and must still be sought, in the block between Ash St. and Johnson Ave.

Thus the problem had simmered down to locating between Nos. 456–414, or the corresponding odd numbers, the house which formerly was known as No. 99. Here the real puzzle began, because I did not know on what side of the street formerly the odd numbers were located. That point neither the directories nor the map made clear, yet on that

---

1. Or, as we might say in English, "had ended up in the wrong pew." — ED.

point the whole success of my research depended. So I decided to hasten to that fascinating block and to interrogate "oldest inhabitants" after looking over the premises. From the coloring of the map it could be deduced that the haunted castle of my birth must have been what were now 447 – 445 *or* 446 – 444, other red-brick houses being too far down the street or too new, as inspection on the spot substantiated. The *or* was the puzzling factor in the situation, and this I decided to remove by first visiting the (horrible) saloon at the corner of Ash St., No. 452. As luck would have it, an elderly workman — the whole block being in-habited now by laborers — was not too far gone alcoholically to take an interest in my "case." After some reflection he decided to take me farther up the street on the other side to a musty greybeard who had lived in the neighborhood for forty years or longer.

The old gentleman's memory was rather weak, but while he could not remember where No. 99 had formerly been, he did know that his own No. 463 had formerly been No. 82! My bibulous friend and I departed in triumph: we now knew that the odd numbers formerly were on that side of Pacific Ave. where now the even numbers are. But with that important discovery luck deserted us. We tackled in vain one of the real-estate dealers in the vicinity; he was too green for my purpose. But he was courteous and referred us to a colleague of an older vintage, a Mr. Schlick, whose mother especially would know all about No. 99, having lived in that block for decades. Unfortunately Mr. Schlick was out of town. There was nothing to do but get his address for inquiry by me, if it should be necessary to "search" old Mrs. Schlick's recollec-tions. I treated my patient collaborator to what proved the vilest beer I ever tasted, in the aforesaid corner saloon, and we parted.

As a last effort for the day, I had a look at Nos. 446 and 444, either of which two houses, I had calculated, might be the historic spot. No. 446 seemed deserted, though not uninhabited. I tried its twin, No. 444. It was opened with reluctance by a workman of patently Slavic origin. He either did not understand me, or else did not understand English, and I was about to give it up as a bad job when another Slav emerged from the rear. He spoke English fluently and was an intelligent chap, but all he could tell me was that he had bought the house from another Slav recently. However, he would look up his deed and if it said any-thing about the former number, he would let me know.

That 446 *versus* 444 left me no peace, and so I decided the next day to bother the city authorities with my problems. First I went to the surveyor's office in the City Hall. The official was very willing and polite, as most officials are if one knows how to handle them; but it became a matter of tactful diplomacy to suggest to him how he might find what he was looking for. To make a long story short, he finally hauled out some surveyors' maps dating from about 1873 and compared them with the recent map. With the result that we found Nos. 446 and 444 to be Lots M and L in Block 2092 and that they corresponded with what had been formerly the double lot 13 in Block 327.

This again was a step forward. There remained only to dig out from the city records which half-lot of 13 once upon a time belonged to "Uncle Graeven." That proved to be more troublesome than I expected. Partly because the city clerk whom I tackled for that job apparently did not put at first much faith in my logic — I, a mere inquiring citizen with a fool notion, and he a politician and official — partly because he evidently was the type of man who will go about a thing in his own way or not at all. Fortunately for me, however, he was not unintelligent, though self-set, and he made up his mind to settle my question without losing many words about it, once he saw that I knew what I was talking about.

As a conscientious politician generally does, he knew a great deal about his ward or district; although at first he denied that there was such a corner saloon, he finally "remembered" the place and the "wop" who owned it. But the Mr. Graeven bothered him. He did not recall any such citizen, though he had known that block for many, many years, etc. It was best to let that sort of mind use its own method of investigation, without antagonizing the man with argument, just at a time when his assistants were out for lunch and he had other, and presumably more important, business to attend to.

Mr. City Clerk (whom I sized up pretty soon as a capable fellow accustomed to doing things) hit upon the same method as I had done the day before: he telephoned to one of the oldtimers, a judge who had lived thereabouts for fifty years. Mr. Justice did not remember anyone by the name of Graeven or Greven. Q.E.D., but at my suggestion that Mr. Graeven might have owned the house without having lived there himself and therefore might conceivably not have been known to the dear old judge of infallible memory, and considering further that my official Jersey City birth certificate showed that I was born at 99 Pacific Ave., and that my mother positively knew the house to have been owned by Mr. Graeven, said city clerk changed his tactics and dragged

The house at 446 (formerly 99) Pacific Avenue, Jersey City

forth from the vaults the terribly dusty tax-assessment books, etc., the only records that could possibly answer my question without useless debate. Once he had gone that far, he kept at it and, turning the leaves of the venerable tome, he found, as I knew he would, Uncle Graeven's name. That he was entered as Theodore Graves — the city clerk pointing out to me with some satisfaction *my* error in the name — made preciously little difference to me, but to put Mr. City Clerk in good humor I conceded my mistake, or rather misinformation. Whereupon he spent another ten minutes comparing the old records and found that, indeed, Theodore "Graves" had owned in 1872–73 a house in the old block 437, *but* Lot 7, not part of Lot 13.

At this contretemps, which threatened to upset all my calculations, I had to laugh. The gentleman resented that, but was pacified when I explained to him the discrepancy and its bearing on the matter. Whereupon he held forth against surveyors' maps, etc., their ignorance in such matters, etc., and made the good point that tax records with their details were a better guide for my purposes than surveyors' maps. It being certain from the records that Mr. Graves owned Lot 7, it could make little difference how the numbering of lots by surveyors differed from the one used by the tax assessor, particularly as surveyors' numberings changed. Mr. Graves having paid his taxes on a Lot No. 7, the only question still to be answered was: what was the present number of that lot?

And after due investigation here is what we learned from the records:

In Block 2092, Lot L, No. 444, is now owned by Mary Rybezyk and Lot M, No. 446, by Carrie Curran. In 1872–73 Lot L had been Lot 6, bore the street number 101, and was owned by George Ellis; and Lot M was now what had been Lot 7, once owned by Theodore Graves. *Ergo Lot M being the same as the then Lot 7 and Lot M being No. 446 Pacific Ave., it was this house that in 1873 bore the street number 99.*

Thus, after much travail and, for me, amusing research, argument, and calculation, I returned to New York City, armed with the incontrovertible knowledge that I was born on October 6, 1873, in Jersey City, at No. 99 Pacific Ave. which is now No. 446.

The expedition, however, had one other result: it made me abandon any desire to rent or purchase my birthplace. Far be it from me.

OSCAR GEORGE THEODORE SONNECK.

Aug. 25, 1922

The American Composer
and the American Music Publisher

As if by historical law, musically weaker nations appear to be invaded by nations musically stronger. The invasion is accepted as a matter of course until native effort stirs. The revolt grows as quantity and quality of the native product clamor more and more for just recognition, and the demand for just recognition is followed by the doctrine of independence. From sensible, reasonable independence to absolute independence is the next step, and the extremists advocate it noisily. A reaction toward saner concepts sets in, and the very ones in whose behalf the whole movement evolved begin to feel uncomfortable and wash their hands of a boosting propaganda that stipulates as the primary consideration not merit but place of birth.

Something of the kind is happening to the American composer. He has become the subject of a somewhat hysterical propaganda literature. With the monotony of repetition, he is pictured as a genius unduly neglected by the wicked foreign musician and the equally wicked native publisher. He is acclaimed the equal, if not the superior, of living European composers. Occasionally, the voice of a gifted, competent American composer like Deems Taylor is raised in protest against such uncritical patriotic hallucinations. Less often the indiscriminate attacks on foreign conductors, singers, and instrumentalists are reduced to tangible evidence. Even more seldom the wicked American music publisher finds

Reprinted from the *Papers and Proceedings of the Music Teachers' National Association,* Forty-fourth Annual Meeting, New York City, December 27–29, 1922, ed. Karl W. Gehrkens, Studies in Musical Education, History, and Aesthetics, 17th ser. (Hartford, Conn.: MTNA, 1923); pp. 122–47.

a defender and then, as a rule, one not sufficiently versed in the intricacies of the publishing industry to gain converts.

As a musician who spoke up for our worthwhile American composers long ago when the sport was not quite so fashionable as now, and who drifted from educational work as a historian of music in America and librarian into the executive realms of the publishing business, I may be credited with some knowledge of the inside facts. That knowledge imposes upon one the duty, both agreeable and disagreeable, to help prevent with a timely note of warning a splendid movement from getting out of control and from being turned into a disorderly show of self-intoxication.

If those who unwisely pamper too many American geniuses with the sweet morsels of martyrdom would draw their data less from inspiration and more from the actual record, they might content themselves with a less vociferous interest in those of us who happen to be native American composers. Again, if they drew up a kind of graded guide to musical genius, setting against the names of European composers the names of American composers of corresponding grade, their disappointment at finding our composers somewhere down the list might not survive the ordeal. Who, in his right senses, would class Edward Mac-Dowell, remarkable as he is and still for me the foremost American composer, with Bach, Handel, Rameau, Haydn, Mozart, Beethoven, Shubert, Schumann, Chopin, Brahms, Wagner, Verdi, Liszt, Mendelssohn, César Franck, Debussy?

Suppose we insisted on giving MacDowell, in such a philistine attempt, the grade of a Bizet — that is to say, a grade considerably below the first few classes. Where would other American composers fit in who compare in artistic importance with MacDowell as Meyer-Helmund or Bohm compare with Bizet or Grieg? And Meyer-Helmund and Bohm, at that, possessed musicianship, and the indefinable sense of *métier,* to a degree immeasurably above that of the similar type of successful *Kitsch* composers in our country, some of whom, in private, are honest enough to admit their inability to work out their ideas (as ideas often winsome enough) without confidential assistance from better musicians.

For our few composers of the caliber of Horatio Parker, Chadwick, Arthur Foote, Whiting, and Mrs. H. H. A. Beach, I have much more respect than have some of our young champions of unpruned self-expression. These American masters of their craft would lose their respect for a critic's balance of judgment if he were to rate them above or as high as a Rubinstein or Raff. Now place in the forefront of American composers those already mentioned, and them alone, together with John Alden Carpenter, Charles T. Griffes, John Powell, Edgar Stillman Kelley, Henry F. Gilbert, Henry Hadley. Triple the number by adding, according to taste, men like Daniel Gregory Mason, Ernest Schelling, Leo Sowerby, Rubin Goldmark, Henry Holden Huss, Emerson Whithorne, David Stanley Smith, and be careful not to forget the eminent septet of naturalized American composers, Charles Martin Loeffler, Ernest Bloch, Percy Grainger, Leopold Godowsky, Victor Herbert, Leo Ornstein, Carlos Salzedo.

Is that enough to challenge the superiority of Europe with her Tchaikovsky, Dvořák, Musorgsky, Richard Strauss, Hugo Wolf, Mahler, Mackenzie, Vincent d'Indy, Ravel, Chausson, Elgar, Schreker, Schönberg, Pizzetti, Malipiero, Rachmaninoff, Nicolai, de Falla, Albeniz, Granados, Pedrell, Medtner, Stanford, Marx, Korngold, Lekeu, Ireland, Goossens, Glazunov, Martucci, Sgambati, Florent Schmitt, Puccini, Pfitzner, Milhaud, Busoni, Rabaud, Ropartz, Fauré, Pierné, Dukas, Charpentier, Nielsen, Sjögren, Casella, Sibelius, Bantock, Massenet, Saint-Saëns, Zandonai, Montemezzi, Zemlinsky, Szymanowski, Braunfels, Bartók, Kodály, Vaughan Williams, Holst, Honegger, Turina, Scott, Delius, de Séverac, Koechlin, Mortelmans, Jongen, Rasse, Gilson, Holbrooke, Parry, Castelnuovo, Magnard, Hindemith, Pijper, Palmgren, Respighi, Weingartner, Du Bois, Duparc, Roussel, Suk, Fincke, Fibich, Smetana, Enesco, Bruckner, Gräner, Alfano, Bax, Bossi, Boughton, Chabrier, Karlowicz, Prokofieff, Rezniček, Reger, Rimsky-Korsakov, Scriabin, Sinding, Wellesz, and many more, of varying styles, modernity, techniques, and talent? Indeed, if we adopt the method of Rupert Hughes in his book on American composers[1] and if our challenge include the American composers too promiscuously, then Europe in such a test of strength would have every reason for crushing us with her inexhaustible reserves of respectable composers of whom the very names would be unfamiliar to many of us.

Certain of our propagandists must have lost all sense of humor if they expect our one hundred millions, on a less favorable esthetic soil, to produce as much good work as four times that number of Europeans on European soil. The actual truth is that we here in America do not know

---

1. The reference is to Rupert Hughes, *American Composers*, rev. ed. (Boston: Page, 1914). — ED.

what is going on in the beehive of Europe's composers. We get an inkling of it if we follow diligently the reports and reviews in our musical news magazines, but for the only test that actually counts, the aural test, our ears have to content themselves with comparatively few new European works by comparatively few composers. And, as is equally inevitable, a not always infallible personal preference by this or that conductor or singer reduces the number of works performed for intrinsic merit and strictly esthetic reasons still further.

Yet there are those extremists who desire even that modicum of acquaintance with modern Europe barred in favor of American works, because some American works happen to be better than some European. Such a policy of exclusion would get us nowhere. Such a wall for the protection of the American composer, who really is no longer an infant, will not make him better than he is. It might indeed make him worse. Though all-American programs in my opinion have their value and place for special purposes,[2] Edward MacDowell's aversion against all-American programs was based on a sound idea: what counts is not comparison between ourselves but comparison with the rest of the musical world. Every self-respecting American composer worthy of the name with whom I have discussed that problem shares MacDowell's point of view. Any other would indicate a confession of weakness and cowardice. And worse, of stagnant ambition. The great majority of works composed in America are utterly dull as music; so are, of course, the majority in every other country, but unfortunately for us the sense of *métier* is nowhere so weak as in our country. Not that technique redeems dullness, but dullness *plus* crudity is hardly a standard by which a healthily ambitious American composer would wish to be judged. For works like Rubin Goldmark's *Requiem*, Loeffler's *Pagan Poem*, Bloch's Viola Suite, Griffes's *Poem* for flute and orchestra, Powell's *Rhapsodie Nègre*, Mason's *Russians*, Gilbert's *Dance in Place Congo*, Carpenter's *Birthday of the Infanta*, Stillman-Kelley's *Pilgrim's Progress* to tower above the dry-as-dust plains and scrubby foothills of American music means little for our pride. That, however, they and other American works move on terms of artistic equality, even

---

2. As an example, I mentioned, when reading this paper, the concerts of the American Music Guild. I said that a program such as that to be rendered on January 3, 1923, with works by Gruenberg, Griffes, Mason, Loeffler, was one of which any American could feel proud and which would command respect everywhere in the world.

superiority, with some of the best European works we have been privileged to hear assigns to them their true measure of significance. Give every American composer who has something of his own to say, provided he says it reasonably well, a chance to be heard, but do not waste the precious energy of patriotic propaganda on the boosting of mediocrity or worse. The propaganda will spend itself ingloriously if it turns its attention uncritically to pretty little prize songs or commonplace effusions in red, white, and blue ink, and does not concentrate persistently on the very best we have to offer, in open international competition. That best we do not hear nearly often enough, but to blame principally foreign-born conductors for this chronic neglect of repetition, for this lack of permanency on the programs, diagnoses the seat of the trouble only in part.

This or that foreign-born conductor may harbor a purblind prejudice against American music good enough to satisfy his requirements for his organization, which he refuses to turn into a laboratory for the tryout of tyros, but emphatically that attitude cannot be imputed to such conductors as a class. The real trouble lies deeper than such trivial argument, if only that fact would be recognized by those who shed tears of patriotic emotion over every composerling accidentally born in America, who accept every phenomenon and institution of American civilization as a sort of eleventh commandment. For the furtherance of the American composer in the larger and more difficult constructive forms, he could not possibly be cursed with a worse organization of musical life than ours. It is not the overseas import of persons and music that stands in his way, but the metropolitan import and transport within our own country from place to place. We have not enough local musical backbone; the best of musical backbone in our make-up is too mobile. This is a subject not germane enough to the present occasion for analysis and proof, so a mere hint must suffice: instead of a dozen first-class and nearly first-class orchestras we should possess competent, professional, and permanent orchestras under competent professional conductors in every city of 100,000 inhabitants or even fewer. The same is true with chamber music organizations and with opera companies. The visits of the "star" organizations would retain the character of festive occasions, but the daily musical bread would be supplied from within.

The problem of the American composer thus resolves itself into an economic problem of music rather than of an affirmative or negative state of mind. Solve that economic problem and his problem, too, will have been solved. Until then his radius of action will remain stunted, and his opportunities for performance will not cease to be comparatively and discouragingly few. Worse than that, until then he will have to go a-begging for (insufficiently rehearsed) performances with score in hand, from conductor to conductor, foreign or native, using "pull" and intrigue as levers. That is the rule, unless he happens to have composed a work of such outstanding merit that even now, under present adverse economic conditions, acceptance by this or that conductor becomes merely a matter of course.

While these defects in the organization of our musical life continue, no propaganda for the American composer will do more than slightly increase the appearances of American works on our programs.[3] That would be a welcomed gain, but it would not be a remedy. If the gain consisted in forcing mediocre American works into a crowded repertory of masterworks, the gain would be one of quantity, not of quality, and therewith actually a loss. Indeed, I sometimes wonder whether the fatal American tendency toward stereotyped, indistinct sameness, toward putting the national mind into a uniform, is not wreaking havoc on the propaganda for the American composer, too. It would be the easiest and most charitable explanation of the singularly frequent absence of differentiation between what is conventional, feeble, and unoriginal in our music and what is unconventional, powerful, and original.

Precisely in that direction I have for some time sensed an alarming weakness of the propaganda. It preaches quality but aims at quantity, and then attributes to the quantity a quality the music does not possess. Under that delusion the fundamentally economic factor of the situation loses attention; the prime responsibility for the plight of truly representative American composers is shifted from general American conditions of society to individual persons. The result is that American composers of only moderate — indeed mediocre — attainments, whose works radiate no significance whatsoever for America's musical progress, receive too frequently the gloriole of martyrdom. Therewith the

---

3. The weakest representation is that of American piano music by both European *and* American pianists; but then, pianists pay as a rule just as little attention to modern European piano music. I hope that the time is not distant when every well-balanced miscellaneous international program may properly contain at least one important American work, not as a result of propaganda pressure but as the natural consequence of artistic supply and demand.

circle completes itself. The virtues of discriminating modesty and discriminating pride both disappear before the vice of chauvinism. The propaganda becomes noisy, shallow, and uncritical; a good American who composes is therefore supposed to be a good American composer; and in John Tasker Howard's pungent phrase, the American composer has become, indeed, the victim of his friends.

This state of affairs is known to be true by every conductor, foreign or native, but prudence forbids public utterance to that effect. Indeed, diplomacy may induce conductors or singers or instrumentalists to express opinions in public that differ essentially from those expressed privately. Well-informed critics often remain silent for the same reason, unless they prefer to speak the truth at the peril of being proclaimed traitors to the cause of the American composer. As for the American music publisher, he too knows the true state of affairs, but he will rarely voice his innermost opinions and then only with a cautious side-glance at his business.

The species of the American music publisher is rather variegated. Here I am concerned only with the publisher who takes an intelligent interest in music as such and gives cultural thought to the problems of music and musical life in America. I do not speak of the mere utilitarian cretin for whom the click of the cash register is the sweetest of all music, or whose musical taste does not rise far above so-called popular music and mushy parlor ballads, or whom the difference between "heart songs" and "art songs" puzzles like an Ephesian [Eleusinian?] mystery, or who sees in every pretty American ditty an imperishable master song and then ostentatiously preaches the gospel of the neglected American composer for the increase of his business in such wares.

If you desire to know the American music publishers who have done and are doing most for the American composer of music that possesses primarily an art value, not commercial value, it will pay you to study and compare their catalogues. Music of this kind is relatively expensive to publish (unless the publisher receives financial help) and it is published as a contribution to American art rather than for commercial profit. A study of publishers' catalogues is the only fair test of the sincerity of their intelligent interest in and propaganda for the American composer, and also of their efforts to increase the composer's commercial viability.

The type of American music publisher whose opinions deserve respect differs from the banausic type just flagellated. Whether an American music publisher belongs to one type or the other, however, the American composer of music *in the smaller forms* has no legitimate grievance against him. The propaganda for the American composer misses its mark if it charges the American music publisher with retaliation or willful neglect in that respect.

Ever since the tender beginnings of the music-publishing industry in our country during far-off colonial days, the American composer has had little to fear from willful neglect by the wicked publishers. Songs, piano pieces, anthems, and the like were produced and published on American soil in ever-increasing quantities; and, whatever the demand of the public for such wares was in any given decade, the publisher acted as the beast of burden to carry the supply from its source to the ultimate consumer.

From its infancy, the industry divided its attention between native products and reprints of foreign music, but not until about the middle of the nineteenth century did the music of our classics, the romantics, and neo-romantics (which means for that period principally German music) assume substantial proportions. In the absence of international copyright protection before 1891, the industry could supply the rapidly growing American demand for the best available European music by reprinting it. Even after 1891 the American music publisher could with impunity reprint whatever had been published abroad before that year. The public domain, so called, was his happy hunting ground, and he made the best of his opportunities, as do publishers everywhere under similar circumstances.

The year 1891, with its first presidential proclamation of special copyright agreements with other countries (the United States to this day not being an adherent to the Copyright Convention of Berne), marks the turning point in the history, theory, and practice of music publishing in America.[4] With that year the further supply of reprintable European material began to be curtailed until it has dwindled down to the remnants of what is presumably in the public domain and commercially still worth reprinting. Certain newer American music publishers clearly perceived the ultimate consequences of our copyright agreements with

---

4. The presidential proclamations were made possible by the copyright act of 1891, which for the first time allowed citizens of other countries to copyright their works in the United States — provided their countries granted reciprocal rights to citizens of the United States. — ED.

foreign countries. They wisely specialized from the start in the publication of American music and did not indulge in the suicidal attempt at competition with older houses whose catalogues owe their far-reaching educational and cultural importance for America to the systematic reprinting of important European music that was in the public domain and free so far as the United States is concerned.

It would be a fatal error to argue from the mass of reprints of the older houses that their ears were bent predominantly on Europe and deaf to the voice of America. The men guiding the destinies of these older firms were by choice or birth Americans. In addition they were farsighted businessmen; and for those two reasons, if for no other, not one of them deliberately slighted the American composer. On the contrary, they outdistanced their predecessors in the industry with their willingness to shorten the interval between the American public and the American composer. In this attitude they have persevered with a liberality that is almost ludicrous, if one applies the acid esthetic tests of intrinsic musical merit to their output. To accuse the American music publisher of indifference toward the American composer simply will not do.

A pilgrimage to the Music Division of the Library of Congress and a mere glance at the American music publisher's mountainous offerings on the altar of American musical "genius" would cure the most doubting Thomas of his doubts. If not, let him glance through the paralyzing pages of the *Catalogue of Copyright Entries;* he will find the wildest dreams of his propaganda for the American composer come true in ghastly fashion.

What the American composer of songs, piano pieces, anthems, and similar music in the smaller forms needs is no longer encouragement by the American music publisher but discouragement. A startling statement, and one, perhaps, that will be deliberately misunderstood. It will not be by those who have worked in a publisher's office and have watched, like Goethe's magician's apprentice, the endless stream of music, good, bad, and indifferent, pouring in on him. Mostly very bad, unspeakably crude, dishearteningly unconscious of a composer's obligations toward Art and of her requirements. Disgustingly often the music is accompanied by letters proving it to have been the ambition of the composer (*sit venia verbo*)[5] to have written his piece less for the sake

---

5. With regard to the word "composer": "You should excuse the expression." — ED.

of Beauty than for making a lot of money. We publishers are staggered by the absence of anything like self-criticism in the bulk of this drivel, by the evident notion that anyone in America so inclined can compose music without knowing the first principles of the art, by the naive expectation that such musical atrocities and imbecilities will forthwith be inflicted on the American public by us. There appears to be a lamentable absence of waste-paper baskets in the homes of composing Americans; at any rate, no conception of the blessings of hospitality dispensed by these useful receptacles. There is too little appreciation of the amount of hard study required to overcome the essential difference between hopeless dilettantism and solid musicianship, as is fortunately displayed in the most casual piece of many an American composer, young and old, who is a trained composer and not merely an unmuzzled apostle of eruptive self-expression.

This fad of self-expression on the part of so many who have nothing to express with any degree of musicianship may be forgiven; but what must one think of music teachers who control music departments in colleges and more or less brazenly give the publisher to understand that the college will withdraw its business from him unless the favor of the account is reciprocated by the favor of publishing that gentleman's music? What is one to say of teachers of composition who, to judge from the results of their teaching, do not master what they pretend to teach, who recommend for publication time and again mere exercises fresh from their classrooms, as if they were heavenly inspirations of *the American composer?* How to reject these conservatory blossoms without offending the professor on whose goodwill we publishers depend as a business asset is a problem — but one not half so critical as to give convincing reasons for nonacceptance of harmless prize-competition songs offered in the flush of victory and endorsed by men or women of reputation. And the innermost recesses of tact — or, if you prefer, hypocrisy — are reached when the publisher with staple, standardized reasons regretfully sees himself unable to publish music of no conceivable merit on which some famous artist has bestowed enthusiastic or merely diplomatic adjectives, competing with us publishers in tact — or again, if you prefer — in hypocrisy.

Happily there emerge with fair frequency from the Fool's Paradise compositions of no particular higher or deeper significance, perhaps, but of sufficient inspiration and charm to arrest a publisher's immediate attention. The experience of drawing in a breath of fresh air after escaping from the dungeons of the subway is not more exhilarating than the discovery of a genuine bit of music, whether prize-composition or not, amidst the rubbish. What of it, if the piece be technically immature? Our music editors will deftly make the piece much better than when it originally reached the publisher. So good, indeed, that much to the amusement of a naturally gifted composer who does not pretend to be an expert in the niceties of compositional technique, one of her songs, so doctored, was quoted in a book on harmony as a most interesting example of harmonic ingenuity.

The American public hardly realizes the extent to which some of its favorite composers lean on such editorial cooperation for the musicianly presentation of their ideas. After all, it is the musical "idea" that counts, and such composers reveal more wisdom and artistic conscience than certain half-illiterate composers so void of every vestige of self-criticism as to resent any helpful suggestion by music editors who are generally their superiors as composers and command the resources of musical technique infinitely more than they. There roam, of course, through the editorial profession pedants and cranks as in every other profession. Occasionally, that species will spoil instead of improve a helpless composer's ideas or will even attempt to tamper with the work of a master because it violates some precious moth-eaten rule. On the whole, however, our best music editors are so hungry for signs of individuality, of originality, of musicianship in the music they editorially prepare for the engraver that they will preserve the composer's intentions intact whenever they possibly can with due respect for the slight difference between what is, in music, "I am not" and "I ain't."

Suppose a manuscript piece has refreshed a publisher like an oasis in the desert; the chances are that he will disregard his conscientious business scruples against overproduction and will accept it with alacrity. The publisher submits the contracts to the composer and promises to publish the piece as soon as his accumulations, his congested publishing program, or whatever else the stock phrases are will permit. Quite often the piece retains its appeal by the time it goes through the process of publication, but quite as often its charms have faded and the publisher would much prefer not to have rushed himself so enthusiastically into a contract with the composer. Why this? Because by that time the piece has been removed from the background of trash from which it had stood out and now has entered into the severer competition with other pieces accepted under similar circumstances. Though still anxious to encourage budding American talent, the publisher is convinced by that acid test that he overestimated the value of the piece, overestimated the promise of the new composer for the future, that the investment will probably not justify itself, and that most probably he has not discovered a new Cadman or a new Nevin in embryo.[6]

In all confidence, how publishers yearn with becoming modesty and sanity, not for a new MacDowell but for a new Cadman or Nevin! But how exasperatingly rare they seem to be among the American composers of a younger generation! Indeed, has the observation ever struck others so forcibly as it has me that the American composers who are musically as well as commercially valuable, composers who not so long ago could be numbered encouragingly, are now either dead or, with a very few exceptions, past their twenties? A singular phenomenon, that, which worries the American publisher for the simple reason that his ultimate salvation depends on the new young American composers rather than on the old. What is the explanation of that disquieting phenomenon? Do the young American composers speak a musical idiom so bold, so unconventional, so ultramodern that we cannot follow it? By no means; with exceedingly few exceptions, their utterances are rather tame and conventional and old-fashioned, if one discounts naive excursions into the whole-tone scale of Debussy or rather rare pilgrimages to the now abundantly charted shores of Stravinsky, Scriabin, Schönberg, and occasional but somewhat futile and clumsy compliments to jazz. Intrinsically, Edward MacDowell's first *Modern Suite for Pianoforte*, composed at the age of less than twenty and published in the year 1883, continues to exhibit a modernity and a craftsmanship far in advance of most of the efforts of present-day American composers twice his age. Among the few really adventurous young American composers whose fairly ultramodern tendencies are the skin and not the shirt, a Leo Sowerby stands forth like a master, because he has both an enviable talent and a conspicuous technique.

The absence of the latter is so noticeable in so many young American composers who come to my notice, as I guide the publishing destinies of the corporation in which I am an officer, that the question weighs heavily on me and on others: is the young American composer under-

---

6. Cadman is of course Charles Wakefield Cadman (1881 – 1946). Nevin no doubt is Ethelbert Nevin (1862 – 1901) of "The Rosary" rather than his younger (and less sweetly sad) brother, Arthur (1871 – 1943). — ED.

trained? If so, the fault lies with his teachers as much as with him and indicates a serious defect in the disciplinary courses in our musical institutions. That is a generalization, of course, but one cannot point to exceptions emanating from this or that conservatory and therewith hope to whitewash matters. Or, has a period of comparative sterility begun in our country? That would be a calamity indeed, after all the systematic efforts by our music journals, by individuals and organizations, foremost among them the National Federation of Music Clubs, to remove unnecessary obstacles from the path of the deserving American composer and to secure a proper recognition for his art in the country of his birth or adoption.

Whatever the explanation, the fact remains that the American publisher who seeks to harmonize musical ideals with commercial enterprise must, nowadays, fall back for his best "wares" on American composers of established reputation. Of course, their new works do not always live up to that reputation, but in such cases the publishers accept them with gratitude for past favors and with hope for better things to come. If the new works measure up to the composer's best, the atmosphere in the editorial office changes as if by magic. All the nauseating trash is forgotten, the publisher and his "readers" give the work their keenest attention and absorb it with admiration. Indeed, I have seen otherwise *blasé* "readers" shed actual tears of delight over beautiful American songs, for instance, and comment on them with expert praise so extravagant as to make me dubious of their prophecies.

If any American composer believes that in reputable publishers' offices, where such experienced and sensitive musicians act as readers, he does not receive fair treatment, he is mistaken. Another absurd notion is that musicians must spend hours over six pages of manuscript of a simple nocturne for piano before they may presume to appreciate the composer's fine points. One does not have to eat the whole omelette to know that a bad egg went into it; generally, it requires just as little time to spot a good or bad composition as it does to taste the difference between a good or bad omelette.

True, a composition may be good and yet may be returned to the composer; for, try as one may to avoid it, the matter of strictly personal taste enters into the problem of critical appreciation. Nevertheless, no really good American composition nowadays is likely to escape publication, if the composer only has the sense to submit it in turn to any one of a half-dozen or more publishers of known standards. Rejection of a composition by a publisher by no means always means that he did not like it. Often enough he would like to accept it, but so many other compositions are patiently waiting for publication that sound business operation demands rejection at the risk even of allowing a promising piece to pass into the hands of a competitor less embarrassed by accumulations.

Granted that all American music publishers issue a lot of things of little or no real musical value, in their totality their publications undoubtedly represent the best the American composer has to offer in whatever field. The teacher, the concert artist, the critic, the public see, as a rule, only what is published; the publisher sees also what is not published, and that outnumbers the published music by at least one hundred to one. Compared with the level of the rejected music, that of published American music is very high, incredible as that may seem in view of some of the stuff inflicted on the public by even the best of us. Hence, if it be wicked not to publish more of the music perpetrated in America, the American music publisher ought to be encouraged to persevere in such wickedness.

Unfortunately, the silver lining has its cloud. That cloud was effectively etched for posterity by Deems Taylor in the musical chapter of that collective inquiry by thirty Americans into *Civilization in the United States*. He says: "Music publishing here is an industry, conducted like any other industry. The Continental type of publisher, who is a scholar and a musician, and a gentleman who is conscious of a duty to music as well as to the stockholders, is almost unknown here. To our publishers, music is a commodity, to be bought cheap and sold dear, and most of them will publish anything that looks profitable, regardless of its quality."[7]

In general, that sweeping charge will withstand refutation; but, in self defense, the American music publisher may point to certain explanatory and extenuating circumstances. Among those circumstances are several important factors that are entirely beyond his control. Furthermore, the Continental type of publisher, adjusted to American conditions, is not yet quite so extinct as Mr. Taylor thinks. As for stockholders (or their equivalents), there exist some who would censure their directors and officers severely if they attempted to forget their duty toward music of

---

7. Deems Taylor, "Music," in *Civilization in the United States*, ed. Harold E. Stearns (New York: Harcourt, Brace, 1922), p. 210. — ED.

nonprofitable quality so completely as to tarnish the family name by publishing, regardless of quality, anything that looks profitable.

This or that high-minded American publisher may share the advanced economic view that the function of an industry dealing in public utilities — and to these we may reckon the sciences and the arts — is not primarily to make money but to render the best public service that incidentally entitles him to a fair profit. Let us assume further that such a publisher recognizes what is implied in the very word publisher, that his profession owes to the public obligations approaching a trusteeship. Grant further that he is fully conscious of a duty to music as well as to stockholders. The fact remains that, in order to live up to these principles, he must "make money." Without it he cannot survive or prosper in the interest of either music or stockholders, and he can make the necessary money only by selling music as a commodity. To publish music, the best of music, and then not be able to sell it means in the long run bankruptcy. He sells it, or tries to sell it, generally speaking, to the ultimate consumer, the public, not direct but through a middleman, the music dealer.

Now, the average music dealer's business in our country is in a rather precarious condition. Very few music dealers can afford to limit themselves to printed music; in the majority of cases the sheet-music business has become an appendix to a business in the larger and more profitable units of pianos, Victrolas, player-pianos, records, etc. The music dealer is supposed to make a living by selling music. As a rule, his resources are limited and he must husband them in the most economical manner. He will follow the lines of least risk, and the least risk consists in concentrating his efforts on music of established commercial value with all possible avoidance of music of as yet unknown commerical quality. The instinct of self-preservation and the undeniably precarious condition of the sheet music business make him essentially a conservative. Along comes the music publisher, however, and tempts him to crawl out of this conservative shell, tempts him to divide his sympathies between "staple musical merchandise," the demand for which he can gauge, and "novelties," which are hazardous. Not one publisher but a dozen or more pour in on him their "novelties," as in trade parlance new publications are called, until the poor man groans in agony, squirms under what he considers an unjustifiable assault on his commercial digestion, curses this inconsiderate overproduction, and hates the very sight of "novelties," especially of the "high-brow" kind. Yet "novelties" may be and are demanded. Inasmuch as the public on which he depends for a fair living prefers, by and large, new "popular" music, fox-trots, mushy home ballads, sentimental heart songs, effeminately virile ballads, stale piano music for the parlor, innocent but musically often harmful easy teaching pieces, etc., to new "classical" music (as almost anything of about the level of Chaminade and above is called), the American music dealer indicates to the publisher the same preference. His shop is his world; that world he hesitates, under present conditions, to turn into a laboratory for publishers' experiments and thereby possibly demolish, to the injury of himself and family.

If the average American musician be ten years behind the times with his taste for modern music, and the average American music lover twenty, the average American music dealer must be forgiven if he limps thirty years behind the procession of events. If in particular he appears to be a Rip Van Winkle in relation to the expansion of intelligent appreciation of "high-brow" music in America (American included), during the last twenty years, again he can produce an alibi, as will be shown later on. Thus, the tendency of the average American music dealer by force of circumstances is distinctly "low-brow," whether outside of his business he enjoys (and often he does) higher musical things or not. As a businessman with his perplexing business problems peculiar to himself he considers "high-brow" music a nuisance, sneers at it, and desires it suppressed, or at least does not desire it inflicted upon him.

From the music dealer's point of view his argument is perfect, but how does it affect the music publisher? To answer that question exhaustively would require a treatise on the history and theory of music publishing, an introduction into the labyrinth of industrial traditions, fictions, and practices, and an analysis of the interrelation of manufacturing costs, overhead expenses, discounts, list prices, competition, and what not. Here only the briefest outline of the fundamental elements of the complicated structure is possible, as they occur to me personally and that without special reference to the potential conditions in Europe, which are so different from ours as largely to deprive Mr. Taylor's compliments to the European publisher of any value as an example for emulation.

The American music publisher, in most cases unconsciously, in some instances with a clear understanding of the philosophical axioms at the bottom of his profession, reacts to a complex of psychological and biological impulses that govern him as they do any other human being or activity. There is, for instance, the creative impulse. The artist creates esthetic values; the publisher creates industrial values. Different as these values are in kind, the psychological impulse back of them is the same. Try as he may to curtail his output deliberately even to the point of nonproduction, that impulse will compel him to violate his pledge, provided he be really a publisher who sells music and not a music dealer who happens to publish music. Just so, no amount of commercial shop-talk, so dear to the hearts of businessmen, with its stereotyped "practical" arguments and fallacies, will ever put the publisher out of reach of an equally important impulse that governs propagation in all Nature: the selective impulse.

The survival of the fittest has a role in the publisher's life as important as elsewhere. Nature plays safe by "wasting" more seeds than she permits to germinate. The publisher cannot, any more than the farmer, predict with certainty which of the seeds he sows will ultimately bear fruit. The best he can do is to use critical and experienced judgment in the selection and care of his wares. For the rest he largely depends on good luck; but precisely because many more seeds must be sown than will germinate, the wise publisher seeks to turn the law of probability in his favor by publishing more "novelties" than the traffic apparently can bear. For that reason overproduction is implicit in the very nature of his profession. Not, of course, an overproduction that smothers, but an overproduction that gives to him a greater number of chances than to the conceited fool who, in the publisher's lottery, gambles on a few numbers as if he can pick the winning numbers without fail by special favors from the goddess Fortuna.

The wise publisher, furthermore, prefers the danger of overproduction to the, for him, greater danger of underproduction. Under the most favorable conditions, only a minority of the works he adds to his catalogue will prove to be commercially valuable; the majority will peter out. Thus the number of profitable works gradually dwindles and the profits from them must float the everincreasing number of those that rapidly become commercially obsolete. The dead wood accumulates alarmingly as the fashions in musical taste change from decade to decade. The residue of permanently valuable publications will not in the long run save him from disaster. He must continually reforest his catalogue, for otherwise his business will die of barren soil as that of every other publisher before him died who disregarded the lessons of musical history. Not a scanty minimum will save him, but a reasonable maximum, for the reasons already stated.

Clearly, such elementary biological observations do not bespeak an identity of problems between the music publisher and the music dealer. This fundamental divergence of practical interests becomes still more serious for the publisher by virtue of a further natural impulse that controls his actions: the impulse to improve his species. Unless he be a creature of abnormally low mentality and spirituality, therefore negligible, he will, consciously or not, aim high rather than low. His commercialized vision may keep his aim low as a matter of daily routine, but he will yield, on festive occasions of his mind, to the uncontrollable ambition to enrich his catalogue with the finer things, though they may not enrich his pocketbook. Those festive occasions become more frequent as his prestige grows. Knowing deserved prestige to be a kind of barometer of a businessman's policy to give to the public superior goods and superior service, hence a business asset of incalculable value, some American music publishers act on the motto of *prestige oblige* more often, and make more frequent sacrifices on this altar of prestige, than the uninitiated appreciate.

At this point the tragicomedy of the whole subject really begins. In publishing the ordinary run of American songs, piano pieces, and the like, the publisher sacrifices nothing except perhaps occasionally his self-respect, the respect of good musicians, and the comfort of the music dealer if the stream of such "novelties" inundates the latter's cellar. Let that be understood without hypocritical self-praise on the part of the publisher, but let also another incontrovertible fact be understood: only the lucrative sale of such minor things permits a publisher in America to indulge in fostering the cause of the American composer's major works. Maybe Carl Engel's cynical remark, that the American music publisher is compelled to publish so much trash because he has laboriously made the public believe it wants trash, contains the essence of truth. The humiliating fact stares at us nevertheless that the publisher, as a rule that fortunately has its exceptions, publishes American music of artistic value at a financial loss and can indulge in that sport only by publishing a lot of lucrative music of no particular artistic value whatsoever. On music in the larger forms he may rarely cover his expenses and does not dream of a profit. If the classic dictum of Simrock that "Bohm must pay for Brahms" holds good for Europe, it certainly applies with a vengeance to America. The American Bohm pays the way for the American miniature Brahms on every excursion of the latter into the costly realms of grand opera, symphonic music, chamber music, everything that spells sonata or other larger forms, and indeed of a good many other things.

Suppose that an American composer produces an opera; does the American publisher who publishes the piano-vocal score derive any direct financial benefit from the performance, as does so often his French or Italian colleague? He does not; he can only reclaim his investment by the sale of the piano-vocal scores.[8] There exist such scores of most of the relatively few significant American operas, those by Parker, Herbert, Cadman, Hadley. Argued *ad hominem,* who in America has bought them? Suppose further that the publisher did derive direct financial benefit from performances, how much would it total from the only two American opera institutions that produce (rather asthmatically) American works? I fear not nearly enough to justify the American publisher in imitating the example of his French colleague who can afford to recognize his duty to music by diverting part of his operatic revenues into symphonic and chamber music channels.

Moreover, in Europe the publisher's potential market for orchestral and chamber music stretches over ten times as many organizations as here, and to these European organizations our miserably few American organizations must then be added. The European publisher has a world market, whereas until the outbreak of the war the American publisher's market was practically restricted to America, if for no other reason than that Europe cared little for American music. Since then there has been an increase of interest, but simultaneously Europe's purchasing power

---

8. That statement is true if the publisher is only licensed to publish and sell; but when the publisher has become the sole or joint copyright proprietor he can (and could in 1922) profit from performances of stage works, or of any works performed "for profit." Helping the publishers and other copyright proprietors do that was then and is now the job of ASCAP (and later SESAC and BMI).

Also, Sonneck ignores the fact that operatic *full* scores, necessary for performances, were and are seldom published and sold; they, like many orchestral materials, were and are supplied by rental only, thus keeping the performance and production costs lower and enabling the publisher to collect what is in effect a performance fee. The drawback to this mechanism, more and more in evidence with the appearance of cheap machine copiers in the 1950s that allowed renting organizations to copy scores and parts and thereafter avoid rental fees — this drawback is countered at least in theory by the Copyright Act of 1976 that declares rentals to constitute publication protectible under the statute. — ED.

has decreased. Among the Central European orchestras, especially, none can now afford to purchase American works. Hence, the American publisher continues to be confined to America and he is cut off from what might have become his best-paying market.

Suppose, however, that undeterred by such an adverse constellation of circumstances, this or that American music publisher, imbued with the proper spirit of his duty toward music as such, embarks within reason and with becoming modesty on the cultural mission of playing the role of a vest-pocket replica of a Durand or the Universal Edition. What facts does he encounter? First of all, the fact that it costs in America today about three and one-half dollars to engrave a page of quartet score, not to mention the cost of the parts. Anyone familiar with the heavenly length of modern quartets or symphonies may thus figure out the initial cost of merely engraving the scores. Add to this the cost of paper, printing, and other labor, editorial and other overhead expenses, and the statement will not come as a shock that the total publishing and business cost of a single work may run anywhere from five hundred to two thousand dollars or more. Against this, place the number of American orchestras that may feel inclined to purchase for performance the score and parts, for, let us say, fifty dollars. The inference is plain: the American music publisher writes off every such investment as a generous contribution to the cause of American music. He certainly does not look upon it as a commercial enterprise for profit, as so often his European colleagues may do.

Exceedingly few American firms can stand the financial strain involved in the publication of a noticeable number of such exorbitantly costly works. More firms find it necessary to content themselves by assisting the American composer of, for instance, songs of serious artistic aim and high artistic quality. But again, what is the controlling fact? Compressed into a few words, the astounding and humiliating answer reads: rarely more than an average yearly sale of two hundred copies, frequently less. True, every prominent publisher has in his catalogue fairly numerous American compositions of absolutely artistic value of which he sells every year thousands of copies; but still the great majority of such compositions enjoy only a regular sale of a few hundred copies, if that. Indeed, several concert programs of American songs could easily be devised in which not one song need fear comparison with contemporary European songs of similar artistic caliber, but in which every single song would be found to sell fewer than fifty copies a year — fifty copies in a country of more than one hundred million inhabitants!

What incentive for publication, if not of speculation combined with idealism and a sense of duty toward music as such and toward American music in particular, can the American music publisher possibly have with such disheartening business prospects before him? He is not starving — far from it — but he would be starving if he adopted the principle of publishing only music of indisputable quality regardless of profits.

By way of contrast, the standard publisher, so called, knows that his *confrère,* the popular publisher, so called, counts the sales of "popular hits" by the hundreds of thousands of copies while the going is good, and that in a few exceptional cases the sales have reached into the millions of copies. Perhaps the standard publisher does not care to descend to the level of "popular" music of the grade of, let us say, "A Perfect Day."[9] While the sales record of that song is dazzling, there exist many pieces of a similar or slightly lower type that reach tens of thousands of people by way of sales. Confronted by such actualities, by the gulf between the commercial allurements of such music and those of art music, even a high-minded publisher can hardly be blamed if in weak moments he loses his courage, turns from the path of rectitude, and prays to the golden calf. It is but human that he begins to heed the anything-but-lofty arguments and example of colleagues who call themselves publishers but think essentially in the terms of music peddlers, who confuse commerce with commercialism; who view art music as a nuisance, as an

---

9. It is natural that Carrie Jacobs Bond and her "Perfect Day" should have come to Sonneck's mind, for about the time he was writing this paper he, as vice-president of the firm of G. Schirmer, was engaged in buying out Mrs. Bond's little firm of Carrie Jacobs Bond and Son, Chicago. For two decades it had published much and profited little; but when "A Perfect Day" came out at just the time Americans were ending an imperfect war and longed for sweet solace, it became a big seller and attracted his business interest. Perhaps it also attracted a bit of envy from the composer in Sonneck, who had tried often and failed often to compose successful songs of quiet beauty and sensitivity. But then Sonneck, the East Coast city boy and intellectual, never watched — as did Mrs. Bond when she was inspired to write "A Perfect Day" — a glorious sunset flood the southern California plain and tint the majestic mountains in the distance. — ED.

illegitimate kind of "business"; who would abolish it altogether as "un-commercial"; or who, at any rate, would publish, instead of as much as is consistent with sound business conduct, as little of it as possible if they were not ashamed of public opinion.

I personally deeply regret and oppose that attitude of mind and its pernicious influence on those to whom the musical world has a right to look for maintenance of their example of the music publishing industry in America above such a debased level. Yet in fairness to the tempters and the tempted it must be said that in the conduct of business affairs the actual conditions of the moment with their violent contrasts cannot but exercise a benumbing effect on lofty theories.

Sales do not merely mean money into the pockets of the publishers; sales also mean distribution, and distribution indicates the degree of concrete interest taken by the public in a composer's works. Therewith the crux of the whole sad matter has been reached. That the American composer to a considerable extent is at the mercy of the American music publisher is obvious; but, as a matter of fact, the publisher has made and persistently does make and will continue to make much if not most of the really artistic music by American composers accessible in print. He therefore needs no defense. It is obvious that both American composer and music publisher are largely at the mercy of the American music dealer, but the latter may with equanimity point the accusing finger at the real culprit: *the American public.* That public is composed of professional and nonprofessional musicians. Considering the enormous growth of an esthetically intelligent public that frequents concerts of good music in our country, it may be said in explanation of that same public's demonstrably stingy response to the rich supply of good American music that it is merely ignorant, that it would respond to the call of duty eagerly if it but knew. Perhaps so, and perhaps the publishers themselves are to blame for not knowing how to create the demand with effective, reliable publicity methods. Still, the miserable sales record of so much neglected artistic American music is so out of proportion to the publicity already given it by reviewers and publishers as to weaken the argument perceptibly.

If the American public (including critics and artists) desires to see the music-publishing industry in America on a higher level, it must exert itself to put it there. The public must cooperate much more than it has done with those American music publishers who cherish the same ambition and have to pay the piper. They will respond quickly enough, for they are businessmen, if they notice that the public wants to buy what it really needs. Then and not until then will their frequent financial sacrifices for the cause of the genuine artists among American composers cease being a burden or an obligation of patriotic conscience, and will be instead a justifiable source of satisfaction to them as American businessmen of musicianly, scholarly, gentlemanly vision.

Recently, Mr. John C. Freund, whom no one can accuse of slighting the American musician, commented shrewdly on some of the reasons for the hold of jazz, ragtime, and "popular" music in general on the American mind.[10] I have resisted the temptation of dragging my own very definite but not at all always antagonistic opinions of these types of music and their publishers into this discourse, except when necessary, but they coincide fully with those of Mr. Freund when he argues that we mistakenly attribute an intelligence to the vast majority that statistics prove it not to possess and that it cannot possess. Those types of music correspond precisely to the cultural and esthetic mentality of the public that caters to them. The fact that some of our most sensitive artists call a bit of jazz fascinating, when it is fascinating musically, must not becloud the general aspect of things. No logic or sophistry about the undeniable musical charm of this or that "popular hit" can obscure the main fact that the public at large gorging itself with such music is just as stupid and vulgar as the bulk of that music itself. That public, whether we like to confess it or not, is the American public. Its vast majority evidently prefers the lower types of American music to the higher types. It will continue to do so until its children have been lifted by an uncompromising musical education into the purer strata of better music where their elders as yet do not and cannot breathe freely.

All the more reason, then, why the intelligent minority ought to remove from itself the opprobrium of palpable neglect of that music. The American composer appreciates, of course, a sane propaganda by word of mouth or the pen in his behalf; he will appreciate it still more if it be reflected in his royalty statement. Not because of the at best moderate increase of his income in dollars and cents, but because with every few hundred copies more sold of a work in which he takes a legitimate pride as composer, the proof lies before him that the interest in him and

---

10. John C. Freund (1848–1924) founded the magazine *The Music Trades* in 1890. In 1898 he founded *Musical America*, which he edited until his death. — ED.

his work has correspondingly and tangibly increased among his compatriots.

Even so the problem of the American composer of music in the larger and more difficult constructive forms will not and cannot be solved while our musical life rests on its present faulty economic basis. Performances of his works depend on opportunity, and those opportunities are circumscribed by the atrophy of actual conditions. Even these few possible performances are made precarious if the works do not exist in print. Their publication throws at present a burden on the American music publishers that only very few of them may assume without undue financial strain. With the best of intentions those few publishers cannot publish more than a few of the works that really merit the record of print.

Because of such considerations I conceived the idea of a society that would lessen the burdens of the publisher and at the same time supplement his labors by undertaking the publication of meritorious American works. Shortly afterward, I helped to found such a society, the Society for the Publication of American Music. Of necessity, that society limited its activities to chamber music, and while no imperishable masterworks have come its way, it has made American chamber music of artistic quality accessible in print, for performance or study, to more than four hundred members, which signifies an immeasurably wider distribution than if the work had been published by professional publishers. Lately the Foundation of Opera in Our Language has begun to be active by financing the publication of American operas, but all this will not suffice to do the American composer full justice. Something additional, something more powerful, something more permanent is needed. With a constructive suggestion in that direction I shall bring this essay to an abrupt end.

We need for our country something akin to the Carnegie United Kingdom Trust Publication Scheme. Under that scheme every year the Carnegie trustees publish a number of British orchestral and other works to which they apply the very highest tests of merit. Chartered only in 1917, already the trust embraces in its "Carnegie Collection of British Music" a most imposing list of published works available for performance. It is a pity that Mr. Carnegie did not think of founding a similar trust for the country of his adoption and success. He did not, and therewith he left the field open for some other benefactor of music. The most logical candidate for such honors is the Juilliard Foundation, and I doubt not that the trustees will give the idea their most serious consideration, if it be endorsed by such national organizations as the MTNA. Perhaps they have already done so, as the idea is one of those that lie in the air. In that case I hope that they have perceived the one fundamental weakness of the Carnegie scheme. That weakness consists in this, that the scheme does not provide for performances.

Frequency of performance is impossible without publication, but publication without performance is still more galling to a composer than sporadic performances without publication. Printed music is merely a jumble of black spots on white paper unless it is heard, and not much more than a souvenir for deaf posterity. In my opinion, then, any American scheme should avoid the weakness of the British Carnegie scheme and should be so broad in scope as to insure not only publication, but also at least first performances of the published works by the principal organizations fit for the task. Such an arrangement could easily be worked out by the publication trustees and organizations located in our music centers and such national organizations as the National Federation of Music Clubs. That organization has already done impressive work for the performance of American music. If the Juilliard Foundation fails us, perhaps the federation will add the project to its fruitful activities. Such a combination of publication and performance opens up vistas of achievement and opportunity for the American composer compared with which the results of the propaganda so far conducted in his behalf — and I am the last to underestimate them — may dwindle into insignificance as to sustaining and propelling public value.

The Communistic Cell:
A Symphonic Hypoblast
By Bill Jones
Op.100

‿

(What follows came to me in the form of a personal letter from my friend, Bill Jones. Of course, you know Bill Jones! No introduction is necessary. The name is so famous, not to say common, that no reader can fail to place its proud owner. His works are manifold, the most famous being *Pigs and Their Progeny.*[1] The letter, be it added by way of essential clarification, came into being as a result of the performance in the presence of the disguised and disgusted Jones and other disgusteds of a symphony so-called by Lord St. Ives, Knight of the Halter and martyr to the cause of Connecticut Modernism — which did not connect, nor was it cut, alas! The Symphonic Hypoblast has already been written. It is now my honor to present it for the first time to the public. — S.W.)

The letter follows:

Dear Si:

Not for publication! Secondly, I apologize for the pencil [The letter is written in pencil. — ED. (S.W.)] but I have come to the conclusion that pencil is the only proper thing for the "modern" composer; it makes it so much easier to rub out music that happens to sound well and substitute something that sounds like h . . . . . . !

But to my op. 100 —

The only praiseworthy thing about present-day composers who affect modernism is that they spit in the face of everything heretofore consid-

---

Reprinted from the *Musical Courier* 94, no. 8 (February 24, 1927): [12].

1. See Mr. Hitchcock, in "After 100[!] Years," below, for a notable piece of detective work and a happy ending withal, disclosing that Bill Jones's alter ego,

ered music. That is all right as far as it goes, but otherwise they are hopelessly antiquated and tamer than a stuffed rhinoceros. They are not modern at all, but belong to the defunct era of musical capitalism, though they may not notice it.

By now it is a universally accepted axiom, or ought to be, that the biological function of a composer is to make noise. But what do we have? Polytonality and Atonality. The very use of the word tonality proves that the gentlemen are still on the beaten track and are straddling. They profess an axiom, but compromise with the leftovers of tradition. The result is that they merely produce music that sounds wrong and hypocritical, instead of noise that sounds right and honest. What we need for the music of the future is honest-to-goodness A-noise and Poly-noise.[2]

Oscar Sonneck, had a surprising affinity for pigs — and here pigs crop up once again! Mr. Hitchcock also explains the double pseudonym used for this hyper-spoof. Being concerned with Sonneck's sunnier side, rather than with his darker insides, Hitchcock did not comment on the cleverly punning and superficially misleading use of *hypoblast* — which is not a Big Noise or a Little Noise but (so the books tell me) an endoderm, the inner layer of an embryo, and so makes good sense here in a nonsensical kind of way. As for the piece being an "attack on ultra-modern music" — well, as such attacks go it's pretty good-natured. No doubt Sonneck felt better after getting it off his chest, the very next day (a Sunday) after a performance of the first and second movements of Ives's Fourth Symphony at Aeolian Hall under Eugene Goossens. But in *Suum Cuique* and elsewhere Sonneck speaks out strongly for the right of every composer to write what he will (even if it means employing "squeaking piglings as orchestral color") *provided* his motives are sincere and his craftsmanship is equal to his imagination. Perhaps it was the latter proviso that gave rise to this mild and tongue-in-cheek diatribe, which Sonneck was careful not to print in his own journal or under his own name. "Noise" to Sonneck was not a matter of loudness but of unorganized, or improperly organized, sound. One person's craftsmanship is another person's cacophony; and from all accounts, including the later history of the Ives Fourth Symphony, one can suspect that what Sonneck had heard was to him not properly organized sound. It was, he implies, neither fish nor fowl, neither satisfactory music nor satisfactory tonal chaos. Had Ives happened to hear some of Sonneck's music, which by that time Sonneck himself did not take too seriously, Ives probably would have reached for some of his ear-stretching epithets. I for one would like to have heard them argue it out face-to-face. Ives (the junior of the two, by the way) probably had the lower boiling point; Sonneck surely would have been the more cuttingly articulate. And Sonneck, after all, had certain credentials as a composer of "new" music: in the mid-twenties he was president of the U.S. Chapter of the International Society for Contemporary Music. — ED.

2. In this quantum jump, Bill Jones points music forward all the way from Wagner's music of the future to that music of the past by twenty-first century

This dire need cannot be satisfied except by one composer: Me! Because no other composer has grasped the truth, the whole truth, and nothing but the truth, that music as heretofore practiced (and including those pitiful compromisers whom I shall not honor by mentioning) is unnatural and absurd esthetically, philosophically, theoretically, economically, politically, biologically, pathologically, medically, penologically, physiologically, psychologically, acoustically, embryonically, etc. (consult Webster's dictionary). Whatever else it was or is, it is not music, but a capitalistic juggling with tones.

That must be as evident to you as it is to me. Now, my discovery of the music of the future really consists in this: it is only that I go back to first principles — in other words, to the cosmic urge. (What all other composers have been doing, one might call by comparison the cosmetic urge.) The whole universe is not bigger than any of its atoms. Conversely, every atom is a universe in itself unlimited by space or time or function. It is the interpenetration of the whole with the part that causes vibration in the form of gas. Sound waves are merely a special materialization of that fundamental principle, but the basic error of music as heretofore made is the futile and, indeed, artificial attempt to separate what belongs together. It simply leads and must lead to an unwholesome capitalistic emphasis on this or that sound wave, academically called tone. The only salvation out of this labyrinth is by way of return, as I just said, to first principles. Logically, we must return to Chaos.

But Chaos is an ideal and, therefore, unattainable. However, though it is not attainable in fact, we ought to strive for it in tendency. Thus the whole problem of the composer becomes one of means. Now, it requires but little intelligence to see that only chaotic order — but not chaos — results if a composer employs all the instruments known to mankind, moves on every conceivable rhythmic, harmonic, dynamic plane in every conceivable key, mode, or scale, and yet prescribes meticulously when and where an instrument enters, what it has to do, and how to do it. Such a procedure smacks of microcosm, not of macrocosm, and I want none of it.

With that sort of absolute procedure, they will produce only a mild,

---

conservatives who will be content to grind out the same A-noisality and Poly-noisality their fathers did, or even the Foundation Noisality of their grandfathers. — ED.

tame kind of bourgeois noise, à la Stravinsky, Varèse, or Ives, but not the Big Noise out of which all creation evolves,[3] and which we must project again on the auditory nerves if music is not to become mummified.

And what an astounding economic waste goes on with the conventional procedure of all composers, me excepted! Astounding and unpardonable when our aim must be the conservation of nature's resources, and in the spiritual realm an unfettered evolution of the cosmic ego! For instance, the harpist sits there and by the time he has an entry for two or three little twangs, the strings have almost gone to rust. Worse, the waste of wood pulp on silly scores of that description! The inhuman strain on the eyes of either copyists or engravers! The absurdity of paying the same salary to the musician who exerts himself powerfully and is heard as to him who barely moves the air and remains inaudible! The farce of the conductor, so called, when he could spend the same energy more profitably for society by shoveling dirt! But politically more criminal than all this, to make of human units mere slaves to the momentary whims of what, with ironical appropriateness, is known as a composer: that is, a put-togetherer or a together-putter! (I do not know which is grammatically correct — but you will understand.)

The above is, of course, a mere sketch of the travail of thought that went into the womb of my op. 100. But, before I present the score to you, just one more observation. Bach, Beethoven, etc., possessed an elementary, stunted sort of talent. The trouble with them simply is they they were born too soon. That is a pity, but their case is not hopeless. Their music can be made to answer the esthetic requirements of the future in a very simple manner. All one has to do is to turn their scores

---

3. *Sic: recte* "evolved." Here Mr. Jones exhibits a prescient proclivity for the Big Bang theory of the origin of our universe. In the next few sentences, Jones likewise shows himself to have been far ahead of his day in many ways. He rails against economic waste even in a time of burgeoning GNP. He views with alarm the failure to conserve natural resources. He recognizes and criticizes male chauvinism (it is a *male* harpist who pettily twangs the strings and hardly stirs the air). He speaks out against inhuman working conditions. He warns against knuckling under to the bourgeois behests of audiences that would pay to see a conductor conduct upside down, against babying the blatant bossism of the conductors themselves, against putting up with the puerile prettiness of most composers — against many of our present evils that in 1927 were no bigger than the flute sound at the beginning of Ravel's *Bolero*. — ED.

and parts upside down and in addition play the music from the end toward the beginning.[4] Of course the noise will not be ideal, but at least it will be a step in the right direction. The music will sound like nothing, but that is precisely what we Chaoticists are aiming at; because music that sounds like something is in a sorry way of lacking creative fluidity and globose relativity of glomerate glonoin.[5] As for the public, it will respond quickly enough to Beethoven, Bach, or Wagner thus revitalized, provided the conductor, as logic demands, conducts standing on his head and uses his legs as he now uses his arms. This will have the further advantage of wiping out deficits, because you can safely count on tens of thousands of applausive subscribers where you now have to reckon with only a few hundred.

As for my own works, no such makeshifts will be necessary because they need none. However, please do not confuse my conceptions with those of any other noisemakers, like Marinetti. They are mere pretenders. The basic difference between them and me is obvious. At their best or worst they strive for noise in chaotic order, what one might call a noisette; I unfold my genius in the ideal of the Noise of Chaos. In fact, I am The Big Noise.

If you have followed me thus far, you cannot fail to understand my op. 100 at first glance or hearing, nor can you fail to appreciate how I am putting music on an economic basis never before dreamed of. The only item in the score that you may not grasp without an explanation is the indication of the Noisometer. That apparatus is to take the place of the conductor (who is entirely done away with, thank God!). It is a simple device, looking like a time-punching clock, which registers

---

4. The sheer brilliance of the man! Knowing that Bach dabbled in both types of mirror canon, by inversion and in retrograde, he perceives sympathetically that Bach can commodiously be modernized, given a shove in the right direction, by combining inversion and retrograde in simultaneous manipulation! Had Bach only lived a few years longer, had he only given a little thought to the esthetic demands of the future, he might himself have composed *Die Zukunft der Fuge.* — ED.

5. This last clause is not at all neologistic in its utilization of etymology but is rather breathtaking in its realization of the relation between human physiology and the higher physics that governs those unheard sounds of which Keats (the mystic poet of early romanticism) spoke so eloquently. The clause means, simply, that under Einstein's third or synthetic law of relativity, music that sounds like something to ordinary human ears perforce travels too slowly through space to achieve the creative fluidity necessary to compress nitroglycerin to the minus degree requisite to its transfiguration into the new ethereal form of acoustical matter known to the ancients as *musica globosa.* — ED.

automatically the degree of noise made at any moment by the orchestra. By looking at the face of the Noisometer, the players know whether they are going below the noise-minimum desired or above the maximum, and they will regulate their dynamics accordingly.

Here is the score of my op. 100. As you will notice, all the space it occupies is ONE page and no orchestral parts are necessary at all!

Dedicated to Si Whiner, Pessimist

THE COMMUNISTIC CELL

Symphonic Hypoblast

by

Bill Jones

Op. 100

MOOD: Like reinforced concrete.

NOISOMETER: Minimum 37, maximum 185, average 119.

DURATION: According to prescription of the house physician.

INSTRUMENTS: Use as few or as many as the treasury of the organization permits.

INTERPRETATION: The instrumentalists play when they damn please, what they please, and how they please, but the composer will appreciate it if the third garbage can, the first baby rattle, and the tenth saxophone avoid jazz in this work.

SPECIAL POINTS: Whenever the Noisometer registers the minimum 37, stop the foghorn for a second, provided the foghornist has no objections, then release barrage of all instruments together, crescendo in three seconds to sustained Noisometer maximum, 185, and release the riveters in 17/19 time through amplifiers.[6] Thank you!

FINIS

New York, January 30, 1927

---

6. Milling around and fuguing as he does in cycles and decibels, and prescribing (even though graciously) precise activities and nonactivities for certain instrumentalists, Bill Jones cannot be said to have surpassed John Cage before his time in the realm of random composition. Yet considering that op. 100 is for full orchestra, including baby rattles and riveters, is there any other work now in being that achieves such radical randomness, such glorious globosity, such preciously prurient perfection? — ED.

An American School of Composition: Do We Want and Need It?

This subject, which I chose from among several suggested, reminds me of Poe's "A dream within a dream." It contains a question within a question. Indeed, more than one. For instance, what is a school of composition? What is an *American* school of composition? If wanted, is it needed? If not wanted, is it needed? If needed, is it wanted? If not needed, is it wanted? And a few more such questions by way of permutation.

A school of composition? The term "school," even in this connotation, implies study. Also, it implies disciples and a master; or, at least, a leader whose esthetic and technical principles and ideals the disciples absorb, emulate, and develop. But just why the singular of school? Might not there be room for more than one school with a corresponding number of masters or leaders? If so, then the plural may be just as legitimate as the singular, an American school of composition, whatever that may be. In other words, perhaps American schools of composition, rather than an American school of composition, ought to attract the inquisitive mind.

History abounds in schools of philosophic thought, of painting, of medicine, of military strategy, and what not. Hence, the concept of a school of composition in itself requires no justification. But when we come to inquire about the qualifications, the characteristics distinguishing one school of composition from another, the ground becomes just a

Reprinted from the *Papers and Proceedings of the Music Teachers' National Association*, 22nd ser., annual meeting of the fifty-first year, Minneapolis, Minnesota, December 28, 29, 30, 1927, ed. Karl W. Gehrkens (Hartford, Conn.: Published by the Association, 1928), pp. 102–10.

The beginning of Sonneck's setting of Poe's "A Dream within a Dream"

little slippery. One courts, for example, the danger of belittling the universal trend of an era — let us say, the Romantic — by attaching to it the term "school." The latter, it seems to me, calls for something more limited, and more specific. Clearly recognizable esthetic or technical principles must govern it and its adherents. In that sense Count Bardi's circle of professional and nonprofessional musicians with its experiments in evolving a *Sprechgesang* (to use Wagner's term) might very well be called a school of composition, while perhaps we stretch things too far if we speak of a polyphonic school of composition. Again, "atonalists," "polytonalists," and similar specialists in composition come more legitimately within the meaning of a school of composition. On the other hand, the mention of Wagner suggests a different type of school of composition — the personal. No composer of outstanding personality during the last fifty years could subtract himself from the influence of Wagner; but it is one thing to absorb and distill that influence, as Debussy did, into something quite personal, another thing to board for the rest of one's life at Wagner's private school and to end, as one began, as an imitator and mere manipulator of Wagner's doctrines and devices. Precisely therein lies the probability of result of any such personal school of composition — a result hardly to be prayed for anywhere.

After having thus sketchily groped through the darkness of my mind for something generally tangible in the idea of a school of composition, I stumble over the concept of an American school of composition. Germans composing music do not constitute a German school of composition, nor do French, Britons, Russians, or Italians constitute a French, British, Russian, or Italian one. Nor can it be sufficient if American composers become imbued with atonality, polytonality, or such more or less generally current doctrines; and still less, if they wrap themselves in the cast-off garments of Wagner, Brahms, or Puccini. In the one case they are simply American Wagnerians; in the other, American atonalists. Yet, if the concept of an American school of composition is to be solid, such a school, whatever it may be and whoever may constitute it, must possess a common denominator. And this postulate forces itself upon us whether we want or need or do not want or need either an American school of composition in the singular or in the plural.

What is, what ought to be the common denominator? As the simplest and also the readiest answer we have the word "Americanism." Admirable, but what constitutes Americanism in music? Is that so definable in words, or may its symptoms be so unmistakably described, that any

American composer can apply the formula and deliver his patriotic soul of a new exhibit for the American school of composition? And, if the matter were really so simple, what would prevent a Russian composer from adroitly mixing the ingredients and graduating with honors from that school? Indeed, would its Americanism save an otherwise hopelessly dull work? Does the American flag proudly flying atop an atrocious, made-in-America sample of French Renaissance impart Americanism to such a building? Even if it did, would that enhance its architectural merits, if any?

Candidly, have so far our many talented, native American composers revolutionized, or, if you prefer, evolutionized to any noticeable extent the trends of music? Have they, beyond creating many more or less personal, talented, and skillful works of musical significance, revealed anything in them that so sets them apart technically, esthetically, spiritually from their colleagues abroad and so bespeaks a "New World" in music as to justify the designation of an American school of composition? To be sure, we may point to certain works by American composers that disclose, in addition to undeniable musical merit and a personal note or flavor, an American note or flavor; but neither note nor flavor suffices as the earmark of an American *school* of composition, if we be asked to take that term seriously. More than a mere American flavor has gone into our "skyscrapers" or into certain types of our suburban homes. Not that our architects and builders have nothing in common with their European colleagues; on the contrary, *substantially* their art and technique coincide, but the conditions and habits of life in America compelled and inspired them to view and solve their structural problems in a different manner — different *essentially*.

If this idea be applied to music composed in America, no time need be wasted on the idiocy of fanatics who pray for an American music that shall have nothing whatsoever in common with European music. To reach their goal they would first of all face the necessity of providing themselves with a specially Americanized brand of acoustics, physiology, and pyschology of tone, regardless of what Nature may wish to say about it; and that is plain nonsense. The musical independence of America will not come about by denying that the same tonal functions inhere in the dominant seventh chord whether it be sounded in Berlin, Iowa, or Berlin, Prussia. Nor is there room in the musical scheme of things for an American fugue *versus* a French fugue. A fugue is a fugue, good or bad, and that notoriously irrespective of the Declaration of

Independence or the Constitution of the United States of America. And those 200-percenters who groan under the suffocating burden of Bach or Beethoven, vampire-like sucking the best of American blood from the American composer of the future, are simply too childish for comment.

Substantially, then, the American composer cannot but employ the raw materials of music very much in the same way as does and will a European composer. Indeed, not only the raw materials, but also the tools and processes of the composer's craft. What is equally obvious, he will have to respond in music to human emotions without which there can be no music, whether American or European, in substantially the same manner. Europeans are human beings, after all, and so if I may put it thus are Americans, separated from their near or distant relations here by water, not by blood. If that be expressed too paradoxically, then in blunt English: racially, white Americans are but transplanted Europeans.

This self-evident fact, far from beclouding the issue, clarifies it, because it delimits the possibilities or impossibilities confronting the American composer. If he forgets that self-evident fact, he will land in a quagmire, chasing jingoistic phantoms; if he remembers it, he will not lose sleep over the futility of shaking off his heritage and of striving for a complete musical independence that, even if attainable, might not constitute a gain. Realizing that in the very nature of music his art must substantially resemble that of his European colleagues, he will be freer to concentrate his talent on what reasonably may be expected to differentiate them both *essentially*. It is a far cry, however, from the composition of works that are essentially American by any one individual to a whole school of American composition.

To repeat, "school of composition" is a senseless term unless those who form the school are bound together by something that they hold characteristically in common technically or esthetically or spiritually. Add the epithet "American"; then the something must be something essentially American. He would be rash who would attempt a convincing definition of what is essentially American, but the difficulty of definition cannot obscure the fact that something tangible or intangible differentiates somehow the typically American from the typically European. One does not need a microscope to notice that Frenchmen differ from Englishmen or Germans. Yet somehow Europeans of contrasting regional traits appear interrelated, in their outlook upon life, more with one another than with Americans. Just so through all the more or less discernible differences between southerners, easterners, westerners, and northerners in our country, there weaves itself a common thread for which only one word seems applicable: "American."

Now, to my way of thinking, it does not necessarily follow that because in our political fabric, in our sociological behavior, or in our outlook upon life we may have added to hitherto known specimens of humanity the essentially new one of *homo Americanus,* we Americans can claim a monopoly of expressing in music either the *homo Americanus* or that for which he stands. Nor does it necessarily follow that by reason of what he is, he or what he stands for must surrender to a sort of obligatory standardized self-portraiture in music. Nothing in logic or esthetic ethics, however, prevents him from voluntarily sacrificing his freedom as a composer to the deliberate mission of helping to base an American school of composition on what is essentially American about him. The only question, granted the premise, is how to go about it, since obviously merely the conviction of the righteousness of his cause will not carry him any farther than will mere patriotic ambition.

If I expressed the doubt that so far our composers have perceptibly revolutionized or evolutionized musical composition, that does not imply that they may not do so in the future. Nor does my doubt imply blindness to the fact that when that Anglo-Saxophon child of Afro-American parentage and Semitic nursing baptized "jazz" was born unto us, all America hugged it as at last something genuinely and vociferously all-American, and the whole world acclaimed it joyously as our very own. Whether one relishes the fact or not, "jazz" is a typically American product and a legitimate one in the musical bargain. That is to say, legitimate within its own boundaries as enticing music for a certain type of dancing, but illegitimate if it sweepingly arrogates to itself beyond its boundaries a greater musical jurisdiction than it inherently possesses. "Jazz" is a musical genre with a technique all its own. Most of it is rubbish, just as most of the music called "classical" to distinguish it commercially from "popular" music is rubbish; but already "jazz" has produced — as music — a few gems and will probably continue to do so. Only it remains to be seen how far such a specialty can stimulate and fructify musical art in general. At any rate, the advocacy of "jazz" as the *sine qua non* of a truly American school of composition seems to me the lamentable confession of an inferiority complex and an insultingly narrow conception of America, as if life in America were confined to the hips downward. Jazz the controlling curriculum of an American school of composition? Of what one might call a night school, yes; otherwise emphatically no.

If not "jazz," then perhaps the music of the American Indian or the American Negro or American folk music in general. I doubt it, though I am a staunch believer in American folk music and have little patience with those who deny to us Americans the possession of American folksong. My patience is equally slight with those who concede that we do have folk music but consider it restricted to music of folk quality by the American Negro. That doctrine held sway for many years, and I was one of the first to help defeat it once and forever. I pointed out many years ago that America, instead of being poor in folk music, in reality may boast of a very respectable body of American folk music, if one but define American folk music properly. It consists of the folk music of the American Indian — not all of his music by any manner of means qualifying as folk music; secondly, of the folk music of the Afro-American; and last but far from least, of the American white man's folk music, whether indigenous to our soil or transplanted from the racial soil of origin and still alive as folk music among the descendents of those who emigrated with it as a priceless heritage from many lands to our shores.

This conception of American folk music now prevails among right-thinking scholars. It provides us with a body of folk music not only rich in volume but in the very nature of things barely surpassed anywhere in variety. That so far it has been explored rather one-sidedly, with emphasis on its Indian or Afro-American or Anglo-Saxon constituents, does not affect the main contention, but the fact does have a bearing on the opportunities of such American composers as feel drawn toward American folk music as the inspirational basis for their composition. While an American composer probably would not hesitate to use for that purpose a Negro "spiritual" or a cowboy or lumberjack tune or even the Kentuckian survival of a British border ballad, he might refrain from using, for fear of violating the proprieties, for instance, some German folk tune that emigrated 250 years ago to Pennsylvania and still exercises the functions of a folk tune in that region or elsewhere.

Our composers have not begun to exhaust the opportunities at their command in the field of American folk music of various types and antecedents, but the utilization of folk tunes in itself does not create or establish a national school of music. Otherwise the American composer who operates with Indian melodies would *eo ipso* become an Indian, and surely a cowboy suit worn by a Hindu at a masquerade ball would not promptly turn that gentleman into an American. The requisites of an American school of composition lie much deeper. They must be sought, as I have already insisted, in that indefinable, subtle, yet indisputable something that all Americans have in common and that distinguishes an American of English, German, Italian, or other descent from a native Englishman, German, Italian, and so forth — in short, in a something essentially American. An American composition, if in essence it be American, will sound American whether or not the composer fashioned it out of a poor theme of his own, instead of helping himself to a perhaps much better American folk tune. Indeed, an American composition, if in essence it be American, very likely will sound American though the composer may have endeavored to write in the latest Italian manner or may have substituted for his own name a Hottentot pseudonym. Just so, Musorgsky's *Boris Godunov* and even Tchaikovsky's Fifth Symphony would be recognized as essentially Russian — the famous *Five* to the contrary notwithstanding — even if not a single Russian folk tune had gone into their making.[1]

Do not misunderstand me: I do not deny — on the contrary I believe — that an assiduous and loving penetration into the characteristics and spirit of really beautiful and musically valuable folk music of one's own country will fecundate the national essence of a composer's art. I do deny, however, that the mere use of folk music as a principle of composition will make a composer great or his music national, unless he possesses other requisites for greatness or nationalism. Brahms would have been a German composer to the core even without his deep study of German folksong. It was not German folksong that made Brahms a great composer, but genius. And in that connection prudence demands we remember how unnecessary it seems to be for a composer to limit himself to his own national history, legends, traditions for the composing of "national" masterworks. There is surely nothing very German about *Tristan and Isolde* or French about *Carmen* or Italian about *Falstaff;* and yet, with all the universality of their appeal, how German, French, Italian the music of these masterworks sounds to their very core!

---

1. "The Five" came to be the designation in English for the five Russian composers (Balakirev, Borodin, Cui, Musorgsky, Rimsky-Korsakov) of Russian nationalist tendencies whom the critic Vladimir Stassov in 1867 dubbed the *moguchaya kuchka,* roughly translatable as "the sturdy little band" or "the powerful little group" or even, perhaps, as "the mighty mites." — ED.

Folksong gives a national aroma to a composition, but to build national schools of music on aromas would be a rather volatile undertaking. Precisely because "jazz" and folksong are "specialities," they may interest American composers sufficiently that the latter may band themselves together into groups of specialists for the common pursuit of that particular kind of musical happiness, just as others might want to specialize in the musical expression of the glories of American prairie sunsets or of the ideals of American democracy. But all such specialities, if overdone (and such things are always overdone sooner or later) will lead to sterile monotony and then "What price American school of composition!"

"An American school of composition: Do we want and need it?" I wonder. The question implies its absence. Perhaps this very absence makes the heart grow fonder. If a true American school of composition is *wanted* badly enough, perhaps our composers will supply the demand. If it really be *needed,* we may rest assured that it will come into existence sooner or later; but I doubt the need of an American school of composition along the lines of specialties, and I further doubt that even in such garden patches its growth can be forced by theoretical propaganda. I propose a much better recipe: let our composers continue to produce the best that is in them, whether they lean toward jazz or folksong or Stravinsky or Wagner or this or that or nothing in particular, but let us who are not composers cease telling them what to do and what not to do. From the growing mass of mediocre stuff will emerge a growing number of essentially American works that command universal respect and admiration. Quite unobtrusively and naturally an American school of composition will then have created itself without having been made to order by chemical formulae, factory methods, dietary systems, or purblind propaganda.[2] Perform the present American composer and stop worrying about the future American composer!

---

2. Sonneck's prediction proved remarkably prophetic. By coincidence, this paper was written and read in the same year that Aaron Copland, who has come to be called the dean of American composers (though not of an American school of composition), first made headlines. His Concerto for Piano and Orchestra, with marked jazz influences, had its premiere in Boston on January 28, 1927, the day before the Ives performance in New York that gave rise to Sonneck's preceding piece. — ED.

The Future
of Musicology in America

Alexander Wheelock Thayer, whose biography of Beethoven still represents America's greatest contribution to musicology, died on July 15, 1897.[1] Had he lived a few years longer, undoubtedly the fitting tribute of honorary membership would have been paid to him when Professor Albert A. Stanley organized the United States Section of the International Music Society (Internationale Musikgesellschaft). With the organization of that body a respectable number of kindred spirits, though with an infusion of unfit elements forced on us by circumstances, had found a rallying center. Not that, under the presidency first of Professor Stanley and then of Professor Waldo S. Pratt, numerous contributions to musicology poured from America into the publishing organs of the IMG — indeed, they were comparatively few and by still fewer scholars — but the yearly gatherings, generally in conjunction with the annual meetings of the Music Teachers' National Association, afforded stimulating personal contacts and fostered cohesion. More important even than this, the monthly and quarterly magazines of the society kept our members in touch with the ideals, objects, and accomplishments of musicology.

However modest our part of the whole, it was at least an organized

Reprinted from *Essays Offered to Herbert Putnam by His Colleagues and Friends on His Thirtieth Anniversary as Librarian of Congress, 5 April 1929*, ed. William Warner Bishop and Andrew Keogh (New Haven, Conn.: Yale University Press, 1929), pp. 423–28.

1. Oscar Sonneck's death on October 30, 1928, left this article — according to Carl Engel — unfinished but at least a complete torso. It shows a whimsical streak unusual in Sonneck's writing for publication, and it makes one wish all the more that he had been granted another ten or fifteen years in which to expand his personal as well as professional capacities. — ED.

movement in the right direction. The war totally demolished the structure, and today the United States Section of the IMG is but a dim memory; most of its scattered remnants are buried in silence or void of enough centripetal magnetism to permit Americans to play much of a part in the new international society of musicologists, the Société Internationale de Musicologie, founded in 1927. Nevertheless, the great compliment was paid America by electing — I am happy to say, at my suggestion — my successor at the Library of Congress, Mr. Carl Engel, into the inner council of this new society that has revived, if not the machinery, at least the idea and ideals of the defunct IMG. Mr. Engel attempted in the spring of 1928, at a meeting called by him at Washington during the music festival at the Library of Congress, to arouse wider interest in a certain musicological project connected with the Library. He failed in his purpose; and — I am not saying this in a spirit of carping criticism — he could not but fail in view of the fact that the mixture of the enthusiasts present was too heterogeneous and because very few of them knew the meaning of musicology.

Just what is musicology? Instead of attempting an answer by way of a definition that, as most definitions do, merely substitutes several words for one, I shall approach the question in the manner of old-fashioned song accompanists who would prelude the prelude of a song with some compositorial notions of their own. Accordingly, first a chord or two on the publication, about a year ago, of a slender volume that was merely a primer of the rudiments of music, but on which the proud author had bestowed the title *Musicology*. Evidently she liked the term, whatever meaning it may have conveyed to her, better than does a certain gentleman who in principle takes an interest in musicology, but whose interest is paralyzed by the term, which he dislikes. Modulating into a neighboring key, I remember that recently a certain benefactor of music felt attracted enough to the mysterious term to desire the addition of a musicological department to the musical institute founded by her. She even announced this intention as a *fait accompli* but, presumably because she had been asked the question with which this paragraph opens, she proceeded to put the same question. She received rather an intelligent answer, whereupon she decided to defer the installation of a musicological department for an indefinite period.[2]

---

2. Reading these lines, one is somehow reminded that the Curtis Institute of Music in Philadelphia was founded in 1924 through the generosity and guidance of Mrs. Mary Louise Curtis Bok (later Mrs. Efrem Zimbalist). — ED.

After this suspension, as we musicians call it, with a harmonically unrelated *arpeggio* into a college town of the Midwest! There a very wealthy and public-spirited gentleman was approached with the urgent plea that he donate to the college one of the most important private collections of music and books on music assembled in Europe during the last hundred years. It was to be had *en bloc* and, prior to auction, at an abnormally low price. Everything went smoothly until the gentleman learned that the collection contained a great many rarities of the kind that gladdens the hearts of musicologists. Thereupon he declined to spend his money on a museum because he abhorred museums.

By way of ending this lengthy prelude to my short song, I turn to an author of a somewhat ambitious book on music.[3] About certain statements in it I found occasion to express my doubts. She in turn expressed her astonishment at my doubts and enumerated about a dozen supporting *authorities* whom she had read in the course of her "musicological research." It so happened, however, that ten of the books were merely commercial compilations and all ten were based on the same two authorities, one of whom is by now superseded and obsolete. At best, then, the twelve apostles of verity dwindled down to precisely one as against the doubting Thomas.

And now, just what is musicology? My answer is, and I shall let it go at that: musicology is to music what philology is to literature or what any kind of "ology" is to its proper sphere of mental discipline; but in these pages I am speaking more specifically of musicology in the narrower sense of history of music, though it may be history as ramified and as broad as one cares to view it. Granted that a multimillionaire, too, enjoys the privilege of spending his money according to his tastes and fancies, nevertheless it is a pity that an idiosyncrasy can so affect an otherwise liberal mind as to deprive America of an opportunity, probably unique, to add a magnificent library to the deplorably few she possesses.

One may concede that, for instance, ichthyology is not a pretty word; but this is hardly a valid reason for adopting a negative attitude toward the scientific study of fish until, and unless, a prettier word be substituted. As for the brand of "musicological research" just mentioned, I question whether any person interested in the study of fish would with

---

3. It may be entirely a matter of coincidence that in 1925 the late Marion Bauer published the first edition of her first book, *How Music Grew*, with Ethel Peyser as co-author. — ED.

equal ingenuousness qualify the copying of fish-stories as ichthyological research. On the other hand, I can hardly imagine that the founder of an academic institution would be so overawed by a definition of philology as to look upon philology as a sort of liability that had better be deferred as long as possible.

The real discomfiture of musicology in America, as I see it, lies in this — that of all the arts music is still supposed to be so mysterious a manifestation of the divine afflatus that its study, in the sense of *"Das Ding an sich,"* is considered almost sacrilegious;[4] and if not that, at least wholly superfluous — for practical purposes. Unless a bit of historical investigation serves some "practical purpose," journalistic scoffers superciliously eye it as of "merely antiquarian interest." But who determines what a practical purpose is and where it begins or ends? Also, why must a practical purpose always underlie a student's historical curiosity? If Beauty be self-sufficient, so is Science and, if you please, even the Science of Beauty. What sets music so far apart from literature that what one might call the philology of music requires the passport of a practical purpose? In the last analysis, such a doctrine would reduce all historical writing on music to a species of advertising copy; and much of it in our country, I regret to say, is precisely that and little more. However, if a practical purpose or result be the test of the right to exist, then the musicologist may rightly insist that he be given at least the benefit of the doubt, on the theory that in other branches of learning, too, sometimes decades pass before a perfectly useless, impractical, abstract piece of research or reasoning transforms itself into gold. And, it not into gold, at least into something helpful to pianists, singers, composers, or others afflicted with the germ of music.

The proof of this pudding lies most enticingly in the eating, when both the cooking and the eating are done by musicians themselves instead of by professional musicologists. This little episode, which I witnessed, may serve to illustrate the point. For years, a very great pianist of a conspicuously keen and intuitive mind had found himself interpreting, with artistic conviction, passages in a sonata by Beethoven very differently from what the supposedly authoritative edition of Beetho-

---

4. *Das Ding an sich* is the Kantian concept of a thing as it exists entirely in itself, with no sense organs of a living being to perceive it and thereby transmute it into something outside of and different from itself. Sonneck uses the term here to mean the pursuit of music purely for its own sake — not for religious, patriotic, pedagogical, or other extra-musical reasons. — ED.

ven's works — authoritative because supposedly based on the master's manuscripts — demanded. He happened to look at those passages in the recently published facsimile of that sonata, and triumphantly he pointed out to a fellow pianist that what both of them had habitually been doing in violation of the authoritative text was plainly, indeed unquestionably, called for by Beethoven himself. The critical and learned editor simply had nodded, thereby falsifying for posterity Beethoven's intentions. The ludicrous part of the episode consists in this: that these two artists had been able to defend themselves against the charge of tampering with Beethoven only by relying on their artistic instincts. Now, let us suppose that they had not seen the facsimile and let us further suppose that some musicologist had made it his business to recompare the "authoritative" edition with the extant manuscripts of Beethoven (or their facsimiles); it is fairly safe to assume that he would have discovered and described the same discrepancies — and discrepancies, be it noted, of quite a "practical" nature — but it is also fairly safe to contend that in that case the two pianists probably would never have seen his discoveries, and would have continued to be on the defensive against colleagues and critics relying on the supposedly authoritative edition. Unfortunately so — and that is precisely my point!

PART 2

Writings about Sonneck

O. G. Sonneck
October 6, 1873 — October 30, 1928

HERBERT PUTNAM

This is not a memorial meeting, deliberately planned, for well-considered expression. It is a tragic impromptu to which we have been summoned, not to appraise Oscar Sonneck, but to take sad leave of him.[1] We are his friends and intimates; and the thought of each of us is engrossed, not with general reflections upon him, but with some phase, some characteristic, some experience of him, or some benefit from him. The thought most personal cannot be uttered here. And if I have been asked to say something of my experience, that is because it relates to a section of his life of high public importance: his fifteen years at Washington.

I recall — constantly — the origin of them; and often cite it as proof that if an administrator can shape *definitely* his purposes, Providence may dispense to him the fit instrument for effecting them.

Among the groups of material that I encountered at the Library, when I went there thirty years ago, was one of Music: some 250,000 compositions, all the result of copyright; and a very meagre representation of the literature.

What was to be our duty to it, and to the subject generally? I swiftly

Remarks by the then Librarian of Congress at the funeral service for Sonneck in New York on November 1, 1928. Reprinted from *The Musical Quarterly* 15, no. 1 (January 1929): 1-4.

1. The funerary leave-taking was in New York; but Music Division folklore recounts how Dr. Putnam and Mr. Engel followed Sonneck's wishes faithfully and interred him in the Library of Congress, strewing his ashes over the quiet inner courtyard adjacent to the then-new Coolidge Auditorium. — ED.

Courtyard outside Coolidge Auditorium and Whittall Pavilion, Library of Congress

satisfied myself that there *was* a duty, positive and appealing; that Music, as one of the noblest of the Arts — most penetrating, most influential — had a rightful claim to recognition from the National Government; that the expression of it, in composition and in literature, should have a rightful place in the National Library; and that the fervor for it among our people was certain to develop a zeal for exact knowledge and understanding, promising studies and research which the National Library might foster as could no other institution.

The duty, then, was to develop the collection on the scholarly side, and to assure a scholarly conduct of it.

But for both of these the indispensable, indeed the prerequisite, was the *man* with the adequate learning and the necessary qualities. The combination required was complicated. He must be a specialist in the subject matter, thoroughly grounded through studies abroad; yet he must, if possible, have some familiarity with our American ways, some sympathies, some faith in what we might do in Music — some appreciation of what we had already done. He must be familiar with the technique of Music as an art, yet prefer to pursue it as a science: the history of it, the theory, the philosophy, even the bibliography. He must be young, for the task would be long; and personally industrious, for his staff would be small. And he must have the urge to gather and interpret for the benefit of others, which is the requisite in a library.

The combination in one person of all these qualifications seemed scarcely credible. Yet I shaped them, and waited.

I waited three years. Then one day (in 1902) there strolled into my office a young man who introduced himself as Oscar Sonneck, and his interest as Music. He had under his arm a packet of manuscript which he proffered to me — without recompense — for publication by the government.

The explanation of it — very simple and modest — induced me to draw from him the facts of his career: that, born in Jersey City, he had been educated at Kiel and Frankfurt and Heidelberg and Munich, specializing in music, which he had pursued further in studies in Italy; that his particular interest was on the historical, philosophic, and critical side; that for the several years preceding he had been writing criticisms and reviews, during the last two, however, concentrating upon the preparation of this manuscript. And the manuscript proved to be "A Bibliography of American Music in the Eighteenth Century"!

Providence, you see, had intervened: do you wonder I thought it?

I talked to him of the task with us, asked him if he would consider it. He thought it might interest him. There were some adjustments — of our roll — involved for which I had to look to the Appropriation Committees in Congress. I sought them, describing the opportunity, and, very frankly, the man himself. They were granted; and he came.

You know what he accomplished there. Laying out a scheme of development by five-year periods, he built up there a ɔllection (now over a million items) which is not merely one of the largest existing, but one of the most important for its scholarly content. Concurrently, and chiefly with his own hand (for he had not a single associate of the scholarship to companion him) — concurrently he produced those prodigies in bibliography — the catalogues (including the Libretti and the Orchestral compositions) and the monographs, which carried the service and repute of the Library — and of our Government — not merely throughout the United States but abroad.

Momentous achievements. Significant also far beyond their immediate dimension, and with consequences to prove far-reaching.[2]

They were the more creditable because he worked under personal difficulties. He was not physically robust; nor temperamentally sanguine or buoyant. He had not the stolidity of nerves which takes with equanimity the inconveniences and annoyances of life. They harassed him. And he lacked the diversions which, with most of us, serve as counterpoise; lacked indeed the *art* of diversion. He did not know "how to play." Often I besought him to — for instance, incidentally, during his trips abroad. But to be "incidental" — effortless — for his own pleasure — was for him in itself an effort. And always, on his return, there

---

2. Among the early ones [were] Mrs. Coolidge's endowments; and the acceptance by Congress, quite complacently, of the role required of the Government under them. It was the solid foundation laid by Sonneck that was, in each case, the warrant. Her Foundation rests on his. — H.P. [Congress's "complacent" acceptance was expressed through Public Law 541 of the 68th Congress, March 3, 1925, "An Act to create a Library of Congress Trust Fund Board." That act enabled the Library to accept Mrs. Elizabeth Sprague Coolidge's gift of the Auditorium and the Foundation endowed by and named after her. Even more far-reaching was the fact that it created the power and the legal machinery by which the Library could accept and use all sorts of gifts and bequests in the future. At the beginning of fiscal year 1983, on October 1, 1982, there were 155 such funds, of which 22 dealt specifically with music, and another 40 that could on occasion include music acquisitions or activities. All of these can be said to rest on Mrs. Coolidge's Foundation and hence, in Dr. Putnam's sense, on Sonneck's "solid foundation." — ED.]

The Librarian of Congress, Dr. Herbert Putnam, and his staff of chiefs of division, on the front steps of the Library, Spring, 1914. Dr. Putnam is in the front row, third from right; O. G. Sonneck is at right in the second row, behind the figure in the white waistcoat. Courtesy of the Library of Congress was the rueful admission that, though the main mission had been achieved, the trip had left him fagged.

So he worked always under obstacles within himself, or at least without the aid of that physical buoyancy and that natural optimism which tonic many men to great accomplishment. And if, in spite of this handicap, he achieved greatly, it was because his conscience forced him on and through. His intense seriousness meant for him personally many deprivations; but it meant in his work that unflagging industry, dogged thoroughness, and persistence toward perfection that not merely reared those monuments of him at Washington, but have influenced wholesomely the standards and canons of an entire profession. The inaccurate was intolerable to him, and the meretricious. Not that he engaged in vehement denunciations of them; he was not an explosive person. But he was too naïf to obscure his opinions, and too sincere in any responsibility to compromise his judgments.

I've no doubt that these qualities, which stamped his work at Washington — and his influence at large — persisted to the advantage of his subsequent work in New York. They certainly appear in *The Musical Quarterly;* and I fancy that Mr. Bauer would declare their value in the affairs of the Beethoven Association.

It is, however, as a colleague that my own thought is of him today. An office such as mine — an administrative office — has not one, but a group of problems. The acquisition, accommodation, and preservation of the material form only one section of them, and that the simplest to deal with. The discovery and acquisition of the *man* who is to bring to them the adequate learning, apply to them the requisite technique, and *animate* them in service, is the major problem of all. Solved, it brings relief and assurance; and also the continuing relish of assisting in the structure which his genius will design and his artistry create.

It is rarely indeed that the ensuing structure proves, as in this case, so complete a realization. But we do not forget, Mr. Engel and I, that the structure itself is no static or inanimate thing: it is an *organism,* which, to serve and to signify, must continually grow and diversify. It will be our task, and that of our successors, to see that in the course of this growth its purpose shall not be thwarted, its essential nature perverted; and that, whatever the development, it shall still embody the ideals, the scrupulous scholarship, and the equally scrupulous artistic conscience of Oscar Sonneck.

A Postscript

CARL ENGEL

⌣

Oscar Sonneck was *The Musical Quarterly*. He created it in his own image. It bore the mark of his scholarship, his honesty, his taste, his catholicity, his whole character. There is no other magazine just like *The Musical Quarterly*, either in Europe or in America, because there is not, and there never can be, another person just like Oscar Sonneck.

He conceived *The Musical Quarterly* as a sound but non-commercial enterprise, as a live but non-topical organ. He saw his magazine, not as a record of current events, but as a store of permanent knowledge. His conception was unique. Without the sympathetic and ready support of Rudolph Schirmer, however, the vision would not have become a reality.

Oscar Sonneck had the courage, in the midst of the world-war, to set about editing a magazine devoted solely to musicology, or to the scientific and scholarly branches of musical art. For an American periodical, the tone and contents of the magazine were a departure. Of musical journalism our country had a great deal; much of it inconsiderable, some of it faddish. At its best, it was sane musical criticism of a high literary order. But very little of it belonged to the domain of musicology.

Carl Engel (1883 – 1944) was born in Paris, was educated in Germany, and emigrated to the United States in 1905, becoming an editor with the Boston Music Company, an affiliate of the New York music-publishing firm of G. Schirmer. Engel succeeded Sonneck in 1922 as Chief of the Music Division of the Library of Congress, in 1928 as editor of *The Musical Quarterly*, and in 1929 as managing editor and officer of G. Schirmer, Inc. (for five years dividing his time between the Library and Schirmer). This tribute to his predecessor is reprinted from *The Musical Quarterly* 15, no. 1 (January 1929): 149 – 51, the issue that began with Sonneck as editor but ended with Engel in that position.

The first article in the first issue of *The Musical Quarterly* (January 1915), by Professor Waldo S. Pratt, was entitled "On Behalf of Musicology." It was obviously a "keynote" article.

The term musicology is still unfamiliar in America; it is looked upon with suspicion. Only recently, the term was decried as "unattractive" by one of our most influential educators, who deemed it an obstacle to the pursuits that it designates. Yet Oscar Sonneck, when he died, left unfinished a memoir on "The Future of Musicology in America."[1] Obstacles were his incentive. He worked for, and he lived in, the future. His zeal for musicology and his faith in America were undying.

For fourteen years Oscar Sonneck edited *The Musical Quarterly*. The beginning, because of the war, was made especially difficult. Suitable contributions were not in abundance. A large part of Europe and some of the most eminent musicologists were temporarily out of reach. In those early days, to make up the requisite number of articles, the editor repeatedly turned contributor — modestly, though, under an assumed name. To such an emergency we owe, for instance, "Kluckhuhn's Chord," by "Frank Lester (St. Louis, Mo.)," in the July, 1916, issue. This delightful little skit is but one example of its author in his lighter vein, applying his wit and gentle irony.

On many, Oscar Sonneck was apt to make the impression of being forbiddingly sedate and short. Occasionally, he appeared irritable and could irritate. He seemed to look on life through the blue glasses of pessimism. Brilliant in everything that he did, endowed with a perseverance equal to any task — even the grind of business cares — he nevertheless drew a happier breath in the atmosphere of a library than in that of an office. The effect was inevitable. Some of us affectionately called him "Oscar Gloom." But there was another side to the man. He had a lively sense of humor; he enjoyed gaiety; he was not merely patient but he possessed unlimited enthusiasm: he believed in beauty and serenity as the supreme comforts of the soul. He was broadminded and generous. Only his sense of duty knew no compromise.

Without this other side, this real side, Oscar Sonneck could not have been the editor that he was. He held to the creed that a competent contributor should be allowed to say what he pleased and say it as he pleased. The editor Sonneck never tried to "dictate" in matters of opinion and style or to enforce an "editorial policy." He considered a diver-

---

1. Reprinted as the last item in Part 1. — ED.

THE MUSICAL QUARTERLY
VOL. I   JANUARY, 1915   NO. I

ON BEHALF OF MUSICOLOGY

By WALDO S. PRATT

PERHAPS the first question is, Do we really need the *word* "musicology?" It is a word not instantly grateful to the ear or to the mind. The eye may confuse it with the botanist's "muscology," and the humorous fancy may even connect it with the ubiquitous *musca* of entomology. Even when we see what it is and that it is etymologically correct, we have to confess that it seems almost as hybrid as "sexology." At all events, it is more ingenious than euphonious, more curious than alluring.

One trouble is that it is extremely recent. It is so new and rare that it is not yet listed in any general English dictionary or in any catalogue of English musical terms. I doubt whether it even occurs in Grove's big "Dictionary of Music and Musicians." Yet it has been creeping in as a twentieth-century innovation. We may guess that it was suggested by the French *musicologie*, or perhaps coined to match the German *Musikwissenschaft*. Like them, it plainly means "the science of music"—a phrase, however, which has often been loosely used, in America at least, for the theory of composition, and which, therefore, does not at all express the proper sense of "musicology," if the latter corresponds to its French and German analogues. Assuming that there is a more general "science of music," for which a single technical term is required, "musicology" offers points of practical convenience. It resembles many other words ending in "-ology" or "-logy." It yields several handy derivatives, such as "musicologist" (or "musicologue"), "musicological," and the like. And, being new, it is free from entangling associations.

We may conclude, then, that the word will take its place in usage if its proper meaning justifies it. We need it if it represents

1

First page of the first issue of *The Musical Quarterly*, January, 1915 sity of views essential to the success of his magazine. He encouraged controversy, civilly waged, because he saw in it a means of arriving at that elusive thing called "Truth." The only aims that really mattered to him were those that are "true, beautiful, and good."

The position now occupied by *The Musical Quarterly* proves Sonneck's wisdom. With his guidance and labor ended, it would seem that the magazine, too, should end. It is not a torso. It will always remain a monument to one of his finest achievements. But he hoped that it might be continued — continued so long as it served the purpose for which it was created, so long as it kept the spirit in which it was conceived and in which he conducted it for fourteen years. On the afternoon of October 23, in the ambulance, on his way to the hospital, with perfect calm he gave me his instructions regarding the final proofreading of this issue of *The Musical Quarterly*. A stoic smile could not belie the pain that contracted his brow. The same evening he was operated on. He died a week later, at 6 o'clock on the afternoon of October 30.

This is not the place nor the time to review Oscar Sonneck's life-work in all its many-sided aspects and stupendous extent. The repute of the scholar will grow, the qualities of the man will be more widely recognized, now that he is dead. At this hour, the eye still sees but a void: the loss, beyond return, of a friend. Over those of us, for whom the bond of friendship made him more wholly ours to love and to appreciate, his going has cast the chill of loneliness. And it has laid on us an obligation. He was a pioneer, a leader, and, in a sense, a martyr. He left us a banner and a cross. Though not one of us have his strength, we must carry them onward.

Oscar G. Sonneck

CARL ENGEL

The present issue of *The Musical Quarterly* might be called a "Silver Jubilee" issue: the first number appeared in January, 1915, twenty-five years ago. The magazine was conceived by the late Rudolph E. Schirmer, music publisher, as a non-commerical enterprise — a periodical devoted to music in all of its branches of higher learning, yet of interest and benefit to the layman. There was to be no appeal or concession to "popular tastes." If "dryness" be an attribute of scholarship, it has its graces. The "lighter touch" need not be excluded, provided it touch the right spot. After all, it should be the editor's business to find the proper leaven for a nourishing and palatable mixture. Chief concern of the publisher's was that the magazine should not be, or even resemble, a "house-organ" for his firm.

Reportage and propaganda were to be left to other and better qualified contemporaries. Schirmer sought for something different and new. His aim was a cosmopolitan publication, in English, giving voice to the commentator upon current trends as well as to the historiographer, but always with a view to the permanent "reference value" of each contribution. He was able to realize so high-reaching a conception only because he chose for his first editor the one American scholar able to give it form and imbue it with life.

In the 438-page "American Supplement" to the Colles edition (1935) of *Grove's Dictionary of Music and Musicians* there are included sixteen full-page portrait-illustrations. Three are of women, and thirteen are of men. Among the latter are six composers, one conductor, one

Reprinted from *The Musical Quarterly* 25, no. 1 (January 1939): 2-5.

piano builder, one theorist, one critic, two pianists, and one a person whose "character" is not easily defined: he is Oscar G. Sonneck. If a photograph of his [shown on p. 63] (not one of his last or best) was admitted to this small but select company, there were probably two reasons: first, that Sonneck's name, through his manifold "works" — his vast research, his monumental catalogs, his pioneering in the musical history of America — had probably become known more widely abroad, especially in certain scholarly circles, than had the names of some of the other pictured "celebrities"; the second reason, very likely, was that the editor of the Supplement, Waldo Selden Pratt, happened to be one of those Americans most keenly and intimately aware on what solid and unique grounds rested Oscar Sonneck's "fame."

It was Pratt who wrote the "key-note" article — "On Behalf of Musicology" — for the first number of *The Musical Quarterly*. There has long existed a foolish and incomprehensible prejudice against the term. Only recently one of our learned friends came out in widely read print, calling the word "ugly and pretentious." Is there greater beauty or modesty concealed in such terms as paleontology, ichthyology, or dermatology? They are legitimate linguistic tools, precise and useful. Musicology in America may have had great-uncles; but Sonneck was its father. And *The Musical Quarterly* was the first American publication to come out boldly on behalf of the ugly and pretentious duckling.

It is not too much to say that from his early youth Sonneck had definitely steered for fame; and it is certain that he reached his goal, despite occasional adverse winds, without ever swerving for a moment from the true course. He may have been ambitious, he may have taken just pride in success; yet he never stooped to sensational tactics, he never succeeded except by fair means and hard work. It was this capacity for close and methodical application which, added to a brilliant mind, was responsible for Sonneck's ultimate renown. And he, himself, was the first to know it.

Among certain letters which Sonneck wrote to his Mother over a number of years, and which, after his premature death in 1928 at the age of 55, she presented to the Library of Congress in Washington, there is one that is exceptionally revealing. He wrote this letter as a young man of twenty, in May, 1894, while studying in Munich. His Mother at the time was living in Frankfurt-am-Main, where she had charge of the household of a wealthy, widowed banker, in whose family Sonneck was brought up like a son. The letter, in German, is long; it comprises 16 closely written pages. We shall quote and translate [it here]:[1]

Munich, May 27, 1894.

Dear Mother:

Just as I was about to write to you, I received your dear letter. Very well, I will confess to you what is the reason for my dissatisfaction.

In considering my whole upbringing, one might really think that I should be the most contented person. I have always been kept in a certain abundance. I lacked nothing that love and money-bags were able and permitted to grant me. Almost everyone of my little wishes, which often were very big ones, has been satisfied.

I am referring here especially to birthday and Christmas presents. What young man of my age and in my circumstances owns his own Blüthner [grand piano], or these quantities of partly very valuable books and scores; what young man, unless he is the scion of rich people, could have traveled as much as I have: certainly, all my wishes were anticipated. I have been petted and spoiled, and, on the other hand, I have been kept under, where it was necessary. Eminent stress has been laid on my education. But why enumerate all the advantages that I have had, and still have, compared with others.

Everything that circumstances, everything that the love of a mother and others could possibly have given me, I have received and have been allowed to enjoy. Consequently I should be the most contented, the happiest person.

But unfortunately this is not so!

Because I should have said instead of "the most contented," the most grateful person. That would better hit the nail on the head. Contentment can be an outer and an inner one. You probably know what I mean, since you yourself, dear Mother, used these expressions in your letter.

Inner contentment I lack. And this for easily comprehensible reasons.

Had I not been reared in these conditions, had from the beginning your and my circumstances of life been different, I should have probably not been placed in the dilemma of being discontented — with myself. I should have become a business man or God

---

1. Engel ended his sentence "only the essential passages" and referred in a footnote to the complete text of the letter he had printed in *The Musical Quarterly* 19, no. 4 (October 1933): 462–65. The complete letter, in Engel's translation, is here reprinted unedited from that source. — ED.

knows what else, and would not, as now, so to speak, have a ticket for the race to immortality.

A clerk has no reason to be discontented with himself, so long as he fulfils the duties of his calling. I am talking of the clerk in general. But as soon as he is pricked by the ambition to become later on independent, or a distinguished merchant, to gain reputation, social position, riches, he will perhaps fall into the same predicament as that of *stud. phil.* O. G. Sonneck.

For in reality it is unsatisfied ambition which daily, hourly, makes me discontented. To be sure, I am not yet 21 and many a one of 24 who also is a student, or even has been one, does not know as much as I know now. But of what avail is industry, energy, and what good is money, luck, and the, in other things so indispensable, love of my relatives and friends, so long as *I* still find a sore spot in myself: and that is, in my case, the obvious want of exceptional talent.

Well, there you have it: "exceptional talent"! I possess industry, energy, educational means, but the chief means are lacking: the talent.

Another fellow, for instance, studies law. If he's in luck, he becomes a lawyer. He knows from the beginning — experience proves it sufficiently — that as such he can be an average [*mittelmässig*] being. His ambition is not a great one, it is healthy and not "false."

My case is different. By nature I have, as I may well say, extraordinary ambition. Instead of damming it up, I have always nursed it, because at times I have really imagined I was a great mind. I saw myself in my imagination now in this, now in that position, but always in a place from which my picture could be taken for the album of immortals. I wanted to become an important, a famous man. So long as one does not have the opportunity more closely to examine one's cranium in that respect, this may be pardonable.

But even now I want to become a famous man. That is my failing.

I could well ask myself: you have a large portion of energy, a considerable share of the necessary diligence, why should you not succeed as others did who had less of these qualities? Then comes the reply: they had eminent talents, you haven't. Yes, dear Mother, I realize it more and more that I am only an average person [*Durchschnittsmensch*] so far as talents are concerned. What is it that I have really more talent for than the great mass? As orator, school teacher, clergyman, stone-breaker, business man, possibly musician, painter, poet, savant, or what? Answer: for nothing. My greatest talent is want of talent [*Am meisten Talent habe ich eben noch zur Talentlosigkeit*].

I could rightfully tell myself: if your talents were commensurate with your industry, energy, and above all your ambition, your name would live more than a hundred years hence. But now imagine a person in whom these qualities are not in the right proportion. Imagine a person in whom ambition gnaws and burns, who has no competitor in building air castles, who holds before his eyes a high, a sublime goal; yes, a goal of which other people would not dare think, a goal which, if he reaches it, would mean honor, fame, and thus inner contentment, self-satisfaction, because he strives for it in the interest of all mankind. Imagine a person actuated by such colossal ambition, but imagine him also as a critical self-observer who knows how to judge his faults as well as his virtues. Imagine him conscious of his lack of talent, of how ambition and ability can not pair themselves in him as an harmonious whole. Imagine him in all his hunger, in all his heart-devouring pain — he is and must be unhappy, he must gradually become sour, pessimistic and, if the torment becomes too great, may be driven to insanity.

If I were only as talented as for instance L. F.! In fifteen years everyone would have to look up to me. But what, after that space of time, will really be the case? *I* shall, as ever, have to look up to *them.*

Unsatisfied ambition, unquenchable ambition, that, in short, is the cause of my discontent. One example may suffice to prove that these self-observations are not self-delusions! Who, among relatives and friends, has ever maintained that mine is a productive nature? I daresay no one. Well, what can I do with all the acquired and acquirable knowledge, if in some other shape, in the form of independent thoughts, it does not flow from the vessel into which I poured it?

Probably, dear Mother, you have for some time had it on your tongue to interject: but you are still so young. To be sure I am so young, so green, so stupid. But all the worse, if as a novice in the field of aesthetics I already realize that, in spite of all my assiduity, I may not get far, because of my lack of talent.

This is the only field in which I could persevere. My dissatisfaction is not caused by my consciousness of lacking talent in certain directions, but by the realization of the disproportion between my general abilities and my ambition.

You suggested to me that I change horses. But that would be falling from the frying pan into the fire. At a time when the germ of my present mood already existed, I chose with full consciousness my present studies. But my real purpose I did not disclose to you. My later activities, my hoped-for eminence, I imagined in a purely artistic field, as a creator and possibly interpreter of music. That I have no talent as a composer, is as good as proved; as a conductor? Time will teach. From the beginning I considered my aesthetic studies as the indispensable equipment of any artist — unfortunately it is not so today in cold reality. Because between an artist and an artisan, and still more an artistic under-strapper, there must be made a sharp distinction.

In accordance herewith I have mapped out yearly the progress of my education. Up to my thirtieth year, every day is taken up with studies, which I have already planned for.

Hence, dear Mother, in this respect you need have no worry. I know what I want, but I do not know what I shall turn out to be, since I know that I cannot achieve what I want.

You see, the reason for my dejection lies deep, very deep. Only very few of my acquaintances know about it, the others need not learn of it. Though time will not heal the wound, it will dull the pain. Time is the best medicine for such ills.

But the main thing is, not to lose courage, even though the head is lost. Even if energetic, constant, conscious striving does not quite lead us to the goal we have set ourselves, after the exertions are over one is none the less pleased with the stretch of way one has covered. At first one looks up to the summit. If one is seized with despair, one looks down again to the valley, far below, and then gathers new hope. Even though at the half-way mark one does not have as beautiful a view as from the summit, one does enjoy, compared with the view from the valley, an incomparably wider prospect of mighty nature. Moreover, willpower is the best hostelry along the arduous way.

In accordance with your wishes, I shall talk over all these things with Uncle Heinrich. I hope that I find him in. You can realize now that my remark, the other day, about some unprejudiced friend to whom I should like to open my heart, was not without reason. Now you have been that friend, dear Mother.

When I sit along with others at the Café Luitpold, nobody notices anything, not even Moritz. They would not understand me; Moritz perhaps, but he could give me only sympathy, not advice.

Many thanks for the piano score. Unfortunately I do not have time enough at present to study it. As regards Bayreuth, we do not yet seem to understand each other. Bayreuth for the present only interests me. Interest without instruction, however, is of no use to your son. In order to appreciate Parsifal, one would have to hear it either six times, or once after thorough preliminary studies. To be sure, most people who have been there say "it is wonderful." That is a cheap opinion. Forty years ago — assuming that Parsifal had existed then — people would have hissed and ridiculed it. Now we know that R. Wagner is a genius, *ergo* everything that he writes is the work of a genius, hence "wonderful." Only very few understand Parsifal, the incorporation of mysticism in the music. And this is fortunate for the art of music! Otherwise, all that existed before R. W. would be considered as childish stuff, though they don't understand even that.

My idea is as follows: I attend here in Munich from August 8 to 20, let us say, the Ring, Meistersinger, Tristan. That is six performances at 6 marks. If I went to Bayreuth it would cost me altogether three times as much. At the same time I utilize these weeks, which fall already into vacation time, for a thorough study of the galleries and museums, for which so far I have had neither sufficient time nor the proper mood.

But I must hurry with the ordering of the tickets.

Let us now take a jump from the music drama to the underdrawers which you sent me. They are rather too wide than too small. I have not grown so terribly fat, only a little rounder. When I come to Frankfurt the superfluous fat can be easily pedaled away in three weeks. But sell, if you can, my bicycle. It may be difficult to do so; because it is very antiquated. In Frankfurt I shall ask A. L. to loan me his bicycle, which he will be glad to do. The few marks that you get for my bicylcle you could exchange at Baer's for paper.

How is Dr. W.?

How is 45 Westendstrasse? Is everybody well? Does *Oma* [grandmother] play sick nurse? Better not, or E. would be spoiled. Have you a new governess? Now C. probably will have to be consulted when it comes to such acquisitions. Ugly governesses are decidedly the greatest aesthetic ruin for a young man. By looking at the beautiful, heart and soul also are beautified. Brr! If I had to look all day at ugly women! Again brrrr! After the storm follows sunshine; but by the broken reeds, the leafless trees, one can still see that the storm has raged.

And so it has been with this letter. I should say, it is by far the longest that you have had in a long time from your son, who sends his greetings to you and the others, and who is yclept [*benamset*]

O. G. SONNECK

You will have to search far before finding a more singular document written by a youngster of twenty. It contains, *in nuce,* the whole man. Compare with the closing paragraph of that letter the *Credo* which, thirty years later, Sonneck placed at the end of his last will and testament:

Without Beauty this world would have been intolerable. In Beauty there is, indeed, more truth and good for Humanity than in all Science and Philosophy.

Ponder this final confession of a man whose training had been largely scientific and philosophical, but who was ever a lover and servant of Art. In this conflict you will find the key to what many may have regarded as a complex and even contradictory nature.

The *Weltschmerz* of his youth tinged the outlook of the mature man with a large measure of pessimism. But under a certain "gloominess" and "grouchiness" Sonneck hid a sparkling sense of humor and a golden heart. He was a man who achieved more than "fame": he won the love and admiration of those who came in closer contact with him and learned to understand him.

This brief sketch — obviously and intentionally — makes no attempt at giving a biographical or critical summary of Sonneck's life and work. Both will have to be dealt with, some day, exhaustively.[2] For in both there is material of uncommon richness and importance. At this moment we have wished merely to evoke a fleeting glimpse of the unusual person and scholar who made possible the creation of *The Musical Quarterly*.

In September, 1916, Sonneck replied to a reader of the young magazine with a letter that began as follows: "Dear Sir — Please don't take the Musical Quarterly so seriously or put it under the microscope in that fashion. My editorial life would become still more miserable. I could point out to you in that number worse things than those criticized by you. Between author, editor, and printer the printer's devil has a merry time." Golden words are these, and consoling to those who would try to uphold the standards set by Sonneck. The miserable life of an editor has its moments of comfort and alleviation. Within the last month we received from one of our subscribers a renewal enclosing a check for thirty dollars covering a ten-year subscription! If the subscriber's apparent confidence was justified, it must be that he rightly sensed the continuing influence of the principles which moved the founder and the first editor of *The Musical Quarterly*. That ten-year subscription would have brightened Sonneck's staid and kindly face with a wise and gratified smile.

---

2. Some fifty-five years have passed since Sonneck's death, over forty since Engel's remark was published; yet Sonneck's very provocative and significant life, and his varied "works," have inspired not a single published monograph, let alone a full biography or critical study. — ED.

Oscar George Theodore Sonneck (1873 – 1928)

OTTO KINKELDEY

Twenty-five years have passed since the death of Oscar Sonneck. If he had lived to the present day he would have been eighty years old. Many of us who knew him personally were quite convinced, long before his death, that his labors were having, and would continue to have, a marked influence on musical life in America. This was especially the case in the field of musicology, and most particularly on those musicologists and on all musical enthusiasts who were interested in the story of musical development in America.

Now, a quarter of a century after these labors ceased, we can see the effect and the significance of his life-work in a somewhat clearer perspective. The high regard in which he was held in his own day has risen higher. The realization of the value of his work has spread over wider circles. His name is held in greater reverence than ever before.

The reference books tell us that he was born in Jersey City, N.J. As a matter of fact his birthplace was a little community called Lafayette, near Jersey City but not at that time a part of this city. It was a station on the line of the Central Railroad of New Jersey which ran from New York to Newark, and the present writer remembers how he often passed through this station on trips to Newark. Sonneck's more intimate friends often chuckled over his account of "Lafayette Revisited." Some years after his return to America after an absence of about thirty years

Reprinted from *Notes* 11, no. 1 (December 1953): 25 – 32, with the kind permission of President Ruth Watanabe of the Music Library Association. © 1953 by the Music Library Association, Inc.

in Europe, he determined to visit his birthplace.[1] But the growing municipality of Jersey City had swallowed up the little settlement. Streets were different. House numbers had been changed; houses had disappeared. And the pilgrim was irritatingly baffled in trying to determine the exact spot of his childhood's games and escapades.

Almost all of the thirty intervening years, which covered practically his entire education, were spent in Germany. For six years, from his tenth to his sixteenth years, he attended a very select elementary school, the *Gelehrten Schule* in Kiel. Then for four years he was a scholar in Frankfurt on the Main in one of those traditional intermediate schools, known in Germany as *Gymnasien.* Here he went through the rigid humanistic curriculum which turned out so many of the famous German scholars of the eighteenth and nineteenth centuries. Whatever one may think today of the value of this conservative, traditional training, there can be no doubt that it laid the foundation and background for the patient, solid, thorough research method which characterizes all of Sonneck's work.

Four years (1893 – 1897, when he was twenty to twenty-four years old) were spent at the University, first at Heidelberg but mostly at Munich. When this period began he thought seriously of making *belles lettres* his calling, and had ambitions to become a poet. He actually published in 1895 a little volume of forty leaves of German verses, to which he gave the typically romantic title of *Seufzer (Sighs).* But his interest in philosophy and still more in musical history and research gained the upper hand. At the same time he studied music (piano, theory, and composition) under private teachers. When his university studies were ended, he continued for another year in the study of instrumentation, composition, and especially conducting. This was followed by a year of free research in Italy (1899).

Then came the return to America. Here he was seized with a true research fever. He determined to attempt for his native land a kind of

---

1. Dr. Kinkeldey's figure of "thirty" here and later must be taken as very "round," for Sonneck could not have left the U.S. before 1875 and we know he was back by early 1900. See the Editor's Preface for documentation. On the other hand, the author's reference three sentences later to "childhood games and escapades" must be septuagenarian extravagancy; in "99 Pacific Avenue" (in Part 1) Sonneck suggests absolutely no recollection of such childhood memories. — ED.

investigation which his historical studies in Europe had revealed to him as a necessary first step toward the establishment of a true record of a national or a local music history. French, German, and Italian musical research scholars had not disdained to spend their time in plowing faithfully and conscientiously through mountains of dusty old archives, records, and account books, through diaries, journals and newspapers, and any other documents and resources that would yield authentic and reliable data upon which one could found a correct and adequate historical presentation.

The American pioneer in this musical field had a decidedly harder task than his European forerunners. State, municipal, church, and school records were much more fully elaborated and better preserved in Europe than in America. There were few or no biographies or autobiographies of musicians in America in pioneer and colonial days. There were no musical journals or magazines in America in the eighteenth century, such as were known in Europe. The young American musical Columbus found only one regular source that covered any appreciable period of time — the ordinary weekly and later daily newspapers. These, in their advertising columns or among their news items, would occasionally — very occasionally — print among their political, commercial, or economic communications, so important to the colonists, a brief reference to something musical. A local or a visiting performer would give notice of a concert. Theatrical performances with music were quite regularly advertised. A music teacher would declare his willingness to accept pupils. A dealer in household goods or furniture, or in books and stationery, would give notice that he had just imported a fine line of flutes and fiddles, later of harpsichords or pianos. A bookseller would announce new imported or domestic publications of musical compositions; and toward the end of the eighteenth century venturesome publishers would devote themselves wholly to the publication of music, which they advertised periodically.

The harvesting of these scattered grains was no inconsiderable task. For two years Sonneck travelled up and down the Atlantic coast from New England to South Carolina and Georgia, visiting libraries and combing through all available American newspapers. The year 1800 was the later limit for his researches. The material thus accumulated formed the basis of some of his important early works, among them *A Bibliography of Early Secular American Music*, published in 1905;

Early Concert-Life in America (1731 – 1800), published 1907; and *Early Opera in America* (1915).[2] It is indicative of American interest in such studies that no publisher could be found for the *Bibliography*. Sonneck had to have it printed at his own expense. It is also indicative of the change which was brought about by the successive publications of Sonneck's works that a new edition of this bibliography was considered desirable. It was published in 1945. Professor William Treat Upton, who was entrusted with the task of revision and addition, found that American libraries and collectors were far more aware of the importance of such material than they were when Sonneck made his first edition. The libraries had overhauled their own neglected holdings and had cataloged more of their material than was accessible to Sonneck. The result was that Professor Upton's bibliography records the holdings of twenty-seven libraries and ten private collections, whereas the first edition covered seventeen libraries and two private collections. Sonneck's entries numbered 1304, Upton's 3533.[3] In addition the new edition has provided a number of valuable indexes, which in Sonneck's time would have made the cost prohibitive to the author. But now the Library of Congress itself sponsored the work. A grant from the Carnegie Corporation helped Professor Upton with the expense of visiting so many collections, and another grant from the Sonneck Fund, established at the Library by the Beethoven Association, covered part of the publication costs, but an even larger share of these costs was borne by the Library itself.[4]

---

2. Complete citations of all Sonneck's works mentioned in this article will be found in Irving Lowens's comprehensive bibliography and list of works that conclude Part 2 of this volume. — ED.

3. Twenty years after Upton completed his revision of Sonneck, Richard J. Wolfe published his *Secular Music in America, 1801 – 1825: A Bibliography*, 3 vols. (New York: New York Public Library, 1964), in effect extending Sonneck-Upton one-quarter of the way through the nineteenth century. As a bonus, Wolfe (who in one way or another explored the pertinent holdings of "about fifty" collections and libraries) added to his third volume three appendixes: I (pp. 1001 – 18) lists 189 new eighteenth-century items not known to either Sonneck or Upton; II (pp. 1019 – 21) names 156 items in Sonneck-Upton that, says the compiler, "for one reason or another I have re-dated into the nineteeth century"; and III cites (pp. 1023 – 33) upwards of 675 items that are in Sonneck-Upton but of which Wolfe discovered additional and hitherto unreported copies. — ED.

4. The Sonneck Memorial Fund of $10,000 was established at the Library of Congress in 1929 by the Beethoven Association (then connected with the New York Public Library). The income from it goes to assist the publication of scholarly works in the field of American music. — ED.

Sonneck's *Early Concert-Life in America* was printed and published by Breitkopf and Härtel in Leipzig. No American publisher was interested, and printing and publishing costs were much lower in Germany than in America. By 1915 Sonneck had become important enough in America to induce the kindly-disposed Rudolph E. Schirmer, then head of the firm of G. Schirmer, Inc., to bear the cost of the publication of *Early Opera in America.*

While Sonneck was making his bibliographical and historical researches before 1902, he of course visited and worked in the Library of Congress. At that time the Library of Congress was faced with a troublesome problem. Not until 1897 had it paid any special attention to music. But obligatory musical deposits with the Register of Copyrights, from which the Music Division (after July 1, 1897) could select all such items as it considered worthy of a place on its shelves, had piled up. With the opening of the new building in 1897, provision was made for a Music Division, but a skilled mind and hand were needed to find a method of dealing with the heterogeneous mass and to forestall chaos.[5]

The Librarian of Congress at that time was Mr. Herbert Putnam, a man of unusually broad interests and wide sympathies, and of infinite tact — a quality much needed in the political atmosphere of Washington. With his keen insight and, above all, his most remarkable foresight, he fully realized the need for a man of peculiar talents, and later he told the story of how Providence had intervened and brought Mr. Sonneck to his office.[6] The assiduous investigator of American music had been working daily in the Library, and having prepared his *Bibliography of American Music in the Eighteenth Century* he offered it to Mr. Putnam — without seeking recompense — for publication by the government. Mr. Sonneck's explanation of his work was so simple and modest that it induced Mr. Putnam to draw from him the facts of his career, and these facts rapidly led Mr. Putnam to the conclusion that here was his man. The upshot of the parley was an offer of a position on the Library staff with the assignment of organizing and developing

---

5. The original provision actually was for a "music department" and it was first headed by — in fact consisted entirely of — a "superintendent" who was none other than the Walter Rose Whittlesey who acted as administrative assistant to Sonneck after the latter's arrival in 1902. — ED.

6. Dr. Putnam's remarks constitute the first article in Part 2 of this volume. — ED.

the Music Division on the best modern lines. Sonneck accepted, and began his career as Chief of the Music Division on August 1, 1902.

One of his first undertakings was to check, in Hugo Riemann's *Musiklexikon,* every book and every composition which the great musical lexicographer had considered worthy of mention in his invaluable encyclopedia. Lists were made, checked as well as possible against the holdings of the unorganized music collection in Washington, and sent to Europe to various dealers. They were asked to make offers to the Library of Congress of all such items as they could find. The firm of Liepmannssohn in Berlin supplied a very large number of the desiderata. The proprietor of the firm, Mr. Otto Haas, transferred his business to London during the Nazi troubles.

In the beginning Sonneck stressed particularly the acquisition of American publications, both music and books about music, and also of British works. In the latter field he succeeded in building up a collection that was second only to the British Museum. In the acquisition of medieval manuscripts and of the now costly rare early printed part-books of music the new Music Division could not compete with the old, long-established national libraries of Paris, London, Vienna, and Munich, nor even with some of the smaller Italian libraries.

Sonneck engaged in an undertaking that was meant to overcome this handicap in one field — the opera. Since by far the greater number of opera scores exist only in manuscript, Sonneck organized a standing procedure by which important operas of many of the great opera composers, for which no printed scores existed, were copied by hand in many scattered libraries in Europe and incoporated with the not insignificant holdings of the Library of Congress. Photostats were little used in those days, and microfilms were not known.[7] The excellence of the expanded collection soon justified the publication of *Dramatic Music: Catalogue of Full Scores* (1908). This catalog includes a number of ordinarily very expensive engraved full scores, and some which were never sold by the publishers but only rented out for a comparatively short period. Many of them came to the Library of Congress by way of the Copyright Office, for the American copyright law required the ac-

---

7. The Library of Congress installed its first photostat machine in February, 1912 (see James B. Wilbur, "The Photostat," in *Essays Offered to Herbert Putnam . . . ,* ed. William Warner Bishop and Andrew Keogh [New Haven, Conn.: Yale University Press, 1929], pp. 520–27). Its first permanent microfilm equipment came only in 1938. — ED.

tual deposit of a copy of the work to be protected by copyright,[8] but others were acquired "for study purposes only" on special contract with the publisher.[9] The 1908 catalog is wholly out of date now, since the collection continued to grow rapidly, and the copyright contributions were correspondingly important.[10] The collection of vocal scores of operas is equally full.

One other highly significant addition in the opera field was engineered by Sonneck. It was the purchase in 1908 of the whole large collection of opera librettos made and owned by Albert Schatz of Rostock in Germany.[11] Several other smaller collections were acquired by the Library of Congress and the whole now represents the largest and most important collection of this kind in the world. The Schatz purchase involved a sum of about $10,000. Such an expenditure would not have been possible from the ordinary annual appropriation for Music Division purchases. A special emergency grant was authorized by the Librarian of Congress. This was not the only special grant for such extraordinary purchases. Sonneck never wearied in acknowledging his debt to the generous support continually afforded him by Mr. Putnam. The special grants were just another proof of Mr. Putnam's foresight.

The same generous attitude led Putnam to recommend the printing, as a Library of Congress publication, of Sonneck's bulky, two-volume

---

8. For operatic scores this statement was very largely true; but publishers of orchestra and band music often got away with depositing only a first violin or lead cornet part instead of a score of some sort or at least a full set of parts. — ED.

9. This clever arrangement Sonneck made with certain foreign publishers of opera scores or other "dramatico-musical" works who were loath to sell such scores to the leading public library in a country where their "grand rights" (covering all performances, whether "for profit" or not) either were not protected (as with Belaiev of St. Petersburg) or could not be properly policed (see note 27 to Sonneck's "The Music Division of the Library of Congress," above). — ED.

10. By 1915 Sonneck had virtually completed a revised and greatly augmented edition of this *Catalogue*. But World War I with its financial repercussions rendered publication "an inopportune expenditure," as Sonneck drily put it in his preface to the volume, the preface being published in the 1921 *Miscellaneous Studies*. — ED.

11. There are approximately 12,200 librettos in the Schatz Collection, several thousand of them dating from before 1800 and therefore included in Sonneck's 1914 libretto *Catalogue*. The entire collection is shelved by Schatz's own numbers, and the ones after 1800 are reached through bound volumes of photostats of his own thin paper slips, inscribed in his elegantly spidery hand. — ED.

Catalogue of Opera Librettos Printed before 1800 (1914), which has approximately 6000 entries with valuable indexes. Based chiefly on the Schatz collection and made with the aid of Schatz's card catalog, this is no mere finding list. Sonneck's comments and added historical data helped to make it a most remarkable bibliographical tool and source book for the opera historians of the whole world.

Before many years had elapsed Sonneck had built up a music library larger and better organized than any other, in spite of the lack of some of the rare, early material. Here, for example, the history of opera could be studied with greater ease than in Europe, where the opera specialist would have to travel to eight or ten different libraries in various countries to study the equivalent material.

One of Sonneck's first assignments on joining the staff of the Library of Congress was to construct a classification schedule for *Music and Books on Music (M, ML, & MT)*. A tentative model was adopted in 1902 and a perfected schedule was put in force in April 1904. All such classification schedules must undergo almost constant revision to keep them up-to-date, but except for the fairly extensive revision in 1917, Sonneck built so well that basically his schedule is substantially still in use in Washington and is gaining wider acceptance yearly with other music libraries.[12] Other published fruits of his activities at the Library of Congress were his *Report on "The Star-Spangled Banner," "Hail Columbia," "America," "Yankee Doodle,"* published in 1909; the revised and enlarged edition of the section of that *Report* on *"The Star Spangled Banner,"* published in 1914; the catalog of orchestral scores (classes M1000 – M1268), prepared under his direction in 1912; and the *Catalogue of Early Books on Music (before 1800)*, compiled by Julia Gregory under Sonneck's direction in 1913. (A *Supplement*, covering the Library's acquisitions in this last field between 1913 and 1942, appeared in 1944.) Sonneck was also much interested in "first editions," and established a special class (M3.3) where all of the first and early editions of certain great masters could be brought together in the locked cases without regard to their medium of performance. It was not very surprising, therefore, that in 1915 he should be involved in catalogs of the first editions of two American composers. He was alone responsible

---

12. The 1917 second edition of the class book (*Library of Congress Classification: Music and Books on Music*) was over the years updated several times with rear supplements of addenda, but a true third edition (of 228 pages) was not published until 1978 (Washington: Government Printing Office). — ED.

for the *Catalogue of First Editions of Edward MacDowell*[13] and worked with his Assistant Chief, Walter R. Whittlesey, on the *Catalogue of First Editions of Stephen C. Foster.*

In 1915 Sonneck persuaded his paternal friend and admirer, Rudolph E. Schirmer, to undertake the publication of an American musical journal, which aimed at a high level of literary, aesthetic, critical, and historical excellence. It was a striking example of lofty aims and true idealism on the part of this sympathetic publisher, for it was quite certain that the new journal, called *The Musical Quarterly,* would not for some time attract enough subscribers to pay the cost of production. But it soon established its reputation in the world of musical *belles lettres,* and the high aim has been maintained by Sonneck's successors up to the present day.

Two years later, in 1917, Sonneck was induced by Rudolph Schirmer to sever his connection with the Library of Congress and to join the staff of the Schirmer publishing house as Director of Publications. Great was the dismay in Washington and among all who knew of the work Sonneck was doing there. But the idea of guiding the course of America's most important music publishing firm was too tempting.[14] In 1921 Sonneck became Vice-President of the Schirmer corporation.

The year before he left Washington, Schirmer's, again with Rudolph Schirmer's active support, published the first of Sonneck's two volumes of miscellaneous essays: *Suum Cuique: Essays in Music* (1916). The second volume, *Miscellaneous Studies in the History of Music,* was published by the Macmillan Company in New York in 1921. Each volume contained eleven essays, and they prove that Sonneck's interests were by no means confined to music in America. Among these interests was a love of Beethoven. When, in 1918, the pianist Harold Bauer founded the Beethoven Association in New York, he found in Sonneck a most enthusiastic supporter and expert aid. As Librarian of the new society Sonneck gathered an outstanding collection of Beethoveniana. The collection was deposited, through the intermediation of Dr. Carlton Sprague Smith, in the New York Public Library, when the Beethoven Association was dissolved in 1940.

This interest in Beethoven also inspired three Sonneck works, which appeared at the time of the centenary of Beethoven's death in 1927.

---

13. The MacDowell catalog actually was published in 1917. — ED.

14. See "Sonneck Person-to-Person III" in Part 1 for his own explanation of his resignation. — ED.

They were: *Beethoven: Impressions of Contemporaries* (Schirmer, 1926); *The Riddle of the Immortal Beloved: A Supplement to Thayer's "Life of Beethoven"* (Schirmer, 1927); and *Beethoven Letters in America: Facsimiles with a Commentary* (Beethoven Association, 1927). The last is a sumptuous publication which gives, in addition to the facsimiles and the commentary, a transcription of the original German text and an excellent English translation. The editor at that time was able to gather thirty-five American-held letters or short notes. Eight of these had not been previously published. There are, doubtless, many more Beethoven letters in America today. Sonneck was also the prime mover in the plan to have Thayer's original English manuscript of his *Life of Beethoven,* which had seen the light only in a German translation, published in its original English form. The task of editing and completing Thayer's unfinished manuscript was entrusted to Henry Edward Krehbiel. The work in this form, in three volumes, was published by the Beethoven Association in 1921.[15]

As was made clear earlier in this essay, Sonneck had had a thorough practical training in music, which is reflected in his compositions. His published works in this field run to Opus 19. The compositions up to Opus 11 belong to his late European period. They include a string quartet, pieces for piano, for violin, and vocal works. Opera 8a and 8b are respectively a *Romanze* and a *Rhapsodie* for violin and piano. They were published in Frankfurt by the "Commissionsverlag" B. Firnberg in the late nineties. Opus 9, issued similarly in 1899, appeared with the title *Cyklus, für Baryton mit Klavierbegleitung, aus "Eine Totenmesse,"* with both words and music by Sonneck. The next work — a "suite blague" for piano — had different titles in its various revisions, but ended as a *Miniature lilipuziane.* The piece remained unpublished, but the autographs, like many of Sonneck's autographs, are in the Library of Congress. Opus 11, which Sonneck had published in Frankfurt at about the same period, consisted of *Drei Concertstücke, für Klavier: Ballade, Capriccio,* and *Interludio scherzoso.* Except for Opus 13 — an *Elegie* for violoncello and piano, which remained unpublished — the subsequent compositions were issued in America. All of them are song cycles. Opus 12, *Vermischte Lieder,* New York, Breitkopf & Härtel,

---

15. The Beethoven Association's edition of Thayer in English was superseded by *Thayer's Life of Beethoven,* revised and edited by Elliot Forbes and published in 1964 by the Princeton University Press (2 vols.). — ED.

First page of Sonneck's autograph manuscript of his setting of Poe's poem "To Helen"

1900, includes a dozen German songs for different registers. Opus 14 consisted of two songs and Opus 15 of four songs from 1902, which were published simultaneously as *Six Songs* by Carl Fischer in 1922. The texts were originally in German, but an English version was prepared for this edition by Theodore Baker. The reverse procedure occurred with Opus 16, a setting of *Four Poems by Edgar Allan Poe* for baritone and piano. Here, the original English poems were used for the Schirmer edition of 1917, and in the same year the Universal Edition brought out an edition with a German translation by R. S. Hoffmann. *Vier pessimistische Lieder, für Bariton and Klavier,* Op. 17, were issued by Universal in 1922; *Ein kleiner Lieder-Zyklus: Sechs Lieder zu Gedichten von Theodor Storm,* Op. 18, were brought out by the same firm in 1921; and the last group, Opus 19, *Studies in Song* — six poems by one English and five different American poets — was published in New York by the Composers' Music Corporation in 1923.[16] The later songs especially reveal a composer of no mean ability with a sensitive soul and clear mode of expression. A glance at the Poe cycle will confirm this. A brief acquaintance with the first of the set: "To Helen" (Helen thy beauty is to me / Like those Nicaean barks of yore) will convince the reader, the hearer, or the singer that he is dealing with a skilled musician, whose own poetic nature has enabled him to clothe Poe's beautiful poem in a dignified, sympathetic, expressive musical vesture not unworthy of the poet's thoughts and words.

When Sonneck died in New York on October 30, 1928, at the age of fifty-five, he was at the full height of his powers. His untimely death was lamented not only by hosts of friends, but perhaps even more by the many beneficiaries of his unselfish labors, who looked forward to a long continuation of his so eminently successful career.

Sonneck could be very brusque and severe with people who sought to use the Library of Congress staff for purely selfish ends, or with would-be composers who made nuisances of themselves in the publisher's office. His friends knew him as a sober, serious-minded man, with a dash of pessimism in his make-up; but also as an essentially just and truly generous, kind-hearted individual, whose serious outward

---

16. The autographs in the Library of Congress reveal that there actually are fourteen songs in this set, but only six were selected for publication. There also is an autograph manuscript of settings of four poems by Heine in translations by Louis Untermeyer, labeled "Op. 20" but left unpublished. — ED.

bearing was often lighted up by unexpected flashes of a dry, whimsical humor, which wiped out all impressions of seeming reserve or aloofness. He never sought, but he most assuredly deserves, the long-continued gratitude of those who live after him.

The Significance of Oscar Sonneck:
A Centennial Tribute

GILBERT CHASE

Oscar George Theodore Sonneck was born in Lafayette, N.J., now a part of Jersey City, on October 6, 1873, and died in New York City on October 30, 1928.[1] Educated in Germany from an early age, he studied musicology and philosophy at the University of Munich from 1893 to 1897.[2] In 1897–98 he studied conducting and instrumentation at the Conservatory of Sondershausen, then spent a year of research in Italy before returning to the United States. With this background, he laid the foundation for "scientific" (the word is his) research in American musical history and bibliography (he always thought of these two disciplines as closely interrelated). His work in this area is so well-known, and his accomplishments so widely acknowledged, that there is scarcely need to use the centenary of his birth as a pretext for reiterating the importance of his achievement as a pioneer in American musical scholarship. My intent is rather to stress the significance of his ideas on musical history, which have perhaps not received as much attention as they deserve.

In my view, "Sonneck's commitment to the 'raw data' of American

Reprinted with permission of the author from the *Yearbook for Inter-American Musical Research* 9 (1973): 172–76. The paper was read in amplified form at the national meeting of the Music Library Association in Champaign-Urbana, Illinois, on February 2, 1974.

1. In later life Sonneck stated that he wanted to be known as O. G. Sonneck, that he was known as such, and that "the insertion of my third initial goes against my grain." (Letter to Carl Engel, then Chief, Division of Music, Library of Congress, dated January 9, 1928.)

2. For later information about the date of Sonneck's removal from New Jersey to Germany, see the Editor's Preface. — ED.

musical history, rather than to an *a priori* aesthetic ideal, is what makes him a truly significant pioneer in American musicology and justifies our placing him within the context of a socio-cultural approach."[3]

What is the basis for such a view? The point of departure is Sonneck's statement that " . . . the interests of a historian of music and musical life ought not to remain confined to matters of musical aesthetics."[4] The quotation is from an address on "The History of Music in America" delivered to the Music Teachers' National Association in 1916. Sonneck's great insight was to recognize the fundamental difference between the critical and the historical approaches, the former concerned with aesthetic values, the latter with cultural values — that is to say, with the manifestations of human behavior in a social and temporal context. When he undertook research on early concert life and opera in America before 1800, he had no illusions of embarking on "adventures of the soul among masterpieces" (to borrow Walter Pater's phrase). He was looking for facts and for patterns of cultural activity, with which to fill an apparent void. History, too, abhors a vacuum.

As Sonneck saw and proclaimed, the urge to fill a historical vacuum is prompted by curiosity:

> Curiosity is the mother of all knowledge, curiosity from its crudest to its most refined forms. The historical instinct, too, is one of curiosity. History but records the inquiry of the curious into the facts of the past and *their logic of friction or mutual support* [emphasis added by G.C.]. This type of refined curiosity is sufficient unto itself without the alluvium of esthetic, ethical, didactic or other mental deposits. Hence the would-be historian need not feel apologetic at all if his curiosity move him to lift the veil of otherwise merited oblivion from facts that the historically non-inclined sneer at as being dry-as-dust and of no value for the furtherance of present musical art. The historian and the esthetician simply work in different mediums that may or may not converge.[5]

---

3. Gilbert Chase, "American Musicology and the Social Sciences," in *Perspectives in Musicology,* ed. Barry S. Brook, Edward O. D. Downes, and Sherman Van Solkema (New York: W. W. Norton, 1972), p. 221.

4. O. G. Sonneck, *Miscellaneous Studies in the History of Music* (New York: Macmillian, 1921), p. 342. — G.C. [Yet it is curious that in his early days as a librarian, a profession that requires sympathy for many disparate sets of values at several levels, he could speak so brashly, even arrogantly, about "undesirable music" and musical "trash." See his 1908 paper for the MTNA, "The Music Division of the Library of Congress," in Part 1 of this volume. — ED.]

5. Sonneck, *Miscellaneous Studies,* p. 331.

Fully to appreciate the significance of Sonneck's rejection of aesthetic criteria for the historian's job of work, we need to bear in mind that up to his time all would-be historians of music in America were motivated by aesthetic considerations. Their view, and hence their evaluations, of American music were dominated by what Sonneck described as "a set of preconceived artistic beliefs."[6] In other words, this represented a "closed system," whose boundaries and goals were fixed in advance according to principles and values derived from the European classical-romantic tradition, conceived as an immutable Aesthetic Ideal. In contrast to this strictly teleological view, of progress toward a pre-determined goal, Sonneck took the view that "music, now as ever, is a realm of unlimited possibilities."[7]

As a corollary to this "open-ended" view of music, Sonneck rejected the notion of "progressive improvement" that was inexorably maintained by earlier writers on American music. In his article on "Music and Progress," written in 1908, he goes straight to the heart of the matter:

> The popular mind believes progress to be an irresistibly steady development from good to better, but progress is rather *the prompt and logical adaptation to the exigencies of changing conditions.* . . . [emphasis added by G.C.] Nor is it at all true that the new is always really *better* than the old. *It is simply different,* the logical result of the modulation into new conditions. . . . [emphasis added by G.C.] All this seems so obvious that I almost feel ashamed of having mentioned it.[8]

As I reread that passage, I realize with chagrin how aptly I might have quoted Sonneck instead of T. S. Eliot in the introduction to *America's Music.*[9] Eliot spoke of the "obvious fact that art never improves, but that the material of art is never quite the same." It is a curious coincidence that both writers used the term "obvious" — though their views were actually considered heretical at the time. Sonneck was a precursor in more ways than one — and somewhat of an iconoclast.

---

6. O. G. Sonneck, *Suum Cuique: Essays in Music* (New York: G. Schirmer, 1916), p. 5.

7. Ibid., p. 8.

8. Ibid., p. 15.

9. Gilbert Chase, *America's Music: From the Pilgrims to the Present* (New York: McGraw-Hill, 1955; rev. 2nd ed., 1966).

Developing his ideas on non-progress in the arts, Sonneck went on to say: "This cold-blooded and perhaps prosaic attitude towards progress does not appeal to those — and they are in the majority — who ultimately expect another Eden. Nor is it a Christian attitude. Still, it is just as stimulating ethically as the 'progress-equal-to-better theory,' and just as sensible. Indeed, if we weigh them both in matters of art and particularly of music, it cannot be doubtful which of the two theories is the more correct and fruitful."[10]

Sonneck's essay on "Music and Progress" is full of good things, among them his refutation of what he calls the "chronological chronic-improvement theory" of musical history. As he writes:

> From whatever quarter the chronological chronic-improvement theory is approached, it fails and must fail because it does not take into account that each age is confronted by different problems which the genius of the age solves at the psychological moment. Once solved, this particular problem defies further solution.[11]

And finally this: "In the fine arts . . . nobody, unless he is a crank, operates with the term 'better' from a shaky chronological observatory."[12] Once again Sonneck reveals his prescience, for the "shaky chronological observatory" has been further undermined by the revolt against chronology in recent historical thought. As stated by Vincent Duckles, for example, "We are just beginning to become aware of the limitations of the chronological view and the degree to which our historical thinking is shaped by it. There are other ways of viewing history. . . ."[13]

Sonneck advanced a "scientific" approach in musical history — and by implication in musicology. In his key address on "The History of Music in America" (1916), after discussing amateurish or self-serving so-called "research" in American music, he said:

> Real research is more neutral, more impartial, more disinterested — in brief, more scientific. That implies a scientific method and the appreciation of the fact that a mere chronological string of

10. Sonneck, *Suum Cuique*, p. 15.

11. Ibid., pp. 18 – 19.

12. Ibid., p. 19.

13. Vincent Duckles, "Musicology at the Mirror: A Prospectus for the History of Musical Scholarship," in Brook et al., *Perspectives in Musicology*, pp. 36 – 37.

dates or names does not constitute history. They are merely bricks with which the historical edifice is reared. . . . The historian is not a bricklayer, but an architect, though often he will have to act in both capacities. The plea then is to apply to the investigation of our musical past, no matter how humble it may be, more of that scientific method and technique, more of that historical analysis and synthesis which still (in a degree) distinguish the best of our historians from the best in Europe.[14]

Although Sonneck did an enormous amount of detailed scholarly work in what he called "the drudgery of historical research," he never lost sight of the larger view of History. He repeatedly insisted that "the mere compilation of facts is not history." As he said, "It is the logical and discriminating interpretation of facts . . . that makes history." For him, the true historian is one who "sees a historical problem . . . and sets out to solve it. . . ."

Sonneck's concept of American musical history was all-inclusive and inevitably leads in the direction of the social sciences. In an important paper on "The Musical Life of America from the Standpoint of Musical Topography," presented to the Congress of the International Musical Society at Vienna in 1909, he called for "a survey of the psychological and economic foundations of music in America."[15] He deplored the fact that "books and articles deal more with the history of music and musicians in America than with *the history of America's musical life*" [emphasis added by G.C.]. Describing the scope of the latter, he mentioned "the development of music in the various states and cities, of church music, chamber music, orchestral music, choral music, opera, music in our colleges, the music trades, the manufacturers of instruments, the music-publishing industry, musical societies and organizations, municipal and governmental interest in and subvention of music, folk music and a host of other subjects."

Only recently has American musicology begun to do its share in the tremendous task of documenting "the history of America's musical life" as proposed by Sonneck. This obviously cannot be accomplished by musicology alone, which is traditionally concerned with "the history of music and musicians." Already there is a large, important, and rapidly growing body of scholarly work in the socio-cultural history and in-

---

14. Sonneck, *Miscellaneous Studies,* pp. 334–35.
15. Ibid., p. 336. — G.C. [See the translation of the entire paper in Part 1 of this volume. — ED.]

terpretation of "America's musical life" that has been done outside the domain of musicology. The field of American Studies has at long last been alerted to the importance of music as a factor of cultural history.

Through the example of his own scholarly research as well as by his broad and deep view of history, Oscar Sonneck stands as a precursor of the socio-cultural approach to musical history, in which scientific method takes precedence over aesthetic considerations. As Sonneck said: "If the vision of history were restricted by the esthetic horizon, historians of music in America would be in a sad plight."[16] If our present outlook is a happy one, we owe this in large measure to the tutelary spirit of Oscar Sonneck.

---

16. Ibid., p. 331. — G.C. [See also the translation in this volume. — ED.]

After 100[!] Years:
The Editorial Side of Sonneck

In memoriam
Oscar George Theodore Sonneck,
1873 – 1928

H. WILEY HITCHCOCK

Oscar Sonneck's life and his contributions to musical scholarship have been summarized by persons much more authoritative than I, notably by Otto Kinkeldey, long a friend of Sonneck and, like him, one of the pioneer American musicologists. Kinkeldey's memoir, published in *Notes* magazine just 20 years ago,[1] when Sonneck would have been 80 years old, cannot be improved upon as a résumé of Sonneck's career and a judicious assessment of his position — very high indeed — in the musicological firmament. Others, too, have written perceptively about Sonneck's achievements, among them Herbert Putnam, Carl Engel, and Irving Lowens.[2] Putnam was the Librarian of Congress who hired Son-

---

Reprinted by permission of Mr. Hitchcock from his Louis Charles Elson Memorial Lecture of the same title, delivered in the Coolidge Auditorium of the Library of Congress on November 15, 1973, and published in 1975 by the Library of Congress, Washington, D.C. © 1974 by H. Wiley Hitchcock.

1. Otto Kinkeldey, "Oscar George Theodore Sonneck (1873 – 1928)," *Notes* 11 (1953): 25 – 32 [reprinted in this volume].

2. Herbert Putnam, "O. G. Sonneck: October 6, 1873 – October 30, 1928," *Musical Quarterly* 15 (1929): 1 – 4 [reprinted in this volume]; Carl Engel, foreword to the posthumously published essay by Sonneck, "99 Pacific Avenue; or, In Search of a Birthplace," *Musical Quarterly* 19 (1933): 456 – 62; Irving Lowens, preface to the reprint of the revised edition of Oscar George Theodore

neck and made him chief of the Music Division in 1902; Engel, a scholarly associate of Sonneck for many years, was his successor in three posts, as Music Division chief, as editor of *The Musical Quarterly,* and as director of publication of the firm of G. Schirmer, Inc.; Lowens has been one of the most notable of Sonneck's scholarly grandchildren, so to speak, as a historian and bibliographer of American music. Still others have made "Sonneck surveys," including Betty B. Buyck, a graduate student at Drexel Institute who in 1954 was awarded an M.A. with a thesis on "Oscar George Theodore Sonneck: The Man and His Works."

Thus it seems to me that any general discussion here of Sonneck or his works might be a rehash — and rehashes are seldom as savory as the original dish. I have chosen instead to speak on a little-noted side of Sonneck, the "editorial" side. That adjective has several meanings, and I should like to view Sonneck in the light of all of them. But I also have a second aim. That can be suggested by my having considered at one point calling this lecture "The Lighter Side of Sonneck" or "Sonneck's Sunnier Side." And, in fact, if I were to choose a motto for the lecture, it would be one or the other of the following remarks by Sonneck: he once wrote, "The searcher after bibliographical and historical data is not always averse to finding a few 'readable' pages in a catalogue," and elsewhere he commented, "We need a little more fun in music."[3]

Sonneck is not exactly famous as a humorist. Those who know his literary work think of him primarily as a "meat and potatoes" scholar, one who produced a substantial body of very solid scholarly fare — highly caloric, not particularly enlivened with sauce, and certainly not spicy. As a historian, Sonneck specialized in documentary history and bibliography. These involve the reproduction of source materials and the compiling of lists of things. They give their practitioner very little room to be belle-lettristic, graceful, witty — personal, in short. Many scholars simply do not have the patience, the stamina, or the selflessness for such documentary and bibliographical work. Sonneck did.

As a librarian, Sonneck's forte lay in similarly impersonal areas. His main literary works were catalogs — impeccable, detailed, monumental, invaluable, but still catalogs. And one of his main achievements in the

---

Sonneck, *A Bibliography of Early Secular American Music* (1905; rev. 1945; rpt., New York: Da Capo Press, 1964), pp. v–x.

3. "A Preface," in *Miscellaneous Studies in the History of Music* (1921; rpt., New York: Da Capo Press, 1968), p. 322; "Guillaume Lekeu," in ibid., p. 213.

Music Division of the Library of Congress was to establish — and brilliantly — that most impersonal thing in a library, a system of classification for its holdings.

Sonneck's personality seems to have matched his inclinations as a scholar and librarian. Those who knew him remarked first on a rather dour, even glacial, manner. Carl Engel admitted that "many who met Oscar Sonneck saw oftenest . . . his serious and occasionally rough or disgruntled side."[4] Otto Kinkeldey said that he and other friends knew Sonneck to be "a sober, serious-minded man, with a dash of pessimism in his make-up [and] of seeming reserve or aloofness."[5] Herbert Putnam remembered Sonneck's "intense seriousness" and claimed that Sonneck "lacked the diversions which, with most of us, serve as counterpoise; lacked indeed the *art* of diversion. He did not know 'how to play.' "[6]

And yet — and this struck me repeatedly as I reviewed impressions of Sonneck by his intimates — he did have a sense of humor. Engel wrote about Sonneck's combination of "all the methodical exactness of the scholar and at the same time . . . the light touch of the ironist."[7] Kinkeldey said that Sonneck's "serious outward bearing was often lighted up by unexpected flashes of a dry, whimsical humor."[8] Irving Lowens and Allen Britton, in a discussion of Sonneck's voluminous manuscript notes, remark on the "pungent comments . . . frequently barbed and witty" which Sonneck made in them; and they cite his note on a German doctoral dissertation: "Ein ganz wischi-waschi Thesis!"[9]

In view of all this, I determined to turn to Sonneck not as one usually does, in search of some specific item of fact or record, but rather in search of his personality, and especially that element of wit and humor claimed for him. What follows is the result of my search.

I was reminded first of all that Sonneck had an uncommon ability at coining *bons mots* — memorable aphorisms, even sometimes virtually frameable epigrams. *Item:* "Some music is suitable for adults; some is suitable only for children. Some is suitable for both — and some is suitable for neither, because merely childish."[10] *Item:* "After all, taste is

---

4. Engel, foreword to Sonneck, "99 Pacific Avenue."
5. Kinkeldey, "Oscar George Theodore Sonneck."
6. Putnam, "O. G. Sonneck."
7. Engel, foreword to Sonneck, "99 Pacific Avenue."
8. Kinkeldey, "Oscar George Theodore Sonneck."
9. "Unlocated Titles in Early Sacred American Music," *Notes* 11 (1953): 35.
10. "Music for Adults and Music for Children," carbon copy of typescript, Music Division, Library of Congress

merely the faculty for distinction."[11] Sonneck found an apt metaphor for those writers on early American music who blindly accepted and preserved the myth of Puritan restrictions on colonial secular music: "As a rule," he wrote, "they make the great mistake of observing things through a New England church window."[12]

Among such trenchant remarks of Sonneck's are a number with an ironic twist of considerable pungency. For example, warning that *Suum Cuique,* one of his two books of miscellaneous essays, might have some inconsistency of opinion in it, he added that in fact he hoped that to be the case, since "chronic consistency is a virtue in mummies only."[13] Or again, defending basic research in music as against mere musical journalism, he made this wicked thrust: "I cannot help thinking that the excavation of some forgotten fact of musical history, trivial in itself perhaps, bears at least as much on the art of music as would the snapshot of a charming primadonna brushing the teeth of her pet monkey."[14]

Sonneck knew several foreign languages, and occasionally he would throw into an otherwise sober, factual account a witty linguistic invention. Thus, in his review of the Haydn Centenary Festival in Vienna in 1909, he wrote: "The trouble really is that so many musicians with *vanitas digitalis* consider musicianship incompatible with a scientific interest in their art."[15]

In a paper on early American operas, Sonneck drew on his knowledge of Italian to coin a word with multiple suffixes — two diminutives plus one pejorative — and even called attention to his coinage in a rare colloquialism: "The peculiarly spectacular and nonsensical character of the American (so-called) comic operas of to-day — veritable operettinaccias,

---

11. *Early Opera in America* (1915; rpt., New York: Benjamin Blom, 1963), p. 161.

12. "Benjamin Franklin's Musical Side" (1903), in *Suum Cuique: Essays in Music* (1916; rpt., Freeport: Books for Libraries Press, 1969), p. 73. Sonneck liked this metaphorical *trouvaille;* he used it again in urging more comprehensive studies of early American sacred music, in "The History of Music in America" (1916), *Miscellaneous Studies,* p. 338: "A historian might well afford to look broadly and deeply into all this instead of gazing contentedly through a New England church window."

13. Prefatory note to *Suum Cuique,* p. [v].

14. "The History of Music in America," *Miscellaneous Studies,* p. 332.

15. "The Haydn Centenary Festival at Vienna — Retrospective Impressions," *New Music Review,* November, 1909, p. 607.

to murder the Italian language — must partly be traced back to the beginnings of operatic life in America."[16]

This playing with language sometimes approaches punning: "If this
concert [in Charleston] was *post*-poned, an irregularity of quite are
[*recte* an] unusual nature happened to a concert with ball which had
been announced for Oct. 27, 1785. It was *pre*-poned to Oct. 26th."[17]

Sonneck's great survey of the early development of our art music,
Early Concert-Life in America, is a kind of bibliography in book form,
essentially a record of concert programs and performers as unearthed by
him in a tireless search through early newspapers. As such, it gave him
little chance for humor or wit of the sort we have been describing.
Nevertheless, he seized what opportunities he could to leaven his account in an understated, deadpan way. Here is his writeup of one New
York concert in 1793:

> . . . Mrs. Hodgkinson was to give an entertainment on June 17th.
> . . . However, [her] personal attendance was rendered impossible
> by her safe delivery of a daughter on June 16th and therefore Mr.
> Hodgkinson saw himself under the necessity of substituting for the
> two songs advertised to be sung by his wife his own new song of
> 'Bow Wow' and a favorite one by Dibdin . . . which he hoped the
> emergency of the occasion would render acceptable.[18]

A very quiet chuckle, that. In another concert writeup, Sonneck simply
let his source material speak for itself. In July, 1786, Philadelphia's leading musician, Alexander Reinagle, went up to New York to organize a
concert. A preconcert announcement in the *New York Packet* carried, as
usual, the titles of the works to be performed and the names of the
performers, but in addition (and exceptionally) it also included the
entire text of the last work on the program. With considerable relish,
one imagines, Sonneck chose to quote the entire announcement, including the text of the song finale, which goes:

> Now the time for mirth and glee
> Laugh, and love, and sing with me;
> Cupid is my theme of story.
> 'Tis his god-ships' fame and glory;

---

16. "Early American Operas" (1904 – 5), *Miscellaneous Studies,* p. 75.
17. *Early Concert-Life in America* (1907; rpt., Wiesbaden: M. Sändig,
1969), p. 25.
18. Ibid., p. 234.

All must yield unto his law:
Ha; ha! ha! ha! ha! ha! ha![19]

The *Massachusetts Centinel* of October 28, 1789, also printed the entire text of a work. It was called *Ode to Columbia's Favourite Son,* and it had been performed at a concert attended by George Washington. Sonneck chose to reprint only the first stanza but, this time, could not resist commenting on it:

> Great Washington the Hero's come
> Each heart exulting hears the sound
> Thousands to their Deliverer throng,
> And shout him welcome around.
> Now in full chorus join the song,
> And shout aloud great Washington!

Said Sonneck: "The President had to submit to seven stanzas of this awful stuff!"[20]

With this last quotation we approach Sonneck's editorial side, for here he is not just giving the facts but also his opinion of them; he is, in short, editorializing. Before looking into this editorial side of Sonneck, we might pause to consider the various meanings of the adjective.

We use the word *editorial,* I think, in at least three different senses. Derived from the noun *editor,* it can refer, of course, to the duties of, say, a magazine or a music editor, who receives or solicits manuscripts, accepts or rejects them, suggests changes in them (or makes them himself). But then, having chosen to publish a manuscript, the editor retires into the background: such articles or musical works appear over the names of their authors or composers only. This kind of editorial work thus results in what we might call an invisible embodiment of self.

On the other hand, we find in the world of scholarship a completely different meaning for the word *editorial.* I mean those occasions when a scholar interpolates in material quoted from original sources his own clarifications, explanations, or annotations. The good scholar always seeks to make perfectly clear any such "editorial" additions or emendations that he has made in the source: he actually makes a point of showing what is his in the otherwise primary source material. This kind of editorial work thus results in a visible interpolation of self.

---

19. Ibid., p. 225.
20. Ibid., p. 283n.

Finally, there is the "editorial we," by which a writer can feign anonymity and impersonality. This usage resembles that of writing under a pseudonym, since it results in a pretended denial of self.

In speaking of the editorial side of Sonneck, I propose to comment on him in all three senses of the word.

Sonneck "editorialized" in the first sense of the word in his position as founding editor of *The Musical Quarterly* and as director of publication for Schirmer's (who published the *Quarterly*). *The Musical Quarterly*'s first issue appeared in January, 1915, with Sonneck's name on the masthead as editor. He was to retain the editorship until his death in 1928. In 1917 he had resigned from the Library of Congress to join Schirmer's in New York as their director of publication. In this post he was effectively an executive editor, reading manuscripts, negotiating contracts with composers, expediting the publication of their works, and promoting performances of them. Alongside of him worked Dr. Theodore Baker, as Schirmer's literary editor and translator, and Carl Deis, as the firm's music editor.

Future scholars will, I hope, make a rounded assessment of this editorial side of Sonneck. Regrettably, two different relocations of the house of Schirmer from the offices that Sonneck knew, at 3 East 43rd Street, have taken their toll of the company's files, but there is still enough in them for a fascinating study, which I can only hint at this evening in turning my attention to the lighter side of Sonneck.

Sonneck's wry, ironic, and often mocking humor shows up in the first exchange he had, as editor of *The Musical Quarterly,* with Edwin Hughes, the American pianist, at a time when Hughes had been living in Germany for some years. Sonneck had sent a circular letter to many musicians inviting them to contribute to the new journal, and Hughes had responded by sending to Sonneck a bulky manuscript of an article on Liszt's songs. Sonneck acknowledged receipt of the manuscript and, wasting no time on amenities, swung into immediate action as editor:

My dear Hughes:
I have received and read your manuscript on Liszt's lieder. Hand auf's Herz, is that article entirely the product of *your* pen and brain? I thought that I knew your English style by this time but this article puzzles me. The English is often singularly German and does

not always read as if penned by an American. If you are losing your grip on your native tongue, for the love of Mike read nothing but English or American literature for a year.[21]

Sonneck then went on to criticize rather severely the second half of Hughes' manuscript, suggested concrete ways in which it could be (and should be) cut drastically, then closed: "Wind up with any kind of codetta that will keep the reader thinking." (Hughes eventually, but very grumpily, accepted the criticisms, and the article was duly published — with cuts — in the October, 1917, issue of the *Quarterly*.)

Some correspondence between Sonneck and Amy Lowell is rather on the serious side (and certainly deserves publication some day). But I cannot resist quoting from a letter Sonneck wrote to the poet-critic early in their acquaintance. Sonneck's secretary had made an appointment for Miss Lowell to see him, forgetting that Sonneck was going to a concert that afternoon. Miss Lowell arrived at the *Quarterly* office and, on learning that Sonneck was not there, had a temper tantrum: she berated the *Quarterly*, G. Schirmer's in general, their office staff in particular; and she left in a huff. When Sonneck returned later that afternoon he heard about the incident and dashed off a letter to Miss Lowell:

Dear Madam: —
. . . I was informed of the embarrassing scene that took place here at Schirmer's between you and my assistants. It goes without saying, of course, that no discourtesy was intended to you by my absence. . . . I do not know whether it is customary in Boston to call some one else's Secretary[,] within the hearing of others, a goose, but I do know that it is not customary in New York. . . .[22]

(Things were patched up between the two, and Amy Lowell's article, "Some Musical Analogies in Modern Poetry," was later published in the *Quarterly*.)

In his position as Schirmer's director of publication, Sonneck was in frequent correspondence with a number of major composers of the

---

21. Letter of April 10, 1915, carbon copy of typescript, Music Division, Library of Congress. I should like to acknowledge gratefully here the aid given me by members of the staff of the Music Division, notably Edward N. Waters, William Lichtenwanger, and Carroll D. Wade.

22. Letter of March 24, 1919, carbon copy of typescript, G. Schirmer, Inc. For access to this and other correspondence in the files of the *Musical Quarterly*, I should like to thank Paul Henry Lang, editor emeritus, and Christopher Hatch, editor.

1920's. His letters reveal him to have been an executive editor with a
sharp and witty pen, great self-assurance, and equally great tough-
mindedness — even combativeness. Let me again just hint at the richness
of this correspondence by reviewing a few of the exchanges between
Sonneck and a single composer, Ernest Bloch.

The correspondence between the two that remains in the Schirmer
files begins in 1919, when Bloch was living in New York and teaching at
the Mannes School of Music — before, that is, he moved to Cleveland in
1920 as the first director of the Cleveland Institute of Music. On December 10, 1919, Bloch wrote to Sonneck to complain about various
matters — about Schirmer's not publicizing his music adequately, about
The Musical Quarterly's not having published an article about him,
about a recent review of his suite for viola and piano (a clipping of
which he enclosed). The review had appeared in the *New York Evening
Journal* (which proclaimed itself "America's Greatest Evening Newspaper"); it was a vicious review, anti-Semitic and anti-Bloch, and it made
much of what it called the "unstinted lamentation," the "conscious
Hebraic cast," and the "wailing wails" of Bloch's music. Bloch told
Sonneck he was considering filing suit against the writer. But he was
even more concerned about urging Schirmer's and the *Quarterly* into
more aggressive action on his behalf; writing in French, he wondered
what he had to do to get more public recognition:

> Un bon petit scandale, par exemple? Divorce retentissant . . . af-
> faire de moeurs? de quoi défrayer la chronique mondaine![23]

Sonneck replied the next day in a long letter, parts of which I quote:

> My dear Mr. Bloch,
>   I have before me your letter of December tenth. I read it once
> and then I read it twice as an encore. . . .
>   The clipping from "America's Greatest Evening Newspaper" I
> am keeping here for future reference, unless you wish me to return
> this . . . vile Wail. . . .
>   The only kind of petit scandale that would give you added pub-
> licity I can suggest is for you to jump off Brooklyn Bridge with the
> tens of thousands of dollars which you have extracted from the
> pockets of New York's millionaires by composing music a la Job.
> Or, perhaps, the desired effect could be made by crouching down

---

23. Manuscript, G. Schirmer, Inc. I am grateful to Schirmer's present director of publication, Mario di Bonaventura, for access to this and other correspondence in the files of the publication department of G. Schirmer, Inc.

in front of G. Schirmer, your publisher, clad in nothing but part of a night shirt, and with a trained monkey passing the hat around to G. Schirmer's customers. . . .

If these two suggestions do not strike your fancy my mind is very fertile in such things and I can sell you a thousand suggestions of that kind either on a 10% royalty basis or for an outright sum of $50 per suggestion. . . .

As a Finale to this letter I must remark again that it has not been my fault that the Musical Quarterly has not yet published about your Oeuvre, once translated by a young lady who studied French in a convent as "rotten eggs." The fact is that all three gentlemen who had been commissioned to write an essay about you fell down on the job and did not deliver the promised goods. . . . [24]

Early in 1923 Bloch urged Sonneck to have Schirmer's get on with the publication of a new piano suite called *Three Poems of the Sea,* in the hope that the pianist Harold Bauer, who had programmed Bloch's *Love Poem* for that season, might also be persuaded to play the suite. Sonneck replied: "My guess is that if H.B. plays the love-tune at one of his concerts before end of season, he will not get around to the three drops of water."[25] Bloch did not take too well to Sonneck's levity and wrote back somewhat frigidly: "I was very pleased with the celerity with which my Love Tune (as you call it) was brought out, and I hope that the Three Drops of Water (as you call them) will have the same good fortune."[26] In the same letter he requested some complimentary copies of the *Love Poem.* Sonneck replied the next day: "In accordance with your request of March 15th I have already given instructions to send you twenty complimentary copies of your 'Love Poem' (as you, I believe, call it)."[27] The *Poems of the Sea* are mentioned only once more in the Sonneck-Bloch correspondence: a few months after the exchanges just quoted, Sonneck remarked in a letter to Bloch that "[Hugo] Riesenfeld has at last inquired about the water pieces with salt in them."[28] Bloch declined to rise to this bait.

One of the few times when Bloch wrote to Sonneck of his personal life and feelings was at the end of a transcontinental train ride he made

---

24. Letter of December 11, 1919, carbon copy of typescript, G. Schirmer, Inc.
25. Letter of January 24, 1923, carbon copy of typescript, G. Schirmer, Inc.
26. Letter of March 15, 1923, typescript, G. Schirmer, Inc.
27. Letter of March 16, 1923, carbon copy of typescript, G. Schirmer, Inc.
28. Letter of August 22, 1923, carbon copy of typescript, G. Schirmer, Inc.

in the summer of 1924. He penned a note from San Francisco saying, among other things: "And what a country! The Grand Canyon! The Yosemite Valls [sic]! And the *Pacific* . . . qui me trouble réellement."[29] Sonneck replied: "Evidently, you are an addition to those who have caught the Bacillus Pacificus. If you now should descend to Los Angeles, the disease will turn into a rash, and furthermore your San Francisco friends will cease being your friends."[30]

That same summer of 1924 saw the climax (but not the conclusion) of a long series of problems besetting the plans for publication of Bloch's symphony with solo voices, *Israel,* which had gone into editorial production at Schirmer's in 1921. Bloch wished a score of the symphony available for performances, so Schirmer's had hired copyists to make a duplicate. This duplicate copy was then sent to Bloch. Two years later, the work still not published, Bloch decided to revise it. In the course of working on the revision, he wrote one day to Sonneck, asking him to have Carl Deis include a note in the publication:

> Kindly ask Mr. Deis to enclose a note that the bass clarinet, though written in the bass clef in the score, has to appear in the parts in the treble (an octave higher than the bass clef) and *loco* when I use the treble, except where I myself have written Octave higher.[31]

Sonneck was predictably befuddled by this request. He wrote back:

> As to Israel, please help me to scratch my head. I happen to see the word *loco* in your letter. This is how I feel. If you do not know what I mean, let a native American explain it to you.[32]

---

29. Letter of June 30, 1924, manuscript, G. Schirmer, Inc.

30. Letter of July 7, 1924, carbon copy of typescript, G. Schirmer, Inc.

31. Letter of January 31, 1923, typescript, G. Schirmer, Inc.

32. Letter of February 2, 1923, carbon copy of typescript, G. Schirmer, Inc. — H.W.H. [Sonneck's loco-emotion here seems a bit much. Bloch simply meant that *most* of his bass clarinet part he had written in his score according to the German system, using the bass clef and writing only a tone higher for the B-flat transposing instrument — this practice being more convenient for those using the score. Bass clarinetists, on the other hand, usually prefer to play from a part written in the French system, using the treble clef and making the notes a *ninth* higher than their actual sounds. The complication was that Bloch in the upper register had himself used the French system to avoid so many ledger lines, so he warned the editor and engraver to follow his instructions in those passages, copying his part exactly where *loco* and an octave higher where indicated. — ED.]

33. Letter of February 5, 1923, typescript, G. Schirmer, Inc.

Bloch replied ingenuously:

> My dear Mr. Sonneck:
> It took me some time, of course, to understand what *loco* meant, in spite of the fact that I am just through reading [Sinclair Lewis's] *Babbitt*, that wonderful picture of American life and ideals.[33]

During the next year, Bloch finished the revision of *Israel*; it was put into publication production at Schirmer's; first proofs went to Bloch; he returned them. Second proofs were drawn in the summer of 1924 — that summer when Bloch began a long vacation with a transcontinental trip to San Francisco; he then went to a resort on Bear Island in Lake Timagami, Ontario. Schirmer's dispatch of the second proofs of *Israel* failed to reach him. No one seemed to know whether they had been sent to Cleveland, to San Francisco, or to Bear Island. Sonneck wrote to Bloch on September 22: "We are trying to trace the score. From our point of view as publishers, summer resorts are a nuisance."[34]

Bloch did finally get the proofs. But he was angry about the whole affair, and on October 7 he wrote to Sonneck complaining about several things — the mixup in the mails of the proofs of *Israel* (which he blamed on Schirmer's), the general slowness with which publication of the work had been proceeding, and finally Schirmer's carelessness in recently sending him a check for royalties not due him. His letter concludes: "From my point of view as a composer, such publishers are a nuisance."[35]

Sonneck whipped a reply back to Bloch, saluting him not with his usual "My dear Mr. Bloch" but rather the chilly "Dear Sir":

> I have just received your letter of October 7, 1924.
> And still, summer resorts are a nuisance, from any point of view, if they involve changes of address, forwarding, etc. . . .
> Mr. Fay [president of Schirmer's] will be delighted to learn that the royalties were not due you. . . . [36]

Bloch retorted with a long, defensive but also aggressive letter ending up with an exculpation of summer resorts and a demand that Sonneck have the courtesy or courage to admit it when Schirmer's had been wrong:

---

34. Carbon copy of typescript, G. Schirmer, Inc.
35. Letter of October 7, 1924, G. Schirmer, Inc.
36. Letter of October 9, 1924, G. Schirmer, Inc.

... The fault was entirely due to you and the notes I have concerning the score of Israel prove that the summer resorts have to be entirely exonerated from every attack. A small word in acknowledgment of an error committed would find me very reasonable but it is true that when people are in the wrong and try to be right and want to be right at any price, it puts me in a very combative mood. . . . [37]

Sonneck came back with this lead:

Well, then, summer resorts are a nuisance only in general and such publishers as we a nuisance only in particular, with extenuating circumstances in both cases. . . . As to the last paragraph in your letter, about mistakes and their acknowledgment, your sentiments work both ways. Perhaps the truth lies in the middle: your manner of complaint irritates me and my manner of explanation irritates you. Looking through our correspondence, I find that whenever and as soon as I found myself actually in error, I conceded the fact. That is a bad habit of mine, bad, because I rarely get credit for it.[38]

When Sonneck dictated this letter, the second proofs of *Israel* corrected by Bloch had not yet reached him, but by the time he signed the letter, they had. He was thus able to close with a characteristic postscript on the lighter side: "P.S. 'Israel' has just crossed the Red Sea."

Israel's problems were not yet over; there were further delays with the engraving, and Sonneck had to write to Bloch on January 14, 1925: "Apparently 'Israel' is pursued by bad luck. The tribes get themselves lost in a most wonderful way."[39] But finally, later that year, the work was published — surely to the relief of both Bloch and Sonneck.

It would be unfair to both men to leave you with the smoke of battle between them still curling in the air. Their last substantive exchange of letters, in midsummer 1927, proves that they came to terms, at least, with their never very warm relationship. Bloch had resigned as director of the Cleveland Institute and was spending the summer in Europe. He wrote to Sonneck an uncharacteristically chatty letter, saying among other things:

After five rather hectic weeks in Paris, and two new doctors to add to my collection of already *ten,* I decided to see a thirteenth one, in Zurich, who, at last, seems to help me. . . . Here I am really finding

---

37. Letter of October 14, 1924, typescript, G. Schirmer, Inc.
38. Letter of October 16, 1924, carbon copy of typescript, G. Schirmer, Inc.
39. Carbon copy of typescript, G. Schirmer, Inc.

my *roots* again — as my father was born, six km. far from this charming little old town. What a pleasure to find slow people . . . with no hurry and no ambition — away from the rush and tension and false values — without thinking of "making a success" . . . simply *living life!*

This alone is a good medicine — for me especially.[40]

Sonneck answered:

> . . . Let us hope that your thirteenth doctor will be the unlucky one not to have been asked years ago to cure you if, as you believe, he at last is able to help you.
>
> I am in hopes that you will find your *roots* again. I should, too, in that region although I have no ancestral connections with it. Apparently we agree that "Bigness" makes for smallness of life.
>
> With best wishes, / Sincerely yours,[41]

Let us turn to a second facet of the editorial side of Sonneck, viewing him as a scholar in the areas of bibliography, documentary history, and catalog preparation, in which he was constantly working with, and often quoting from, primary source materials.

Sonneck had got his scholarly training in Germany, fountainhead of modern documentary historiography and bibliography, and there he had learned a cardinal principle about the scholarly use of source material: it must be given as found in the source, in every detail. A phrase torn out of context, a punctuation mark omitted, a word respelled may alter completely the meaning of a source document; hence the need for absolute punctiliousness in presenting primary source material. The late Sir Donald Francis Tovey liked to tell a story that is a particularly horrible example of the misuse of sources. It is about "the minister who, wishing to inveigh against a prevalent frivolity in head-gear, preached upon the text, 'Top-knot, come down!' — which he had found in Matt. XXIV.17 ('Let him which is on the housetop not come down')."[42]

Sonneck never thus misused his sources; we can count on him to "tell it like it is." On the other hand, whenever he feared that the reader's credulity might be strained by a source's spelling or punctuation or date or fact — that the reader might think that Sonneck either could not

---

40. Letter of July 12, 1927, manuscript, G. Schirmer, Inc.
41. Letter of July 22, 1927, carbon copy of typescript, G. Schirmer, Inc.
42. *Essays in Musical Analysis,* 6 vols. (London: Oxford University Press, 1935–39), 1:141.

transcribe documents correctly or did not proofread carefully — he used
a conventional scholarly device to indicate that "Yes, that is the way it
is in the source." In scholarly American writing today, the conventional
way of doing this is to follow the dubious word or date or passage of
the source with the Latin word *sic* — meaning "thus" — enclosed in
square brackets. But in Germany Sonneck had been trained in a slightly
different convention — he used an exlamation mark enclosed in square
brackets: [!].

As we might imagine, given the vagaries of early printers of newspapers, librettos, and the like, Sonneck constantly ran into typographical
errors, and the pages of his publications are liberally sprinkled with
[!]'s: Haydn's named spelled "Heyden [!]"; Handel cited as "G. H. [!]
Handel"; a Baltimore soprano whose name is spelled three different
ways on a single concert program ("Miss Tiesseire [!]," "Miss Tiessier
[!]," "Miss Teisseire [!]"); a song in *Young's Vocal and Instrumental
Musical Miscellany* entitled "The Reconsaliation [!]"; another song title
given as "Yanke [!] Doodle"; the first line of yet another appearing in
the source as "Tell me babling [!] echo why"; a 1739 imprint with a
lengthy title beginning *Promiscuous singing no divine institution; having neither president* [!] *nor precept to support it* — all the offending
words are signaled with Sonneck's semaphore.

Sonneck added a footnote — and with considerable relish, we can
imagine — to one such typographical goof (or gaffe). Baltimore's *City
Gazette* reported early in 1793 on the opening of Shield's ballad opera,
Highland Reel. Mrs. Bignall, in the role of Miss Moggy M'Gilpin, was
lauded for her "comic powers, gaiety, and *naivette* [!]." Sonneck foot-
noted this:

> Dr. Theodore Baker, to whom I am indebted for relieving me of
> much of the labor of seeing this book through the press, here made
> the following marginal remark: "Dear Author: Very likely
> 'naivette' was the local pronunciation! Up-State in New York, at
> the present time, they pronounce *décolleté* deck-o-leet!!"[43]

If most appearances of [!] in Sonneck's works are intended merely to
alert the reader to a palpable error in the sources, some are not. Unlike
[*sic*], the bracketed exclamation mark is not concretely meaningful; it
does not necessarily mean only "thus." It is literally only a symbol for
an exclamation, and there are exclamations of various kinds. With Son-

---

43. *Early Opera*, p. 169n.

neck, in fact, the simple sign has a variety of meanings; it is an extraordinary chameleon, now meaning this kind of exclamation, now that. In sum, in Sonneck's writings [!] is an expressive editorial device.

I have made a tentative classification of the varied meanings of [!] in Sonneck. In order of decreasing frequency, according to my tabulations:

1. [!] = [*sic*]
2. [!] = A surprising fact! (or Aha!)
3. [!] = Unlikely!
4. [!] = Impossible!
5. [!] = Ha! ha! (or That's a good one!)
6. [!] = Ugh! (or Yecch!)

Let me present a few specimens of each type, other than the most common one ([!] = [*sic*]), which we have already observed in action.

First, [!] as indicator not of an error in the source but of a surprising fact in it. Sonneck reports on a concert organized by the Van Hagen family at Salem, Mass., in the summer of 1798. It was a subscription concert, and Sonneck quotes the terms on which persons were admitted: "A subscriber for a ticket to admit a lady and gentleman, 1 dollar 50 cents; *do.* for one person 88 cents [!]; a non-subscriber, 1 dollar."[44] Here, Sonneck's [!] really amounts to an expression of surprise over the ticket-price differential: if a subscriber's ticket admitting a *couple* cost $1.50, how on earth did Peter Van Hagen arrive at a price of 88¢ for a single admission?[45]

Puzzled surprise must also lie behind another such (!) that we find in Sonneck's discussion of early concert life in Providence. He writes:

---

44. *Early Concert-Life*, p. 315.

45. Probably each one of a couple was charged six bits (75 cents), whereas a single was penalized by being charged an extra bit. Drastically short of silver coins from about 1760 until after the Napoleonic wars, the British made do with thousands of Spanish-milled dollars captured from Spanish ships. With a bust of King George superimposed on the Spanish design, these "pieces of eight" were distributed as coin of the realm especially in the North American colonies and the West Indies. To fill the need for smaller change, the dollars were often broken into halves, quarters, and "bits," which were quarters halved. The value of the bit varied from time to time and place to place (Thomas Jefferson mentions it about 1782 as being worth a tenth of a dollar) but nominally in the States — before, during, and after the Revolution — it was worth 12½ cents; hence seven bits would be figured at 88 cents. The coin was used, especially in the South, well into the last century; and the word still lives in "Shave and a haircut: two bits." See *The Oxford English Dictionary*, s.v., and Mort Reed, *Cowles Complete Encyclopedia of U.S. Coins* (New York: Cowles Book Co., 1972), pp. 12–13. — ED.

"Providence . . . was not blessed with overly many concerts [although] to be sure, as early as August 1762 'Concerts of musick' were advertised in the Boston Evening Post (!) [*sic*] to take place . . . at the new Schoolhouse."[46] I take it that Sonneck is calling attention to the surprising fact that a concert in Providence was advertised in a Boston paper.

One last sample of this type of [!]. By now everyone spells the name of a certain great Italian composer as "Monteverdi," but in Sonneck's time there were many who insisted on "Monteverde." Sonneck tended to side with Emil Vogel, who, referring to the composer's manuscripts, argued for the *i* ending. Thus, with some satisfaction Sonneck noted, in his catalog entry for a libretto of *Arianna* published within the composer's lifetime, the surprising fact that the name was spelled twice with an *i*:

> L'Arianna del Sig. Ottavio Rinuccini. Posta in musica dal Sig Claudio Monteverdi. [!] Rappresentata in Venetia l'anno 1640. . . . [Sonneck quotes later, from the dedication:] L'Arianna . . . ritorna à veder le scene in Venetia, per opra del Signor Claudio Monte Verdi [!] celebratissimo Apollo del secolo. . . . [47]

A subcategory of the "surprising fact" usage of [!], found very rarely, is the double exclamation mark: [!!]. Sonneck very seldom lets himself go that far, but when he does it marks a super-surprising fact, and the reader should take special notice. Thus, in his commentary on the libretto of Ottavio Rinuccini's *L'Euridice*, printed in Florence in 1600 after the successful performance of the opera in Jacopo Peri's setting, Sonneck remarks on the dedication: "In this dedication Peri speaks of his 'Euridice' as '*le nuove musiche* [!!] fatte da me nello sponsalizio della Maestà Vostra.' In other words," says Sonneck excitedly, "Peri used this famous term, at least in print, prior to Caccini."[48]

Some sources provoke from Sonneck bracketed exclamation marks with the meaning of "Unlikely!" or even "Impossible!" In one concert notice from Philadelphia dated June 15, 1787, he found the following list of instrumentalists: "Messrs. Hopefield[,] Wolfe, Mucke, Homann, Brooke, Shetky, Petit, Oznabluth [!], Morel, De Clary, etc."[49] (We can

---

46. *Early Concert-Life*, p. 317.
47. *Catalogue of Opera Librettos Printed before 1800*, 4 vols. in 3 (1914; rpt., New York: Burt Franklin, 1967), 1:141.
48. Ibid., 1:460n.
49. *Early Concert-Life*, p. 102.

hear Sonneck snorting, "Oznabluth indeed!") And in a New York program of June 16, 1800, he noted another unlikely name; whether composer or performer, the man was of doubtful existence, at least under this sobriquet:

Sinfonie ....Sterckel
Song "Ellen or the Primrose girl"..........................Mr. Hodgkinson
Andante..Monchausen[!][50]

An attribution to Mozart of a certain march seemed "Impossible!" to Sonneck, and that of another to one "Moyard" seemed "Unlikely!" in two items in an advertisement for *The Gentleman's Amusement,* a New York collection of music of the 1790's:

Grand march from the opera of the Prisoner. *Mozart* [!]
Grand march from the opera "the Pirates," composed by Moyard[!][51]

One concert program in New York (July 8, 1797) drove Sonneck to scatter editorial exclamations on the page like birdshot.[52] First comes a surname of doubtful accuracy, "Wiska [?]." Later in the program appears the composer "Canabichi [!]" obviously a typo for *Cannabich.* The Finale is said to have been composed by "Mustcropo [!]" — and certainly Sonneck's [!] represents an outraged exclamation of "Impossible!"

In a few instances Sonneck clearly wanted to communicate his amused reaction to a source by using the [!] in the sense of "Ha! ha!" or "That's a good one!" "Handle's [!] Celebrated Water Music" could be argued as just another typo, the [!] equaling [*sic*], but there is less doubt about "Six Favorite German Waltzen [!]," and even less about the "two eminent masters [of the flute], *Florio* and *Tacet* [!]," mentioned in the *New Instructions for the German Flute* (Philadelphia, [1795 – 97]).[53] Equally amusing to Sonneck was a notice in New York of a new symphony, apparently notable for its seaworthiness: it was billed as a "Symphony, just received from Europe per the *Eliza,* Capt. Armour [!]."[54]

My classification of the varied meanings implied by Sonneck with [!] ends with an *unicum* which can only mean "Ugh!" or some other such

---

50. Ibid., p. 221.
51. *Bibliography of Early Secular American Music,* rev. ed., p. 159.
52. *Early Concert-Life,* p. 212.
53. *Bibliography of Early Secular American Music,* pp. 176, 164, and 291, respectively.
54. *Early Concert-Life,* p. 228.

expression of digust. In his research on New York's early concert life, Sonneck found the first specific concert announcement in 1736. But in a 1733 issue of the *New York Gazette* he found evidence of a still earlier concert. This was in the form of a poem entitled "Written at a Concert of Music where there was a great Number of Ladies." Unable to resist documenting precisely this indication of a pre-1736 New York concert, Sonneck printed the whole poem; at the same time, unable to suppress his aesthetic opinion of it, he appended an editorial comment:[55]

> Music has Power to melt the Soul:
> By Beauty Nature's sway'd
> Each can the Universe controul
> Without the other's Aid:
> But here together both appear
> And Force united try
> *Music* inchants the listning Ear
> And *Beauty* charms the Eye.
> What cruelty these Powers to join!
> These transports who can beat!
> Oh! Let the Sound be less divine
> Or look, ye Nymphs, less fair. [!]

There remains for us to consider the editorial side of Sonneck in a third and final sense of the word *editorial*. This sense is typified, as we have noted, by the so-called "editorial we," in which a writer or a speaker, by using the first person plural, depersonalizes his remarks — pseudonymizes them, so to speak. Indeed, the "editorial we" is simply carried a step further when a person writes under a pseudonym, or when he publishes without any byline at all.

Sonneck published several articles of this sort, at least two of them under pseudonyms. The pseudonymous articles were probably published as such because of their content, which is quite harshly satirical. One appeared in an early issue of *The Musical Quarterly;* it is entitled "Kluckhuhn's Chord."[56] The other came out in *The Musical Courier* of February 24, 1927, under the title "The Communistic Cell: A Sym-

---

55. Ibid., p. 158.
56. *Musical Quarterly* 2 (1916): 418–24. Sonneck is identified as the author in the index to vols. 1–9 of the journal.

phonic Hypoblast."[57] What interests me, in the context of our approach to Sonneck's "sunnier side," are the pseudonyms he chose for himself.

One must remember that after growing up and being educated in Germany (where he spent virtually all of the first thirty years of his life) Sonneck became an East Coast urbanite: Washington, D.C., and New York City were his domestic domiciles, and one wonders whether he ever went west of the Hudson River or at least the Appalachian Mountains. But, as we have seen, Sonneck liked to play the "middle American" — as evidenced by his use of colloquialisms such as "loco" and "for the love of Mike." This aspect of him is also revealed in the postscript of a letter he wrote near the end of his life to a Mrs. Parker of Philadelphia. She was the key figure in the Pennsylvania Society of the Colonial Dames of America, which sponsored (with Sonneck's urging and support) a monumental publication on *Church Music and Musical Life in Pennsylvania in the Eighteenth Century*.[58] Mrs. Parker had sent Sonneck a complimentary copy of Volume 2 of the book, and Sonneck wrote to thank her. Having congratulated the Society on its publication, he signed off, but then added a postscript (as so often he did):

> P.S. May I point out on p. 155 a "misprint" which pursues me everywhere? I am not a "Dr.", but justaplain "Mr."[59]

The pseudonyms Sonneck chose for himself are those of "justaplain Mr." Sonneck. Both articles actually offer two pseudonyms: in each, there is an author's byline, but then the "author" recounts what he has heard from an alleged friend: the "friend" is thus a Doppelgänger, and his name is also a pseudonym for Sonneck.

The article "Kluckhuhn's Chord" is attributed to "Frank Lester" of St. Louis, Mo. The article is "Frank Lester" 's account of the search for a kind of lost chord by one "Cyrus Kluckhuhn" (with a capital "K," and the surname might be translated as "Clucking Hen"). "Cyrus Kluckhuhn" is described as a "middle-aged gentleman [who] invariably busied himself with pad and pencil."

---

57. Sonneck identifies himself as the author in a penciled note on a copy of this article in the Music Division, Library of Congress; next to the name "Bill Jones" in the article's title is written, in Sonneck's hand, "That's me! OGS."

58. See note 4 to "Sonneck Person-to-Person I," above, for some intimation of how Mrs. Parker figured in the lives of a number of persons associated with this volume. — ED.

59. Letter of November 28, 1927, carbon copy of typescript, Music Division, Library of Congress.

The author of "The Communistic Cell: A Symphonic Hypoblast" is "Si Whiner," who begins by saying:

> What follows came to me in the form of a personal letter from my friend, Bill Jones. Of course, you know Bill Jones! No introduction is necessary. The name is so famous, not to say common, that no reader can fail to place its proud owner.

The article is an attack on ultramodern music. (And, as president of the Charles Ives Society, I regret to say that it was inspired by a performance of "a symphony so-called by Lord St. Ives, Knight of the Halter and martyr to the cause of Connecticut Modernism — which did not connect, nor was it cut, alas!")[60] "Bill Jones," purportedly a composer, tells in his letter to "Si Whiner" about the genesis and general nature of his ultramodernistic Opus 100, *The Communistic Cell: A Symphonic Hypoblast*, which he has dedicated to "Si Whiner, Pessimist."[61]

Related to these Sonneckian pseudonyms is a private joke embodied in a Latin phrase that underlay an article of 1908 in *Die Musik;* Sonneck titled the essay "Jedem das seine," an accurate German translation of "Suum cuique." Later he reprinted the article — but now titled in Latin — in an English translation by Theodore Baker, as the lead piece in a book of miscellaneous essays published in 1916; and for the book as a whole he used the essay's title: *Suum Cuique.* The article "Suum Cuique" is a plea for critical tolerance, specifically tolerance of the many kinds of new music that were being composed in the early years of the century, each with its ardent and often dogmatic adherents. Sonneck argued for the right of a composer — any composer — to use any means whatsoever to express his ideas, if only he were motivated sincerely and were craftsman enough to know how to handle the new means. "He may frame quadruple fugues," wrote Sonneck, "or fashion a musical projection of the Leaning Tower of Pisa, should the spirit urge him irresistibly thereto."

For this essay the title "Suum Cuique" or its German equivalent, "Jedem das seine") was a natural, since the Latin phrase means "To

---

60. This would have been the Fourth Symphony, or at least its first two movements, which were performed in New York, with Eugene Goossens conducting, on January 29, 1927, slightly less than a month before Sonneck's pseudonymous article appeared. See John Kirkpatrick, ed., *Charles E. Ives — Memos* (New York: W. W. Norton, 1972), pp. 12, 332.

61. See the reprinted article in this volume. — ED.

each his own." Less clear by far, however, is the appropriateness of the phrase as a title for the later book of miscellaneous essays. As I worked at the preparation of this lecture, realizing increasingly how often Sonneck's tongue was in his cheek, I began to wonder whether besides the literal meaning of the phrase *Suum cuique* Sonneck might not have intended something else. I began asking about among friends and colleagues, particularly those who had studied Latin in Germany, as, of course, Sonneck had. One evening I inquired of a designer friend, Kim Hoffmann (born Joachim Hoffmann), who completed his *Gymnasium* studies just before the Nazi years, what the phrase *Suum cuique* meant to him. Without any hesitation he snapped back, "The pig oinks." "What?!" said I. "Well," he said, "actually it's 'The pig squeaks,' but here in America we would say, 'The pig oinks.' " He then went on to explain that in Germany, in his youth, one technique used in teaching Latin was to set students to learning aphorisms, such as *Ars longa, vita brevis, Iacta est alea,* and the like. *Suum cuique* was one aphorism he learned that way. Now, as with foreign-language students everywhere, a favorite game in Germany was to coin outrageous mistranslations for such aphorisms — "fractured Latin" translations. Out of this came, as a translation for *Suum cuique,* "The pig squeaks" from *sus,* Latin for "pig" and the German verb *quiecken,* "to squeak."[62]

How characteristic it would be for Sonneck to refer to himself as "the pig," and his essay — later his book of essays — as the "oinks"! But could it be true? I went back to Sonneck's essay. It is true. In his plea for letting the modern composer use any means at all to express himself, as long as he is strongly and honestly motivated, Sonneck wrote the following: "He must not even be forbidden to employ squeaking piglings as orchestral color."

Cyrus Kluckhuhn, Frank Lester, Bill Jones, Si Whiner! Cyrus, Frank, Bill, and Si! The clucking hen and the oinking pig! These are the alter egos of Oscar George Theodore Sonneck. How revealing they are of his

---

62. Mr. Hoffmann kindly made available to me the textbook from which he and his fellow students learned Latin aphorisms (and those in other languages as well): Georg Büchmann, *Geflügelte Worte,* 19th ed. (Berlin: Haude & Spener'sche Buchhandlung, 1898). My colleague Siegmund Levarie, whose *Gymnasium* schooling was in Vienna, reported several similar fractured-Latin translations out of his experience. One related to *suum cuique,* in that it too is a play on *sus,* is "My mother is a bad pig," as a translation for *Mea mater sus est mala* (*recte* "Run, Mother, the pig is eating the apples").

"editorial" side, one which in many ways offsets the anonymity, the impersonality, and the sobriety which were inherent and inevitable in the kinds of work he performed so superbly — bibliography, librarianship, documentary history, magazine editing, music publishing. And how perfectly they suggest the lighter side of "Justaplain Mr." Sonneck, who did, after all (*pace* Mr. Putnam), know "how to play."

(That, of course, is the logical conclusion of this lecture. But I cannot resist adding a Sonneckian P.S. For the few who may not have guessed it by now, the first half of my title — "After 100[!] Years" — is a quotation from a primary source, but the [!] calls attention to an error in it, or a fact especially to be exclaimed over. The source is the title of a short editorial Sonneck wrote as *The Musical Quarterly* ended its first decade of publication under his editorship. His title was, of course, "After Ten Years."[63] But in view of the centenary we are commemorating — that of Sonneck's birth — perhaps even he would excuse the misquotation, granted that I have duly signaled it with a careful [!]. After all, it was Sonneck who wrote, "We need a little more fun in music.")

---

63. *Musical Quarterly* 10 (1924): 459–62.

Oscar George Theodore Sonneck

His Writings and Musical Compositions
With a List of Portraits and of Writings about Him

A Bibliography

IRVING LOWENS

Books and Articles

1894

1. "Recension und Kritik: Ein Kapitel in der Reform des modernen Musikwesens." Unpublished.

> No. 1 on Sonneck's MS checklist of his writings, in the LC Music Division.

2. "Referat über Méhuls 'Joseph.'" Unpublished; read [where?] December 5.

> No. 2 on Sonneck's MS checklist of his writings, in the LC Music Division.

1895

3. "Referat über Spontinis 'Vestalin.'" Unpublished; read [where?] January 30.

> No. 3 on Sonneck's MS checklist of his writings, in the LC Music Division.

4. *Seufzer* (Frankfurt-am-Main: Gebrüder Knauer).

Poems. No. 97 of 100 copies printed is in the LC Rare Book and Special Collections Division.

1896

5. "Geschäft, Zopf und Clique in der Musik der Gegenwart," *Neue Musik-Zeitung* 17: 133–34, 148.

6. "Münchener Komponisten," *Kieler Zeitung*, February 12, 13 (in two parts).

7. "La nuova rappresentazione del 'Don Giovanni' di Mozart a Monaco," *Rivista Musicale Italiana* 3: 741–55.
Translated by Luigi Torchi from the original German; holograph MS of the latter in the LC Music Division. English translation by Theodore Baker printed in Sonneck's *Miscellaneous Studies* (1921), pp. 1–15.

8. "Die sogenannte Unsterblichkeit in der Musik," *Kieler Zeitung*, April 12.

9. "Wechselströme in der Musik," *München Allgemeine Zeitung*, July 24.

1897

10. "Das Bayreuth Mozarts," *Kieler Zeitung*, September 28.

11. "Die Klassiker als Zukunftsmusiker," *Kieler Zeitung*, December 22, 23 (in two parts).

12. *Ein kritisch-polemisches Referat über die Musik-ästhetischen Streitfragen u.s.w. von Friedrich Rösch, als Protest gegen den Symbolismus in der Musik* (Frankfurt-am-Main: Gebrüder Knauer).

13. "Rote und gelbe Musik," *Frankfurter Zeitung*, October 23.

1898

14. *Eine Totenmesse* (Frankfurt-am-Main: Gebrüder Knauer).
Poems.

1899

15. "Italienisches Provinzpublikum," *Kieler Zeitung*, September 21, 22, 23 (in three parts).

1900

16. "Der Anti-Bayreuth-Unfug," *Musikalisches Wochenblatt* 31: 653–54.

17. "Benjamin Franklin's Relation to Music," *Music* 19: 1 – 14.
A revised version, read as a paper in 1903 under the title "Benjamin Franklin's Musical Side," was published in Sonneck's *Suum Cuique* (1916), pp. 57 – 84.

18. "Don'ts for the Public," *Etude* 18 (April): 124.
Holograph of "Don'ts for Pupils and Public" in the LC Music Division; submitted in the *Etude* contest for the three best sets of "don'ts," it was one of the three prize winners. Reprinted as "Prize Don'ts for the Public" in *Oscar Sonneck and American Music* (1983).

19. "Ein Indianer-Konzert," *Kieler Zeitung*, April 19.

20. "Italian Composers: A Correction," *Music* 18: 79 – 81.

21. "Im Konzertsaal nur Konzertmusik: Eine Anregung," *Zeitschrift der Internationalen Musikgesellschaft* 1: 121 – 26.
Typescript of English translation by Theodore Baker, with ink corrections by Sonneck, in the LC Music Division; also tear sheets with ink corrections by Sonneck.
Reprinted in *Rheinische Musik- und Theater-Zeitung* 9, no. 40 (1908).

22. "Die musikalische Zeitschriften-Litteratur: Ein bibliographisches Problem," *Zeitschrift der Internationalen Musikgesellschaft* 1: 388 – 90.

23. "Notes on a Renaissance in Italian Literature." Unpublished.
No. 24 on Sonneck's MS checklist of his writings, in the LC Music Division.

24. "Zum Verständnis des amerikanischen Musiklebens," *Die Zeit* 23: 136 – 38.

25. "Zum Wiederaufschwung des italienischen Musiklebens," *Sammelbände der Internationalen Musikgesellschaft* 1: 630 – 70.
English translation by Theodore Baker in Sonneck's *Suum Cuique* (1916), pp. 215 – 71.

1901

26. "Alte Musik in altem Gewande," *Zeitschrift der Internationalen Musikgesellschaft* 2: 264 – 67.

27. "Bemerkungen zum 44. Jahr des Worcester Music Festival." Unpublished.
No. 42 on Sonneck's MS checklist of his writings, in the LC Music Division.

28. "Critical Notes on the Origin of 'Hail Columbia,'" *Sammelbände der Internationalen Musikgesellschaft* 3: 139–66.

29. "European Fallacies and American Music," *Music* 19: 220–25. Reprinted in *Oscar Sonneck and American Music* (1983).

30. "Italienisch oder Muttersprache?," *Zeitschrift der Internationalen Musikgesellschaft* 2: 158–59.

31. "Musicians, etc., Mentioned in Directories of New York, Philadelphia, and Boston." Unpublished.

No. 40 on Sonneck's MS checklist of his writings, in the LC Music Division.

1902

[It is not surprising that the year 1902 shows no publications by Sonneck: it saw the end of his youthful wanderings and the beginning of his career. On August 1 he became chief of the Music Division at the Library of Congress in Washington, D.C. He himself provided no account of 1902 at the Music Division, as he did over the next fifteen years, for the fiscal year 1902 had ended a month and a day before he took charge; but Dr. Herbert Putnam did not draft his *Report of the Librarian of Congress . . . for the Fiscal Year Ending June 30, 1902* until late in that calendar year, and he took obvious pride in announcing (on pp. 13–14) Sonneck's appointment. He described Sonneck's exceptional qualifications for the post, and he stretched the fiscal year a bit so that he could write proudly of Sonneck's activities during his first months on the job. — ED.]

1903

32. "Francis Hopkinson (1737–1791): The First American Composer," *Sammelbände der Internationalen Musikgesellschaft* 5: 119–54.

33. "Hie nationale Tonsprache—hie Volapük," *Die Musik* 3 (October): 47–53.

Tear sheets with ink corrections by Sonneck in the LC Music Division.

English translation by Theodore Baker in Sonneck's *Suum Cuique* (1916), pp. 23–34.

34. "Mendelssohn's 'St. Paul.'" Unpublished. Paper read before the Choral Society of Washington.

No. 43 on Sonneck's MS checklist of his writings, in the LC Music Division.

35. "Music: Accessions," in *Report of the Librarian of Congress
... for the Fiscal year Ending June 30, 1903* (Washington: Government
Printing Office), pp. 32–33; "Select List of Recent Purchases . . .
1901–1903: Music," ibid., pp. 190–251 [all categories of music and
books on music; Sonneck's name is not mentioned, as it came to be
after 1906, but he was the responsible official].

36. "A Plea for Home Products," *Musician* 8: 239.
Reprinted in *Oscar Sonneck and American Music* (1983).

37. "Samiel hilf—'Parsifal' in New York," *Musikalisches Wochenblatt* 34: 354–55.

38. "To Be or Not to Be—a Critic," *Musician* 8: 321.
Tear sheet with Sonneck's pencil corrections in the LC Music
Division.

1904

39. "Cataloging Special Publications and Other Material: 2.
Music," in Charles A. Cutter, *Rules for a Dictionary Catalog,* 4th ed.
(Washington: Government Printing Office), pp. 138–40.
Reprinted in *Reader in Music Librarianship,* ed. Carol June
Bradley ([Washington, D.C.: Indian Head Editions, 1973]), pp.
146–47.

40. *Classification: Class M, Music; Class ML, Literature of Music;
Class MT, Musical Instruction. Adopted December, 1902; as in Force
April, 1904* (Washington: Government Printing Office).
Original typescripts, with ink corrections and additions by Son-
neck, in the LC Music Division.

(a) Revised edition printed 1917 under the title *Classification:
Music and Books on Music.*

(b) Second edition, with supplementary pages, printed 1957.

(c) Third edition, newly integrated, printed 1978 with 1917
title.

41. "Music: Accessions," in *Report of the Librarian of Congress
... for the Fiscal Year Ending June 30, 1904* (Washington: Government
Printing Office), pp. 72–73; "Select List of Recent Purchases" [in all
music categories], ibid., pp. 310–20.

42. "Nordamerikanische Musikbibliotheken: Einige Winke für
Studienreisende," *Sammelbände der Internationalen Musikgesellschaft*
5: 329–35.

43. "The Teaching of the History of Music," *Etude* 22 (February):
54.

1905

44. "Amerikanische Studenten," *Die Zeit,* August 11.

45. *Bibliography of Early Secular American Music* (Washington: Printed for the author by H. L. McQueen).

(a) New edition, *A Bibliography of Early Secular American Music (18th Century),* revised and enlarged by William Treat Upton, printed 1945 for the Music Division, Library of Congress, Washington.

(b) The 1945 edition was reprinted in 1964 by Da Capo Press, New York, with a new preface by Irving Lowens.

(c) The 1945 edition is in effect supplemented by Appendixes I–III of Richard J. Wolfe's *Secular Music in America 1801 – 1825: A Bibliography,* 3 vols. (New York: New York Public Library, 1964). Appendix I, pp. 1001 – 18, provides an additional 190 "unrecorded eighteenth-century imprints located during the course of [Wolfe's] work." Appendix II is "a list of [156] works in the Sonneck-Upton *Bibliography* which have been re-dated [by Wolfe] into the nineteenth century" (pp. 1019 – 21). Appendix III (pp. 1023 – 33) gives "locations of newly-discovered copies of [an estimated 675] works in the Sonneck-Upton *Bibliography.*"

Many of the MS notes of both Sonneck and Upton are to be found in the LC Music Division.

46. "Early American Operas," *Sammelbände der Internationalen Musikgesellschaft* 6: 428 – 95.

Reprinted in Sonneck's *Miscellaneous Studies* (1921), pp. 16 – 92.

47. *Francis Hopkinson, the First American Poet-Composer (1737 – 1791), and James Lyon, Patriot, Preacher, Psalmodist (1735 – 1794): Two Studies in Early American Music* (Washington: Printed for the author by H. L. McQueen).

Reprinted 1969 by Da Capo Press, New York, with a new introduction by Richard A. Crawford.

48. "Music: Accessions," in *Report of the Librarian of Congress . . . for the Fiscal Year Ending June 30, 1905* (Washington: Government Printing Office), pp. 63 – 65, 82.

49. "Suggestions for the formation, etc., of a library for James Loeb's conservatory." Unpublished.

No. 60 on Sonneck's MS checklist of his writings, in the LC Music Division. James Loeb was an Anglo-German art collector; whether his conservatory that Sonneck mentions had to do with music is not evident.

1906

50. "The Bibliography of American Music," *Proceedings and Papers of the Bibliographical Society of America* 1: 50–64.
Reprinted in *Oscar Sonneck and American Music* (1983).

51. "Early Concerts in America," *New Music Review* 5: 952–57.
Reprinted as part of the introduction and chapter 1 of Sonneck's *Early Concert-Life* (1907).

52. "European Musical Associations," *Papers and Proceedings of the Music Teachers' National Association* 1: 115–38.

53. "Music: Accessions," in *Report of the Librarian of Congress . . . for the Fiscal Year Ending June 30, 1906* (Washington: Government Printing Office), pp. 48–50.

54. "Washington's March," *Zeitschrift der Internationalen Musikgesellschaft* 7: 273–74.

55. "Zwei Briefe C. Ph. Em. Bach's an Alexander Reinagle," *Sammelbände der Internationalen Musikgesellschaft* 8: 112–14.

1907

56. "After-Dinner Music," *New Music Review* 7: 17–18.

57. "Der Ausbau von Musik-Bibliotheken," in *Bericht über den zweiten Kongress der Internationalen Musikgesellschaft zu Basel vom 25.–27. September 1906* (Leipzig: Breitkopf & Härtel, 1907), pp. 6–7 (abstract only).

58. "Division of Music," in *Report of the Librarian of Congress . . . for the Fiscal Year Ending June 30, 1907* (Washington: Government Printing Office), pp. 46–49.
"From the report of the chief, Mr. Sonneck" (p. 46).

59. *Early Concert-Life in America (1731–1800)* (Leipzig: Breitkopf & Härtel).
Holograph in the LC Music Division.
(a) Reprinted 1949 by Musurgia Publishers, New York.
(b) Reprinted 1969 by M. Sändig, Wiesbaden.

60. "Edward MacDowell," *Zeitschrift der Internationalen Musikgesellschaft* 9: 1–13.

61. "The Musical Side of Our First Presidents," *New Music Review* 6: 311 – 14, 382 – 85.

(a) Reprinted in Sonneck's *Suum Cuique* (1916), pp. 35 – 55.

(b) Reprinted in part in *George Washington as a Friend and Patron of Music* (Washington: Government Printing Office, 1931).

(c) Reprinted in the George Washington Bicentennial Commission's *History of the George Washington Bicentennial Commission* (Washington: Government Printing Office, 1932) 2: 259 – 64.

62. "Pre-Revolutionary Opera in America," *New Music Review* 6: 438 – 44, 500 – 506, 562 – 69.

Reprinted as part 1 of *Early Opera in America* (1915).

63. " 'Yankee Doodle' nicht 'made in Germany,' " *Allgemeine Musik-Zeitung* 34: 381.

1908

64. "Division of Music," in *Report of the Librarian of Congress . . . for the Fiscal Year Ending June 30, 1908* (Washington: Government Printing Office), pp. 38 – 40, 56.

"From the report of the chief, Mr. Sonneck" (p. 38).

65. *Dramatic Music (Class M1500, 1510, 1520): Catalogue of Full Scores* (Washington: Government Printing Office).

Reprinted 1969 by Da Capo Press, New York.

66. "Jedem das seine," *Die Musik* 7: 203 – 9.

Tear sheets with Sonneck's ink corrections in the LC Music Division.

English translation by Theodore Baker in Sonneck's *Suum Cuique* (1916), pp. 1 – 12, where it is the title essay. For the full explanation of that typically enigmatic title, see pp. 232 – 34.

67. "Music and Progress," *New Music Review* 8: 11 – 13.

Reprinted in Sonneck's *Suum Cuique* (1916), pp. 13 – 21.

68. "The Music Division of the Library of Congress; Methods, Policies and Resources," *Papers and Proceedings of the Music Teachers' National Association* 3: 260 – 87 [followed on pp. 288 – 89 by a partial catalog of the Exhibition of Music and Books on Music Arranged in Honor of the Music Teachers' National Association in the Great Hall of the Library of Congress].

(a) Reprinted as a separate, for the author, by the Association at Hartford, Conn.

(b) Reprinted in *Oscar Sonneck and American Music* (1983).

69. "Musical Libraries: A Rhapsody in Minor," *Musician* 13: 258–59.

70. "Opera in America from 1783 to 1800," *New Music Review* 7: 502–6, 554–57, 598–603.
   A summary of what became part 2 of Sonneck's *Early Opera in America* (1915).

1909

71. "Anton Beer-Walbrunn," *New Music Review* 8: 269–71, 321–23.
   Reprinted in Sonneck's *Suum Cuique* (1916), pp. 155–74.

72. "Deutscher Einfluss auf das Musikleben Americas," in Max Heinrici, *Das Buch der Deutschen in Amerika* (Philadelphia: Walther's Buchdruckerei), pp. 355–67.
   Original typescript in the LC Music Division.

   English translation in *Oscar Sonneck and American Music* (1983).

73. "Division of Music," in *Report of the Librarian of Congress . . . for the Fiscal Year Ending June 30, 1909* (Washington: Government Printing Office), pp. 35–39.
   "From the report of the chief, Mr. Sonneck" (p. 35).

74. "The Haydn Centenary Festival at Vienna — Retrospective Impressions," *New Music Review* 8: 605–11.

75. "How to Use a Music Library," *Musician* 14: 486–87.

76. "Das Musikleben Amerikas vom Standpunkte der musikalischen Länderkunde," in *III. Kongress der Internationalen Musikgesellschaft, Wien, 25. bis 29. Mai 1909: Bericht vorgelegt vom Wiener Kongressausschuss* (Vienna: Artaria & Co.), pp. 446–58.
   (a) Selected excerpts were reprinted in the *Oesterreichisch-ungarische Musiker-Zeitung* 17 (1909): 189–91, 196, 201–2, 213, 221–22.

   (b) Sonneck included one long paragraph from this interesting survey, a paragraph pointing out the lack of primary sources for the writing of a history of music in America, in his 1916 paper entitled "The History of Music in America: A Few Suggestions" (no. 117 below), which was in turn reprinted in his 1921 *Miscellaneous Studies* (no. 130). No credit was given for the translation, so it presumably was by Sonneck himself; by 1921 he obviously was thinking more fluently in English than in his earlier years, when he felt the need of a translator.

(c) English translation of the entire paper, by the editor and colleagues, in *Oscar Sonneck and American Music* (1983).

77. *Report on "The Star-Spangled Banner," "Hail Columbia," "America," "Yankee Doodle"* (Washington: Government Printing Office).

Reprinted 1972 by Dover Publications, New York.

78. "Should Our Government Establish a National Conservatory of Music?," *Musical America* 10 (September 4): 1, 22.

With a portrait photograph, side view, of Sonneck, showing him at an earlier age than any other this editor has seen.

Reprinted (without the portrait) in Sonneck's *Suum Cuique* (1916), pp. 105 – 18, titled "A National Conservatory: Some Pros and Cons."

1910

79. "Bibliographie [générale des publications consacrées jusqu'à ce jour à la musique des Indiens de l'Amérique]," a supplement to Julien Tiersot's "La Musique chez les peuples indigènes de l'Amérique du Nord (Etats-Unis et Canada)," *Sammelbände der Internationalen Musikgesellschaft* 11: 223 – 31.

80. "Division of Music," in *Report of the Librarian of Congress . . . for the Fiscal Year Ending June 30, 1910* (Washington: Government Printing Office), pp. 48 – 53, 67.

"From the report of the chief, Mr. Sonneck" (p. 48).

81. "Galuppi oder Perez?," *Sammelbände der Internationalen Musikgesellschaft* 11: 312.

82. "The Music Division of the Library of Congress," *New Music Review* 9: 74 – 78.

1911

83. " 'Caractacus' Not Arne's 'Caractacus,' " *Sammelbände der Internationalen Musikgesellschaft* 12: 297 – 315.

Reprinted in Sonneck's *Miscellaneous Studies* (1921), pp. 241 – 68.

84. "Ciampi's 'Bertoldo, Bertoldino e Cacasenno' and Favart's 'Ninette à la cour': A Contribution to the History of Pasticcio," *Sammelbände der Internationalen Musikgesellschaft* 12: 525 – 64.

Reprinted in Sonneck's *Miscellaneous Studies* (1921), pp. 111–79.

85. "A Description of Alessandro Striggio and Francesco Cortecia's Intermedi 'Psyche and Amor,' 1565," *Musical Antiquary* 3: 40–53, 116.
> Reprinted in Sonneck's *Miscellaneous Studies* (1921), pp. 269–86.

86. "Division of Music," in *Report of the Librarian of Congress . . . for the Fiscal Year Ending June 30, 1911* (Washington: Government Printing Office), pp. 41–48, 86.
> "From the report of the chief, Mr. Sonneck" (p. 41).

87. "MacDowell versus MacDowell: A Study in First Editions and Revisions," *Papers and Proceedings of the Music Teachers' National Association* 6: 96–110.
> Reprinted in Sonneck's *Suum Cuique* (1916), pp. 85–103.

88. "Was Richard Wagner a Jew?," *Papers and Proceedings of the Music Teachers' National Association* 6: 250–74.
> Holograph in the LC Music Division.
> Reprinted in Sonneck's *Suum Cuique* (1916), pp. 175–212.

89. "Yankee Doodle," in *Grove's Dictionary of Music and Musicians,* 2nd ed., ed. J. A. Fuller-Maitland, 5 vols. (London: Macmillan, 1904–11), 5: 574–77.
> This article obviously was a spinoff from Sonneck's work on the 1909 *Report* (no. 77 above). So little further work had been done, and the topic no doubt seemed so trivial in British eyes, that it was retained — although greatly cut in size — through the third, fourth, and even fifth editions of *Grove*. — ED.

1912

90. "A Contemporary Account of Music in Charleston, S.C., of the Year 1783," *New Music Review* 11: 373–76.
> Reprinted in *Oscar Sonneck and American Music* (1983).

91. "Division of Music," in *Report of the Librarian of Congress . . . for the Fiscal Year Ending June 30, 1912* (Washington: Government Printing Office), pp. 70–78, 98–100.
> "From the report of the chief, Mr. Sonneck" (p. 70); pp. 98–100 include a hearty commendation of Mr. Sonneck by his boss.

92. "Italienische Opernlibretti des 17. Jahrhunderts in der Library

of Congress," *Sammelbände der Internationalen Musikgesellschaft* 13: 392–99.

93. "Notiz zu Eugen Schmitz's Aufsatz über Spohr's *Alruna*," *Zeitschrift der Internationalen Musikgesellschaft* 13: 406.

94. *Orchestral Music (Class M1000–1268) Catalogue: Scores* (Washington: Government Printing Office).
    Reprinted 1969 by Da Capo Press, New York.

1913

95. *Catalogue of Early Books on Music (before 1800)*, by Julia Gregory of the Catalogue Division; prepared under the direction of O. G. Sonneck, chief of the Division of Music (Washington: Government Printing Office).

    (a) *Catalogue of Early Books on Music (before 1800): Supplement (Books Acquired by the Library 1913–1942)*, by Hazel Bartlett. With a list of books on music in Chinese [compiled and annotated by K. T. Wu] and Japanese [compiled and annotated by Shio Sakanishi]; plus a list of books from the Dayton C. Miller Collection from the catalog of the Collection compiled by Mr. Miller (Washington: Government Printing Office, 1944).

    (b) Both volumes, of 1913 and 1944, reprinted together 1969 by Da Capo Press, New York.

96. " 'Dafne,' the First Opera: A Chronological Study," *Sammelbände der Internationalen Musikgesellschaft* 15: 102–10.

97. "Division of Music," in *Report of the Librarian of Congress . . . for the Fiscal Year Ending June 30, 1913* (Washington: Government Printing Office), pp. 78–82, 105.
    "From the report of the chief, Mr. Sonneck" (p. 78).

98. "Die Drei Fassungen des Hasse'schen 'Artaserse,' " *Sammelbände der Internationalen Musikgesellschaft* 14: 226–42.

99. "Il giocatore," *Musical Antiquary* 4: 160–74.
    Original typescript and proofs in the LC Music Division.

100. *A Survey of Music in America;* read before the "Schola Cantorum" at New York City, April 11, 1913 (Washington: Privately printed for the author by the McQueen Press).
    Reprinted, in part, in Sonneck's *Suum Cuique* (1916), pp. 119–54.

101. "Zu Georgy Calmus' Notiz 'L. Vinci, der Komponist von Ser-

pilla e Bacocco,' " *Zeitschrift der Internationalen Musikgesellschaft* 14: 170–72.

With rejoinder by Calmus, pp. 172–73.

1914

102. *Catalogue of Opera Librettos Printed before 1800,* 2 vols. (Washington: Government Printing Office).

(a) Reprinted 1967 by Burt Franklin, New York.

(b) Reprinted 1968 by Johnson Reprint, New York.

103. "Division of Music," in *Report of the Librarian of Congress . . . for the Fiscal Year Ending June 30, 1914* (Washington: Government Printing Office), pp. 82–93, 114.

> "From the report of the chief, Mr. Sonneck" (p. 82). On pp. 114–16, Dr. Putnam awards Mr. Sonneck a second commendation to go with that of 1912. He was happy about the very favorable reviews — in Europe as well as in this country — gained by the Library's recent publications, the opera libretto catalog and the centennial report on "The Star-Spangled Banner."

104. "Noch etwas über Opernlexika," *Die Musik* 13: 140–43.

105. *"The Star Spangled Banner"* (revised and enlarged from the "Report" on the above and other airs issued in 1909) (Washington: Government Printing Office).

> Reprinted 1969 by Da Capo Press, New York. [Through some mishap in the photocopying process, Plate VIII of the reprint shows not the very first Longman & Broderip issue of "The Anacreontic Song" as does the 1914 Sonneck (and as the 1969 caption proclaims) but the second one of several years later. — ED.]

1915

106. *Catalogue of First Editions of Stephen C. Foster (1826–1864),* by Walter R. Whittlesey, Assistant in the Music Division, and O. G. Sonneck, Chief of the Division (Washington: Government Printing Office).

> Reprinted 1971 by Da Capo Press, New York.

107. "Division of Music," in *Report of the Librarian of Congress . . . for the Fiscal Year Ending June 30, 1915* (Washington: Government Printing Office), pp. 91–94, 119.

> "From the report of the chief, Mr. Sonneck" (p. 91).

108. *Early Opera in America* (New York: G. Schirmer).
Reprinted 1963 by B. Blom, New York.

109. "The Music Division of the Library of Congress," *Library Journal* 40: 587–89.

110. [*The Musical Quarterly,* O. G. Sonneck, Editor, made its appearance with vol. 1, no. 1, of January, 1915. For fourteen solid years and fifty-six straight issues Sonneck was its editor. As such he did not play so active a role as editor-contributor as did his successor, Carl Engel, who instituted an editorial section for each issue in which he commented on topical matters and reviewed books. Sonneck, on the other hand, did not hesitate to publish his own articles from time to time — seven under his own name, at least two (nos. 118 and 148 in this bibliography) under pseudonyms, and two to which no name is attached but for which editorial responsibility can be assumed (nos. 111 and 150). — ED.]

111. "Pauline Viardot-Garcia to Julius Rietz (Letters of Friendship)," *Musical Quarterly* 1: 350–80, 526–59; 2: 32–60.

112. "A Preface [to *A Catalogue of Full Scores of Dramatic Music*]," in Sonneck's *Miscellaneous Studies* (1921), pp. 296–323.

> The *Catalogue* was in manuscript and was (according to Sonneck) "practically completed" in December, 1915. It was never published, sad to say — certainly because of financial problems at the Library of Congress raised by the war, and perhaps also because of Sonneck's anomalous position as a German sympathizer (see his 1921 letter to Carl Engel printed earlier in this volume) in spite of himself.

1916

113. "Appreciation," in *Gustav Mahler: The Composer, the Conductor and the Man* (New York: Society of Friends of Music), pp. 29–30.

> Appreciations by distinguished contemporary musicians, collected and published by the Society of Friends of Music on the occasion of the first performance of Mahler's Eighth Symphony in New York, April 9, 1916.

114. "Creed" [of the Committee on the History of Music and Libraries], *Papers and Proceedings of the Music Teachers' National Association* 11: 47–49.

115. "Division of Music," in *Report of the Librarian of Congress . . . for the Fiscal Year Ending June 30, 1916* (Washington: Government Printing Office), pp. 70–79, 113, 119.

"From the report of the chief, Mr. Sonneck" (p. 70).

116. "The First Edition of 'Hail, Columbia!,' " *Pennsylvania Magazine of History and Biography* 40: 426–35.

> Reprinted in Sonneck's *Miscellaneous Studies* (1921), pp. 180–89.

117. "The History of Music in America: A Few Suggestions," *Papers and Proceedings of the Music Teachers' National Association* 11: 50–68.

> Reprinted in Sonneck's *Miscellaneous Studies* (1921), pp. 324–44.

118. "Kluckhuhn's Chord," *Musical Quarterly* 2: 418–24.

> Published under the pseudonym of "Frank Lester."

119. "Mahler's achte Symphonie," in *Gustav Mahler: The Composer, the Conductor and the Man* (New York: Society of Friends of Music), p. [2].

> A poem in German.

120. *Suum Cuique: Essays in Music* (New York: G. Schirmer). Collected reprints of:

> *Suum Cuique (1908), pp. 3–12
> Music and Progress (1908), pp. 13–21
> *National Tone Speech versus Volapük — Which?
>   (1903), pp. 23–34
> The Musical Side of Our First Presidents
>   (1907), pp. 35–55
> Benjamin Franklin's Musical Side (1900), pp. 57–84
> MacDowell versus MacDowell (1911), pp. 85–103
> A National Conservatory: Some Pros and Cons
>   (1909), pp. 105–18
> A Survey of Music in America (1913), pp. 119–54
> Anton Beer-Walbrunn (1909), pp. 155–74
> Was Richard Wagner a Jew? (1911), pp. 175–212
> *Signs of a New Uplift in Italy's Musical Life
>   (1900), pp. 213–71

*Translated from Sonneck's German by Theodore Baker

Reprinted 1969 by Books for Libraries Press, Freeport, N.Y.

1917

121. *Catalogue of First Editions of Edward MacDowell (1861–1908)* (Washington: Government Printing Office).

Typescript of prefatory note with Sonneck's ink corrections in the LC Music Division.

(a) Reprinted 1971 by Da Capo Press, New York.

(b) Reprinted 1971 by Arno Press, New York.

122. "Division of Music," in *Report of the Librarian of Congress . . . for the Fiscal Year Ending June 30, 1917* (Washington: Government Printing Office), pp. 56–58.
"From the report of the chief, Mr. Sonneck" (p. 56).

123. "Music in Our Libraries," *Art World* 2: 242–44.
(a) Reprinted in Sonneck's *Miscellaneous Studies* (1921), pp. 287–95.

(b) Reprinted in part as an appendix to *Music Departments of Libraries,* prepared by a committee of the Music Teachers' National Association (U.S. Bureau of Education Bulletin 1921, no. 33) (Washington: Government Printing Office, 1922), pp. 49–51.

(c) Reprinted in *Reader in Music Librarianship,* ed. Carol June Bradley ([Washington, D.C.: Indian Head Editions, 1973]), pp. 5–9.

124. "Special Memorandum on the Music Division." Unpublished. Submitted to the Librarian of Congress on July 25, 1917. The original probably is somewhere in the files of the Librarian's Office, which for that period are virtually unorganized and in dead storage. A carbon copy of the original typescript is in the LC Music Division, along with a copy of Sonneck's formal note of resignation. Several paragraphs are quoted in the *Report of the Librarian of Congress . . . for the Fiscal Year Ending June 30, 1917,* pp. 66–68.

1918

125. "Liszt's 'Huldigungs-Marsch' and Weimar's Volkslied," *Musical Quarterly* 4: 61–73.
(a) Reprinted in Sonneck's *Miscellaneous Studies* (1921), pp. 93–110.

(b) Reprinted in *The Musical Quarterly* 22: 326–38.

1919

126. "Francis Hopkinson: Some Corrections and Additions," *American Organist* 2: 337–38.

127. *Francis Hopkinson: The First American Poet-Composer, and Our Musical Life in Colonial Times.* Address to the Pennsylvania Society of the Colonial Dames of America, Philadelphia, November 12, 1919, by Oscar G. Sonneck (Philadelphia: Pennsylvania Society of the Colonial Dames of America, [1919]).

> Reprinted in *Church Music and Musical Life in Pennsylvania in the Eighteenth Century,* ed. William Lichtenwanger, 3 vols. in 4 (Philadelphia: Printed for the Pennsylvania Society of the Colonial Dames of America, 1947), vol. 3, part 2, pp. 427–36.

128. "Guillaume Lekeu (1870–1894)," *Musical Quarterly* 5: 109–47.

> Reprinted in Sonneck's *Miscellaneous Studies* (1921), pp. 190–240.

129. "Rudolph E. Schirmer," *Musical Quarterly* 5: 451–52.

> A tribute to Sonneck's great friend and supporter, the son of the founder of the music-publishing firm, Gustave Schirmer.

1921

130. *Miscellaneous Studies in the History of Music* (New York: Macmillan).

> A second collection (the first was *Suum Cuique* in 1916) of articles first published, with one exception, in the years cited following each title and entered under those years in this bibliography. In his prefatory note, Sonneck thanks his colleague at G. Schirmer's, Theodore Baker, for having translated the first study from German into English, and especially "for his remarkably able translation of the rather difficult early Italian text [from 1565] of Il Lasca's *Descrizione*" in the eighth article. The eleven studies are:
>
>> The New Mise en Scène of Mozart's "Don Giovanni" at Munich (1896), pp. 1–15
>> Early American Operas (1905), pp. 16–92
>> Liszt's "Huldigungs-Marsch" and Weimar's Volkslied (1918), pp. 93–110
>> Ciampi's "Bertoldo, Bertoldino e Cacasenno" and Favart's "Ninette à la Cour": A Contribution to the History of Pasticcio (1911), pp. 111–79
>> The First Edition of "Hail, Columbia!" (1916), pp. 180–89
>> Guillaume Lekeu (1870–1894) (1919), pp. 190–240

"Caractacus" not Arne's "Caractacus" (1911), pp. 241 – 68

A Description of Alessandro Striggio and Francesco Corteccia's Intermedi "Psyche and Amor," 1565 (1911), pp. 269 – 86

Music in Our Libraries (1911), pp. 287 – 95

A Preface [written in 1915 – q.v. – but not published], pp. 296 – 323

The History of Music in America: A Few Suggestions (1916), pp. 324 – 44

(a) Reprinted 1968 by Da Capo Press, New York.

(b) Reprinted 1970 by AMS Press, New York.

1922

131. "The American Composer and the American Music Publisher," *Papers and Proceedings of the Music Teachers' National Association* 17: 122 – 47.

(a) Reprinted in *The Musical Quarterly* 9 (1923): 122 – 44.

(b) Reprinted in part in *Music News* 15 (February 9, 1923): 1 – 2.

(c) Reprinted in part in *Sackbut* 3 (1923): 195 – 201.

(d) Reprinted in *Oscar Sonneck and American Music* (1983).

132. "Heinrich Heine's Musical Feuilletons," *Musical Quarterly* 8: 119 – 59, 273 – 95, 435 – 68.

Original typescript with Sonneck's ink corrections in the LC Music Division.

133. "Prefatory Note," in Amy Fay, *Music Study in Germany,* ed. M. Fay Peirce (New York: Macmillan), pp. [iii – vi].

In the LC Music Division: (a) carbon copy of original typescript with Sonneck's ink corrections; (b) uncorrected page proofs.

1923

134. "The First American Composer: Hopkinson or Lyon?," *Musical America* 37 (February 17): 9, 40.

135. "Letter to Mrs. Edgar Stillman Kelley," *National Federation of Music Clubs Bulletin* 2 (March): 10.

Tear sheets with Sonneck's pencil corrections in the LC Music Division.

136. "On the Value of Music and Its Appreciation." Unpublished.

In the LC Music Division: (a) original typescript, much revised; and (b) retyped copy with Sonneck's further corrections.

137. "The Use of the Music Library for the Appreciation of Music," *Journal of Proceedings of the . . . Music Supervisors National Conference* 16: 132–40.

Carbon copy of the original typescript with Sonneck's ink corrections in the LC Music Division.

1924

138. "After Ten Years," *Musical Quarterly* 10: 459–62.

139. *Modernists, Classics and Immortality in Music,* an address . . . under the auspices of the Philharmonic Society of Philadelphia [March 23] (New York: G. Schirmer).

Carbon copy of original typescript with Sonneck's ink corrections in the LC Music Division.

Reprinted in *The Musical Quarterly* 11 (1925): 572–90.

1925

140. "Footnote to the Bibliographical History of Grétry's Operas," in *Gedenkboek aangeboden aan Dr. D. F. Scheurleer* (The Hague: M. Nijhoff), pp. 321–26.

Carbon copy of original typescript in the LC Music Division.

1926

141. *Beethoven: Impressions of Contemporaries,* compiled, annotated, and in part translated by O. G. Sonneck [From the preface: A few translations were made by Theodore Baker but the majority by F. H. Martens] (New York: G. Schirmer).

Reprinted 1967 by Dover Publications, New York, under the title *Beethoven: Impressions by His Contemporaries.*

142. "Some Impertinent Remarks." Unpublished.

"Written for the A.S.C.A.P. Jan. 1926." Carbon copy of original typescript with Sonneck's ink corrections in the LC Music Division.

1927

143. "An American School of Composition: Do We Want and Need It?," *Papers and Proceedings of the Music Teachers' National Association* 22: 102–16.

Carbon copy of original typescript with Sonneck's ink corrections in the LC Music Division.

Reprinted in *Oscar Sonneck and American Music* (1983).

144. "Beethoven," *American Mercury* 10: 316 – 20.
In the LC Music Division: (a) tear sheets bearing Sonneck's ink notation: "originally written as: An apology for anti-Beethovenians"; and (b) a carbon of the original typescript with Sonneck's ink corrections.

(a) Reprinted in the *New York Times*, March 6, 1927, section 7, p. 12.

(b) Reprinted in *Musical Courier* 94 (March 24, 1927): 14 – 15.

145. *Beethoven Letters in America: Facsimiles with a Commentary by O. G. Sonneck*, in commemoration of March 26, 1927 (New York: Beethoven Association).
Holograph in the LC Music Division. March 27, 1927, was the centenary of Beethoven's death.

One chapter reprinted as the next entry, no. 146.

146. "Beethoven to Diabelli: A Letter and a Protest," *Musical Quarterly* 13: 294 – 316.
A chapter from *Beethoven Letters in America* (1927), no. 145.

147. "Centenarian Perplexities," *Journal of Proceedings of the Music Supervisors National Conference* 20: 211 – 16.
Carbon copy of original typescript with Sonneck's ink corrections in the LC Music Division; also there is an unauthorized typed copy with Sonneck's marginal notes.

Reprinted in *Music Supervisors Journal* 14 (1927): 25, 27, 29, 31.

148. "The Communistic Cell: A Symphonic Hypoblast," *Musical Courier* 94 (February 24): 12.
Communication from a pseudonymous Bill Jones addressed to an equally pseudonymous editor, one Si W.

Reprinted in *Oscar Sonneck and American Music* (1983).

149. *The Riddle of the Immortal Beloved: A Supplement to Thayer's "Life of Beethoven"* (New York: G. Schirmer).
Holograph in the LC Music Division.

150. "Sayings of Beethoven," *Musical Quarterly* 13: 183 – 207.
Compiled by Sonneck, according to his MS checklist of his writings, in the LC Music Division.

1928

151. "Music for Adults and Music for Children," *Journal of Proceedings of the Music Supervisors National Conference* 21: 124–28.

Reprinted in *Music Supervisors Journal* 15 (December 1928): 21–27.

Carbon copy of original typescript with Sonneck's ink corrections in the LC Music Division.

152. "Yankee Doodle," in *Grove's Dictionary of Music and Musicians*, 3rd ed. (London: Macmillan), 5: 766.

This article is an abbreviated version of the one written in 1909 for the second edition of *Grove* (see no. 89). That article was an offshoot of the work done by Sonneck in preparing his 1909 *Report* (no. 77). This abbreviated version apparently was thought sufficient, when coupled with Sonneck's *Report,* for it was carried again in the fourth edition of 1940 and even in the fifth edition of 1954. There is no article under the song title in the recent sixth edition of 1980.

Posthumous

153. "Foster, Stephen Collins," in *Encyclopedia Britannica*, 14th ed. (London and New York: Encyclopedia Britannica, 1929), 9: 550.

Carbon of typescript with Sonneck's ink corrections in the LC Music Division.

154. "The Future of Musicology in America," in *Essays Offered to Herbert Putnam*, ed. W. W. Bishop and Andrew Keogh (New Haven, Conn.: Yale University Press, 1929), pp. 423–28.

Sonneck's original manuscript draft is in the LC Music Division.

(a) Reprinted in *The Musical Quarterly* 15 (1929): 317–21.

(b) Reprinted in *Oscar Sonneck and American Music* (1983).

155. "Heinrich, Antony Philip," in *Dictionary of American Biography* (New York: Scribner, 1932), 8: 504–5.

156. ["Letter to Mrs. Julia Sonneck, May 17, 1894"], *Musical Quarterly* 19 (1933): 462–65.

Reprinted in *Oscar Sonneck and American Music* (1983).

157. "99 Pacific Avenue; Or, In Search of a Birthplace," *Musical Quarterly* 19 (1933): 456–62.

Reprinted in *Oscar Sonneck and American Music* (1983).

Written in 1922. With a snapshot of Sonneck on the porch of

his Washington home, ca. 1913, and in a group photograph of the Librarian of Congress and his staff of chiefs of division on the front steps of the Library in the spring of 1914.

158. "Oscar Sonneck Writes to Carl Engel," *American Music* 1 (1983): 60–69.

> Written September 21, 1921. With an introductory note by William Lichtenwanger.

> Reprinted, without the introductory note, as "Sonneck Person-to-Person III: Letter to Carl Engel" in *Oscar Sonneck and American Music* (1983).

159. [Miscellaneous writings in various publications of various dates, some signed and some unsigned. Sonneck was active in many organizations throughout his career in this country; he was an officer at G. Schirmer's for eleven years; he may well have published articles under pseudonyms that have not been spotted and recorded here. As a member of the Washington Choral Society during most of his stay in Washington he was often cited as an officer and committee member, and over the period 1907–10 he sometimes contributed program notes to its *Bulletin*. He no doubt sent communications to foreign periodicals that have not been noticed. His writings and activities seem infinite, whereas this bibliography is finite. — ED.]

160. *Oscar Sonneck and American Music*, ed. William Lichtenwanger (Urbana: University of Illinois Press, 1983).

> Of the Sonneck writings cited in this bibliography the volume reprints nos. 18, 29, 36, 50, 68, 72, 76, 90, 131, 143, 148, 154, 156, 157, and 158. Two communications are printed for the first time: a talk on musical research procedures to a committee of the Pennsylvania Society of the Colonial Dames, and his report as a reader for a publisher on a book manuscript submitted for publication. There are articles about Sonneck's life and works by Herbert Putnam, Carl Engel, Otto Kinkeldey, Gilbert Chase, and H. Wiley Hitchcock, together with this comprehensive bibliography and a foreword by Irving Lowens.

Musical Compositions
With opus numbers

4. String Quartet. Unpublished.
   Location of holograph unknown.

8. Romanze and Rhapsodie, für Violin und Klavier (Frankfurt: B. Firnberg, 1899).

9. Cyklus, für Baryton mit Klavierbegleitung, aus *Eine Totenmesse* (Frankfurt: B. Firnberg, 1899).

10. Suite di miniature, for piano solo, 1899. Unpublished.
    1. Fanfara
    2. Danza russa
    3. Marcia dell' oche
    4. Intermezzo nero
    5. Arietta
    6. Un sogna
    7. Finale

    Holograph in the LC Music Division. Revised 1917 (revised holograph also in the LC Music Division) and given the title *Miniature lilipuziane: Suite blague,* with six movements:
    1. Fanfare
    2. Camminato scolastica dell' oche
    3. Intermezzino nero
    4. Ballata pastorale
    5. Sogno (R.-K.)
    6. Marcia-Finale

11. Drei Concertstücke, für Klavier (Frankfurt: B. Firnberg, 1900).
    1. Ballade
    2. Capriccio
    3. Interludio scherzoso

12. Vermischte Lieder (New York: Breitkopf & Härtel, 1900).
    1. Freudvoll und leidvoll (Goethe)
    2. Der du von dem Himmel bist (Goethe)
    3. Es ragt ins Meer der Runenstein (Heine)
    4. Zu spät (Detlev Freiherr von Liliencron)
    5. Jugend (Franz Evers)
    6. Nachtgeschwätz (Franz Evers)
    7. Herbstlied (Fritz Cassirer)
    8. Nelken (Theodor Storm)
    9. Ueber die Haide (Theodor Storm)
    10. Elisabeth (Theodor Storm)
    11. Bettlerliebe (Theodor Storm)
    12. Oktoberlied (Theodor Storm)

13. Elegie, für Violoncello und Klavier. Unpublished.
    Holograph in the LC Music Division.

14-15. Six Songs (New York: Carl Fischer, 1922).
    Op. 14, no. 1. Liebeserfüllung (Sonneck)
               2. Tod in Aehren (Detlev Freiherr von Liliencron)

Op. 15, no. 1. Die Nachtigall (Theodor Storm)
    2. Juli (Theodor Storm)
    3. Die Tote (Theodor Storm)
    4. Sommermittag (Theodor Storm)

16. Four Poems by Edgar Allan Poe, for baritone (New York: G.
Schirmer, 1917).
    1. To Helen
    2. Thou Wouldst Be Loved
    3. El Dorado
    4. A Dream within a Dream
An edition of the Four Poems with German text only (transla-
tions by R. S. Hoffmann) was published in 1917 by Universal-
Edition. Holographs of Nos. 1, 3, and 4 in the LC Music Division.

17. Vier pessimistische Lieder, für Bariton und Klavier (Vienna:
Universal-Edition, 1922).
    1. Nachtigall (Ludwig Scharf)
    2. Stirb (J. H. Ma[c]kay)
    3. Blätterfall (Heinrich Leuthold)
    4. Mit dir am Abgrund (Karl Bleibtreu)

18. Ein kleiner Lieder-Cyclus: Sechs Lieder zu Gedichten von Theodor
Storm (Vienna: Universal-Edition, 1922).
    1. Noch einmal
    2. Nun sei mir heimlich zart und gut
    3. Im Sessel du
    4. Schliesse mir die Augen beide
    5. Es ist ein Flüstern
    6. Ich weiss es wohl
Holograph sketches in the LC Music Division.

19. Studies in Song. [Nos. 2, 4, 6, 7, 8, and 9 published in 1923 by
Composers' Music Corp. of New York; the others unpublished].
    1. The Moon (P. B. Shelley)
    2. Serenade (T. L. Beddoes)
    3. Portuguese Sonnet (E. B. Browning)
    4. Wild Swans (E. St. V. Millay)
    5. Elegy (E. St. V. Millay)
    6. Caliban in the Coal Mines (Louis Untermeyer)
    7. Night (William Rose Benét)
    8. To a Golden-Haired Girl (Vachel Lindsay)
    9. Voices (Witter Bynner)
    10. Lethe (H.D.)
    11. I Shall Not Care (Sara Teasdale)

12. Love and Liberation (J. H. Wheelock)
13. The Hills of Home (Witter Bynner)
14. Lullaby (Witter Bynner)
   Holographs of Nos. 1, 3, 5, 10, 11, 12, 13, and 14 in the LC
Music Division.
20. Poems of Heine; translated by Louis Untermeyer. Unpublished.
   1. Death Is But the Long, Cool Night
   2. Like a Pelican
   3. Away
   4. It Makes a Man Feel Happy
   Holograph in the LC Music Division.

Without opus numbers

A Mother's Song, for piano solo, 1909. Unpublished.
   Holograph in the LC Music Division.

1848 – 1898. Melodramatische, programmatische und aromatische
Schauerballade, von Anton Notenkopf. Unter gütiger Mitwirkung des
berühmten und berüchtigen Recitators: Professor Maestro Chevalier
Otto Weber und seinen unübertrefflichen Musikautomaton.
   Holograph in the LC Music Division. Referred to by Betty B.
Buyck in her thesis (see below) as "a mockingly grandiose orchestral
work by Sonneck, written for Schröder's fiftieth birthday . . . [and]
performed in November of 1898." Carl Schröder, conductor of the
orchestra at Sondershausen, was Sonneck's teacher in conducting.

Symphonischer Satz, for small orchestra. Unpublished.
   Location of holograph unknown.

Portraits

1. *Musical America* 10 (September 4, 1909): 1.
   The earliest portrait of Sonneck known to have been published: a profile, with his pince-nez and youthful earnestness
quite evident.
   Reproduced in *Oscar Sonneck and American Music* (1983).
2. *American Review of Reviews* 51 (March 1915): 370.
   Same photograph as no. 1.
3. *Grove's Dictionary of Music and Musicians, American Supplement*

(New York: Macmillan, 1920), facing p. 364.
Same photograph as no. 1.

4. *Music Trade News* 7 (November 1928): 20.
A full-length but close-up photograph not seen elsewhere, possibly the last of those known.

5. *Musical Quarterly* 15 (January 1929): facing p. 1.
The *Musical Quarterly* portrait of the mature Sonneck. Used twice more in later years (nos. 6 and 9 below).

6. *Musical America* 49 (October 25, 1929): 4.
Same as no. 5.

7. *Musical Quarterly* 19 (1933): facing p. 456.
Sonneck on the porch of his Washington home, ca. 1913.
Reproduced in *Oscar Sonneck and American Music* (1983).

8. *Musical Quarterly* 19 (1933): facing p. 457.
The Librarian of Congress, Dr. Herbert Putnam, with his staff of chiefs of division, on the front steps of the Library of Congress, spring, 1914.
Reproduced in *Oscar Sonneck and American Music* (1983).

9. *Musical Quarterly* 25 (1939): facing p. 2.
Same as no. 5.

10. *American Music* 1 (1983): 62.
The Sonneck Society portrait. Individual prints have been distributed by the Society, and the portrait has been used in promotional material by the University of Illinois Press. Obviously taken at the same sitting as no. 5, but with Sonneck looking directly at the camera. The original is framed and hangs in the office of the Chief of the Music Division, Library of Congress.
Reproduced as the frontispiece of *Oscar Sonneck and American Music* (1983).

About Sonneck

Aldrich, Richard. [Book review of *Francis Hopkinson . . . and James Lyon*, 1905], *New York Times*, July 8, 1905, part 2, p. 48.

[Baker, Theodore]. "Sonneck, Oscar George," in *Baker's Biographical Dictionary of Musicians*, 3rd ed., rev. and enl. by Alfred Remy (New York: G. Schirmer, 1919), p. 889.

Barini, Giorgio. "Un musicologo americano," *Nuova antologia* 264 (1915): 100–111.

"Beethoven Association Presents Sonneck Memorial Fund to National Library," *Musical Courier* 49 (October 19, 1929): 9.

[Book review, unsigned, of *Miscellaneous Studies*, 1921], *Booklist* 18 (1922): 109.

[Book review, unsigned, of *Suum Cuique*, 1916], *Review of Reviews* 55 (February 1917): 219.

Britton, Allen P., and Irving Lowens. "Unlocated Titles in Early Sacred American Music," *Notes* 11 (1953): 33–48.

    Includes a description of Sonneck's 132 working notebooks of the years 1899–1903 in the LC Music Division (pp. 34–35).

Broder, Nathan. "Sonneck, Oscar George," trans. by Johannes Hennesen, in *Musik in Geschichte und Gegenwart* (Kassel: Bärenreiter Verlag, 1965), 12: cols. 911–13.

Brodsky, Adolph. [Obituary notice: Oscar G. Sonneck], *Musical Times* 70 (February 1, 1929): 174–75.

Buyck, Betty B. "Oscar George Theodore Sonneck: The Man and His Work." A study submitted in partial fulfillment of requirements for the degree of Master of Science in Library Science, Drexel Institute of Technology School of Library Science, Philadelphia, June 12, 1954. [iii, 82 pp., typewritten]

Chase, Gilbert. "The Significance of Oscar Sonneck: A Centennial Tribute," in *Yearbook for Inter-American Musical Research* 9 (1973): 172–76.

    Reprinted in *Oscar Sonneck and American Music* (1983).

"Contemporary American Musicians, No. 258: Oscar George Sonneck," *Musical America* 37 (January 13, 1923): 29.

Curzon, Henri de. [Book review of *Dramatic Music*, 1908], *Guide Musical* 54 (1908): 586–87.

Downes, Olin. "A Scholar Passes," *New York Times,* November 11, 1928, section 8, p. 8.

Elson, Louis C. [Book review of *Francis Hopkinson . . . and James Lyon*, 1905], *American Historical Review* 11 (1906): 419.

Engel, Carl. "O. G. Sonneck: Ein Charakterbild," in *Studien zur Musikgeschichte: Festschrift für Guido Adler* (Vienna: Universal-Edition, 1930), pp. 216–20.

————. "Oscar G. Sonneck," *Musical Quarterly* 25 (1939): 2–5.

    Reprinted in *Oscar Sonneck and American Music* (1983).

————. "A Postscript," *Musical Quarterly* 15 (1929): 149–51.

    Reprinted in *Oscar Sonneck and American Music* (1983).

————. "Sonneck, Oscar George Theodore," in *Dictionary of American Biography* (New York: Scribner's, 1935), 17:395–96.

Finck, Henry T. [Book review of *Early Opera in America*, 1915], *Nation* 101 (August 26, 1915): 270.

———. [Book review of *Suum Cuique*, 1916], *Nation* 105 (November 15, 1917): 546.

Foss, Hubert J. "Death of Mr. Oscar Sonneck: An American Music Publisher," *London Times*, November 20, 1928, p. 18.

Goldmark, Rubin. "O. G. Sonneck," *Musical Quarterly* 15 (1929): 4–5.

Tribute by the vice-president of the Beethoven Association at Sonneck's funeral service, November 1, 1928.

Gurlitt, Wilibald. "Sonneck, Oskar George Theodore," in *Riemann Musik-Lexikon*, 12th ed. (Mainz: B. Schott's Söhne, 1961), 2:699–700.

Henderson, W. J. [Book review of *Francis Hopkinson . . . and James Lyon*, 1905], *Atlantic Monthly* 96 (1905): 854.

Hitchcock, H. Wiley. "After 100[!] Years: The Editorial Side of Sonneck. *In Memoriam* Oscar George Theodore Sonneck, 1873–1928" (Washington: Library of Congress, 1975).

The Louis Charles Elson Memorial Lecture delivered at the Library of Congress on November 15, 1973; published with the Lowens bibliography cited below.

Reprinted in *Oscar Sonneck and American Music* (1983).

Howard, John Tasker. [Book review of Sonneck-Upton, *A Bibliography of Early Secular American Music (18th century)*, 1945], *Musical Quarterly* 31 (1945): 536–38.

"In Memoriam: Editorial Note on O. G. Sonneck," *Musical Courier* 101 (November 1, 1930): 22.

Kaiser, Rudolf. "Von Katalogisierung von Textbüchern," *Zentralblatt für Bibliotheksweisen*, 1915, pp. 137–45.

Kinkeldey, Otto. "A Notable Scholar Passes On: Oscar G. T. Sonneck, Musicologist and Editor, Enjoyed a Brilliant Career," *Musical America* 48 (November 10, 1928): 18.

———. "Sonneck, Oscar George Theodore," in A. Eaglefield Hull, *A Dictionary of Modern Music and Musicians* (London: J. M. Dent, 1924), pp. 468–69.

———. "Oscar George Theodore Sonneck (1873–1928)," *Notes* 11 (December 1953): 25–32.

Reprinted in *Oscar Sonneck and American Music* (1983).

——— and Waldo S. Pratt. "Tributes to the Memory of Oscar George Theodore Sonneck (1873–1928)," *Papers and Proceedings of the Music Teachers' National Association* 23 (1928): 257–63.

Kinkeldey: pp. 257–61; Pratt: pp. 261–63.

Lowens, Irving. "Oscar George Theodore Sonneck: His Writings and Musical Compositions, with a List of Portraits and of Writings about Him. A Bibliography," published with H. Wiley Hitchcock's "After 100[!] Years" (Washington: Library of Congress, 1975), pp. 20–38.
> Reprinted, with some updating, in *Oscar Sonneck and American Music* (1983).

Newsom, Jon. "Sonneck, Oscar G(eorge) T(heodore)," in *The New Grove Dictionary of Music and Musicians*, ed. Stanley Sadie (London: Macmillan Publishers, 1980), 17: 525.

[Obituaries of Sonneck: A Short Index], *Jahrbuch der Musikbibliothek Peters* 35 (1928): 63.

"Obituary: O. G. T. Sonneck," *Musical Courier* 97 (November 8, 1928): 39.

"O. G. Sonneck Dies," *New York Times*, October 31, 1928, p. 31.

"O. G. Sonneck Passes," *Musical Leader* 55 (November 8, 1928): 8.

"O. G. T. Sonneck, Prominent Musical Authority, Passes Away," *Music Trade News* 7 (November 1928): 20.
> With portrait not seen elsewhere.

[Patterson, Frank]. "Personal Recollections of Oscar G. Sonneck," *Musical Courier* 97 (November 15, 1928): 8.

Putnam, Herbert. "O. G. Sonneck (October 6, 1873 – October 30, 1928)," *Musical Quarterly* 15 (1929): 1–4.
> Reprinted in *Oscar Sonneck and American Music* (1983).

Slonimsky, Nicolas. "Sonneck, Oscar George Theodore," in *Baker's Biographical Dictionary of Musicians*, 6th ed. (New York: Schirmer Books, Macmillan, 1978), p. 1629.

Smith, Warren Storey, and Gustave Reese. "Sonneck, Oscar (George)," in *Grove's Dictionary of Music and Musicians*, 5th ed. (New York: St. Martin's Press, 1954), 7:965.

"Sonneck, Oscar G. T.," in *Who Was Who in America* (Chicago: Marquis – Who's Who, 1942), 1:1156.

"Sonneck Memorial Fund of $10,000 Created by Beethoven Association. Library of Congress to Administer Gift for Advancement of Musicology," *Musical America* 49 (October 25, 1929): 3–4.

Thorpe, Harry Colin. "Interpretive Studies in American Song," *Musical Quarterly* 15 (1929): 88–116.
> Includes a study of Sonneck's "To Helen," Op. 16, no. 1, on pp. 111–16.

Unger, Max. [Book review of *Beethoven Letters in America,* 1927], *Die Musik* 19 (1926 – 27); 504 – 5.

Upton, William Treat. *Art Song in America* (Boston: Oliver Ditson, 1930).

On page 151 a paragraph is devoted to Sonneck as a song composer.

Index

OSCAR GEORGE THEODORE SONNECK, the "father of American musicology," was born October 6, 1873, in Lafayette, New Jersey, but was brought up and educated in Germany. After returning to the United States in 1900, he devoted himself to research in American music, a field in which he was a pioneer historian and bibliographer. In 1902 he was appointed the first Chief of the Music Division of the Library of Congress; in 1915 he became the founding editor of *The Musical Quarterly;* in 1917 he resigned from the Library of Congress to join the New York music-publishing firm of G. Schirmer as editor. He died in New York on October 30, 1928. The Sonneck Society was established to celebrate the centenary of his birth in 1973.

WILLIAM LICHTENWANGER was born in Asheville, North Carolina, on February 28, 1915. He received a B.M. in 1937 and an M.Mus. in 1940, both from the University of Michigan. From 1960 to 1974 he was Head of the Reference Section, Music Division, Library of Congress. In addition to serving as editor of *Notes,* he has edited and contributed to many other publications, including a catalog of the music of Henry Cowell (in progress), and is archivist for the Sonneck Society. Currently he lives near Berkeley Springs, West Virginia.

Books in the series *Music in American Life:*

Sing a Sad Song: The Life of Hank Williams
ROGER M. WILLIAMS

Long Steel Rail: The Railroad in American Folksong
NORM COHEN

Resources of American Music History: A Directory of Source Materials
from Colonial Times to World War II
D. W. KRUMMEL, JEAN GEIL, DORIS J. DYEN, AND DEANE L. ROOT

Tenement Songs: The Popular Music of the Jewish Immigrants
MARK SLOBIN

Ozark Folksongs
VANCE RANDOLPH
EDITED AND ABRIDGED BY NORM COHEN

Oscar Sonneck and American Music
EDITED BY WILLIAM LICHTENWANGER